Diet Free!

Lose Pounds And Inches The Activetics Way

Charles T. Kuntzleman, Ed.D.

Arbor Press: Spring Arbor, Michigan

ISBN 0-940040-00-X

Designed by Esther Ann Cryderman

Manufactured in the United States of America

1   2   3   4   5   6   7   8   9   0

ACTIVETICS—A NEW APPROACH TO WEIGHT CONTROL

This book is based on the premise that the best way to lose pounds and inches is to engage in a program of increased physical activity. Hence the term ACTIVETICS. The Activetics Plan will help you look and feel better and is a lot more fun than dieting. Developed by the author, Charles T. Kuntzleman, Activetics has been used throughout the United States and Canada as a part of the YMCA's adult fitness program. Over 100,000 men and women have used Activetics to help them reduce their amounts of body fat while increasing their overall fitness levels.

In 1980, the Campbell Soup Company incorporated Activetics into their own fitness program called The Turnaround. The Turnaround is a fitness program focusing on three vital public concerns: weight control, nutrition, and exercise. The philosophy of The Turnaround is based on the behavioral modification approach. Simply stated, once you understand your problems with food and exercise, you can make changes in your daily life to correct these problem areas.

When you incorporate the principles of Activetics outlined in this book, you will enjoy gradual, *permanent* weight loss. Best of all, the activities recommended will give your body that firm, youthful look you always thought was impossible to achieve.

Contents

Acknowledgements

Everytime I write a book I realize just how much I depend on others. My office staff shares in every phase of a book and are really great people to work with. They include Lyn Cryderman who edited the book; Dan Runyon who provided excellent criticism; Esther Cryderman, the art director; and Wendy Ware, the artist. And of course, Lynette Van Alstine, my typist who did all the typing and correspondence on this book, as well as on ten previous books.

Moreover, I have been fortunate enough to have an understanding spouse and family who have encouraged me to keep writing until the task is completed. Special recognition must go to my wife, Beth, who's not only an excellent wife and mother, but a respected health and fitness professional as well. My children, Debbie, John, Tom, Lisa, and Becky, are a constant source of inspiration and enjoyment. Without their encouragement, it would be difficult to write.

To each of these wonderful individuals, I extend my heartfelt appreciation.

Charles T. Kuntzleman

PROLOGUE

Warning: This Book Can Change Your Life

A trim, sexy body. You want it. This book will show you how to get it. If you are serious about losing pounds, inches, and fat, the following chapters will help you—no matter how out of shape, fat, or old you are. No matter how many times you have failed in losing weight. No matter how depressed you are with your lot in life. This book will forever change not only the way you look, but also your attitudes about weight, fat, food, and activity. The program outlined will make you feel good, look healthier, and be more energetic.

This book is not just for obviously fat people. It is also for those of you who give the appearance of cutting a mean figure. You who select your fashions well to hide your fitness faults. You look trim, but you're not. You have rolls of fat where your skin used to be taut and your muscles firm. You may even weigh the same as you did at high school graduation. Deep down, however, you know your figure is not what it used to be, or what it could become.

The trim and fit will also get something from this book. Throughout you'll find reinforcement for what you already do. You'll learn the value of many of your favorite physical activities for weight and fat control. You'll find new information on why and how your fat must be kept low for optimum living.

Here is a plan that works. Over the past 10 years I've worked with thousands of people who have benefited from the plan outlined. I've seen hundreds of research reports supporting this concept. This plan works because it:

- Treats the cause of obesity and extra pounds, not the symptoms;
- Points out the wrongness of scales in determining your best weight;
- Shows you that eating is okay;
- Demonstrates that dieting is filled with psychological hangups, physiological roadblocks, and cultural bugaboos;
- Proves that *real* physical activity is the key to weight control;
- Proves that fat is the issue, not pounds, in a better looking body and health;
- Highlights once and for all the "best" activities for permanent fat and weight loss; and
- It demonstrates that anyone can lose fat.

You'll also find that losing weight and fat via exercise can be pleasant, rewarding, and stimulating. A promise few authors can back up.

I know what you are thinking: Another stairway to heaven. Charlie's plan for life, liberty, and the pursuit of happiness.

If you have extra pounds of fat or you don't like your figure, I don't blame you for being skeptical. You've probably been burned a dozen times with promises of a new you for only $10. Most likely, you have a closet full of diet books, body wraps, and health club membership forms. Your teeth may still be shaking from paranoia-producing diet pills.

Believe me, nothing turns me off more than high pressure salesmen pushing phony weight loss devices or plans. I too dislike their lack of knowledge and misguided enthusiasm. I also feel many newspaper and magazine editors should know better than print ads which promise you a program which will burn fat right off your body or help you burn more fat than 96 miles of running.

I'm not selling you anything. You needn't spend another penny in your quest to lose weight. This plan is simple, cheap, and effective. Thousands of YMCA members in over 500 cities across the United States and Canada have put the principles of this book into practice. They have lost weight, inches, and fat. They've gained improved health and fitness. They've increased their energy and self-concept. They've proven that it works.

I have both personal and professional reasons for writing this book. First the personal: like everyone else, I want a good looking body. I want a low amount of fat and muscles that are well toned. I want to be able to look at myself in the mirror and not be embarrassed. So does my wife. Narcissistic? I don't think so. I'm just honest and I'm a physical person.

During my professional career (18 years in 1980) I have worked with the obese, unfit, the fit, and the athlete. For the fit person and the athlete I know that top performance is contingent upon a low amount of body fat. For the unfit and obese, it is important that they reduce their body fat for health and beauty reasons. As a result I have developed programs and consulted with people to help them achieve their goals.

My advanced degrees focused on weight and fat loss. My master's thesis investigated the effectiveness of different weight control programs for college age men. My doctoral dissertation examined the amount of exercise necessary to improve a person's cardiovascular fitness and reduce body fat and weight.

Currently, I'm not doing experimental research in the area of adipose tissue, cellular physiology, dietary eating patterns, or psychological tendencies toward food. Instead, I'm using my previous research and the work of other experimenters to develop weight control programs—trying various programs and concepts on for size with many people, throwing out things which don't seem to work, accepting those things which do, and trying to figure out why certain techniques work for some individuals some of the time and fail miserably at other times.

As a result, during the past six years I've written, developed, and field-tested two programs for the National Board of YMCAs and developed a program for Phillips Petroleum Corporation in Bartlesville, Oklahoma. One program is Feelin' Good—a heart health program for children. Here obesity and its relationship to all other coronary risk factors are explored. Making exercise fun for the obese child is a focal point of this program. The second program is Activetics—a weight control program for adults. This program demonstrates to adults that regular vigorous exercise (and even small amounts of exercise) are significant in reducing body fat. This book serves as a text for that YMCA program. The third program I developed, Living Well, is a complete wellness plan which helps people lead more positive lives by improving their own general well-being.

All this experimentation has brought me to the conclusion that over-fatness is a complex issue. It is also a highly emotional one. I trust that I have been sensitive to these considerations in this book. And while I am biased, I think this book will prove to you that *proper* types of exercise are mandatory in weight and fat control programs.

Working with people who have fat and weight problems is both rewarding and frustrating. It's rewarding to see people reduce their body fat, change their personalities, and become new and better people. But it's also frustrating, because some people start to make progress and then slip back into their old ways. I feel for them greatly, and I'm constantly trying to help them along.

Solving fat and weight problems is an intensely personal issue. I hope that you will read this book carefully and thoughtfully, and that you will apply the principles set forth. If you do, the result will be a drop in body fat and weight.

I trust that you will be patient. For most of us, weight comes on slowly. Then, when a certain weight is reached which we thought we would never attain, our reaction is: "I've got to lose these pounds now—regardless of the consequences." That type of thinking is fuzzy. Anyone can lose weight. The mark of a successful program is: Does it stay off and do you look good afterwards? This plan promises you both. If you're willing to take the time.

The information to follow represents the consensus of scientific opinion of professionals working in this area. Fifty percent of what I say is based on solid facts. Another 25% is based upon the trend of current research. It's not proven, but it's certainly a workable practice for you to follow. The other 25% is my best guess: the way the research seems to fit or the most logical explanation.

This is not another "diet revolution" book. Instead, it's a program based on increasing your physical activity level and making healthful but not drastic changes in your diet. The program takes you through three necessary steps to improve your body's appearance.

The first section will get you to *admit your problem*. Surprisingly, this can be the most difficult thing for some people.

The second step is to *plan the attack*. Here you'll learn how to design a program for your body's own needs.

Finally, you'll learn how to *stick with it*. Hints will be given to help keep you from being a weight control dropout.

In this book I can show you the way. The rest is up to you. You are going to have to decide for yourself how long, how often, and how frequently you must exercise. It's also your job to decide the types of exercise which are going to be best for you.

Most experts agree that 30 minutes of exercise, four times a week is enough to get your body into fairly respectable condition. It's possible, of course, that some of you will see results with less; some of you will need more. The important thing is that you get started now and do it regularly. Good luck and God bless.

1

Fat: How Does It Get On Our Bodies?

Fat is America's heartbreak. Self-concepts, relationships, and health have been destroyed by unwanted bumps, bulges, and pounds. It seems that the fatter people get, the sadder they get. Life is a real drag for the obese. It's tragic.

Americans hate fat. At least we talk like we do. "Got to cut down. I'm getting too fat. Gonna go on a diet. Better watch your calories, dear. Why is it that everything that tastes good is fattening? I look at food and I gain weight. My New Year's Resolution is to lose 20 pounds."

Let's face it. We're just too fat. No matter how much we try to girdle, shake, or roll it away, we are still too fat. Our clothes are too small. We need king size beds. Our belts are too short. It seems like everyone is trying to starve, steam, medicate, and meditate their fat into oblivion. But, it still sneaks up on us and violates us. Few escape its wrath.

The next time you're in a supermarket look around you. Count 10 people at random. Note how many need to do something about the size of their stomachs, arms, legs, or jowls. If you find less than five, you have a unique group. That's because even the most conservative estimates indicate that 50% or more of the adult population carry too much fat. Another 25% of the population are able to control their weight but are worried about it. That means if you don't have a problem with fat, the person sitting or standing next to you probably does.

If fat was something like baldness, it wouldn't be such a problem. We could just buy wigs and then lead normal lives. No one would have to know of our condition. The problem is that fat is far more serious and can neither be hidden nor ignored. Eventually, it is noticeable both visibly and physically. It increases our waistline and robs us of good appearances. It expands our body and sabotages our supply of energy. Worse, it clogs our arteries and leads to disease conditions that can kill us. It should be considered public enemy #1.

Fat does not discriminate. It affects both rich and poor, old and young, male and female, black and white, and all shades in between. We see fat in Congress and in our coffee klatch. The car salesman may be fat. And probably the lady buying the car is too. Celebrities spend weeks every year at fat farms trying to shed, while ordinary Janes and Johns settle for diets and sauna belts.

Not only are we too fat, but it looks like we're getting fatter. Some of my own testing shows that over the past 10 years, college freshmen women have more body fat than their predecessors. The American Seating Company says that derrieres of United States citizens have expanded more than two inches in the past 30 years. They ought to know. The company must now provide chairs with larger seat bottoms to accommodate spreading hips. Clothing manufacturers for the military report that individuals of both sexes, and all ages, have shown an increase in girth of arms, chest, and other body parts over the past few years. Government reports show that each decade we are getting fatter. Americans gain an average of one to two pounds a year from age 20 to 50.

Americans are heavier than any other population in the world. Why? It cannot be solely attributed to an increase in height. Nor can we blame it on the fact that we're eating more calories. Study after study has shown that Americans are not eating more. In fact, if anything, we are eating fewer calories than previous generations. Government calculations show that on a per capita basis Americans are eating 200 calories per day less than did their counterparts 20 to 30 years ago.

All of this is happening in spite of the fact that millions of Americans seem to have a fascination with healthful living. Organic foods, "diet best sellers," revealing fashions, memberships to health clubs, jogging, TV health experts, and magazine articles on fitness pervade our culture. We're told to shape up, lose those unwanted pounds, and get the body we've always wanted.

Yet something's wrong. People keep getting fatter. The reason is that Americans are not as active as we used to be. Oh I know, Americans are more active socially, politically, and domestically than any other population that has walked the face of this planet. But when it comes to real physical activity, it just isn't so. Don't confuse busyness—shopping, housework, office work, yard work, occasional rounds of golf, picking the kids up at school, etc.,—with sufficient physical activity.

My grandfather and I serve as perfect examples. My grandfather was a true physical being. He was up every morning at 4 o'clock. He spent two hours in the barn milking cows and doing farm chores. From there he then walked to work where he slaved away in the coal mines for a good 12 hours. That was pick and shovel work. In the evening he returned home— walking, did a few more farm chores, and collapsed into bed.

Compare that with my life. I'm up by 6 or 7 in the morning, eat my breakfast, drive to work, and sit at a desk four hours in the morning. Then I take a lunch break, sit again for another four or five hours in the afternoon, and finally return home for some more sedentary activities.

To offset this problem, I run. But I'm still really a sedentary person who happens to spend additional time running every day. I'm sure I could run circles around my grandfather, even when he was in his prime. But he could work me under the table.

Everything he did in life demanded a tremendous expenditure of physical energy. Obesity was not a problem for him, but it is a potential problem in my life. I'm just not active enough.

I'm not suggesting that we go back to the dark ages or even slip back a couple of decades. I like it right here in modern-day America. But I think we all have to recognize that because we live in modern-day America we must pay the rent. We have to pay for all the labor-saving devices we have. We can pay for it with increased physical activity through such things as walking, running, biking and swimming, or we can choose to be fat. It's that simple.

The Real Key To Weight Control

Activity—using your body the way it was meant to be used—is the key to weight and fat control. Fat accumulates not so much because of overeating, but because of *underdoing*.

We all know someone who claims to "eat like a bird" but gains weight anyway. And someone else who "eats like a horse" but never puts on an extra ounce. There's a tendency to disbelieve both stories, because up until very recently in our society, the accepted "cause" of overfatness has always been "eating too much."

Chances are, however, that both these people are telling the truth about how much they eat. We now know that many people who are too fat eat no more than the "lucky" ones who have no problem with their weight, and that most people—fat or thin—eat somewhere between 2,000 and 2,300 calories* worth of food per day. So, it's beginning to look as though the reason one person gains weight while another doesn't has less to do with the relative amounts of food eaten than was previously suspected. Authorities in the fields of health and nutrition are finally making the right connection between obesity and the sedentary lives we lead.

*Every man, woman, and child in America has 3,000 to 3,300 calories set before him or her each day. But approximately one-third is thrown away.

The sitters of the world have always run to fat. I don't think it's any coincidence that throughout literature and history we find the recurring image of the sedentary, rotund merchant in contrast to the lean and muscular hunter or warrior. Somehow, it doesn't make much sense to assume that soft, round people are just naturally attracted to sedentary occupations; while lean, wiry people like to be active. It seems more logical to conclude that when people sit around a lot, they get fat, and people who are active stay lean.

Several studies bear this out. A particularly interesting one was made of an industrial population in Calcutta. At one end of the scale were the sedentary workers—office personnel, merchants, etc.—who sat during most of their working hours. Next came the mechanics, drivers, weavers, and others whose work called for an average amount of activity. Finally, there were the ashmen, coalmen, and blacksmiths—extremely active people who were forced to carry their body weight for eight or nine hours daily. The results were fascinating. The sedentary merchants and clerks ate about the same as the moderately active people, but weighed considerably more. And while the very active blacksmiths, ashmen, and others ate as much as the sedentary workers, they weighed significantly less.

A world-famed nutritionist, Jean Mayer, Ph.D., formerly of Harvard University, has also concluded that inactivity is a primary cause of obesity. His study of overweight high school girls indicated that they ate no more and some ate less than their classmates of normal weight. But they exercised far less and went in for "sitting" activities. In fact, they spent *four times* as many hours watching TV as the others. Similar studies done with boys revealed the same pattern.

It's obvious to me and to a lot of others who have a professional interest in fitness and health that the reason dieting so seldom works is that it merely treats a symptom, not the problem itself. People gain weight not because they consume too many calories, but because they're inactive and don't burn off enough.

The "Good Life" And How It Makes Us Fat

Fat, it seems, is one of the prices we pay for having achieved the "good life"—by which is meant an existence of physical ease and inactivity.

One of the country's biggest health problems, "creeping obesity," used to be blamed on affluence. But we now know it has more to do with indolence. With all our appliances and gadgets and gizmos, our power this and automatic that, we can do with a flick of a switch or the push of a button what once would have taken body power—and lots of it—to accomplish. We're great at conserving energy—our own physical energy—and the question arises: what are we saving all that energy *for*?

As I said before, I wouldn't be especially happy at the prospect of going back to the days when everything had to be done by hand or foot. But at least our grandparents, unless they had servants to do all the dirty work for them, didn't have to contend with obesity and its related problems in the same way we do.

Sixty or seventy years ago, before the technological revolution, people used their bodies in a way very few of us do now. Most of the population lived in small towns or on farms, but even city dwellers did a fair amount of walking—footing it to work, to the market, to visit friends, to parties and dances. Indeed, strolling to and from an evening's entertainment was usually considered *part* of the entertainment.

Vertical houses were the rule rather than the exception and there was a good deal of walking or running up and down stairs. Garden tractors didn't exist and lawns were cut with hand mowers. Snow was shoveled, leaves were raked (neither was sucked up by one of those power-driven vacuum devices). Wood was cut and stacked for the fireplace. In coal heated homes, the furnace had to be stoked and the ashes carried out regularly. Rugs were beaten. So was cake batter. Whipped cream was cream that was whipped—by hand, not something that got squooshed out of an aerosol can. Clothes were scrubbed clean on a washboard, hung out on a line to dry, then dewrinkled with an iron that probably weighed seven pounds or more.

I could go on and on, but that would belabor the point which is, of course, that they had to work awfully hard back then. So hard that fat was a luxury only the leisure class could afford. These are far more democratic times. All but the very poor can own the labor-saving devices that program activity right out of our lives.

Inactivity is so much a part of our culture we actually have to go out of our way to burn off calories. But unless we do, do you know what happens to all that "saved" energy—the calories that don't get burned off? It gets deposited in the "bank," the fat cells of our bodies.

The trends that encourage obesity are likely to continue. The more labor-saving devices we acquire—and it seems as though someone comes up with a new one every day—the fewer calories are burned away and the greater is the weight gain. Short of passing a law banning the sale of all mechanical and electronic gadgets and gizmos (including autos and TV sets), there's only one way to reverse the trend: we absolutely must become more physically active.

The Truth About Exercise

I'm very well acquainted with the argument that says, in effect, that stepping up one's physical activity is an ineffective way to fight excess poundage; that the only *real* way to lose weight is to diet.

I'm not quite sure why such a pro-diet, anti-activity bias should exist. The diet people are surely not in cahoots with the manufacturers of labor-saving devices. But the bias does exist. I only wish I had a dollar for every magazine and newspaper article, every pamphlet and book, stating the rationale behind this kind of thinking. Usually, it's presented something like this: "In order to burn off a pound of fat—3,500 calories—you'd have to walk 35 miles, split wood for 7 hours, or play volleyball for 10 hours."

Sounds pretty discouraging, right? Strictly speaking, the equations are correct. But it's as misleading as saying that in order to lose 10 pounds by limiting your food intake, you'd have to fast for 15 days.

In other words, the pro-diet argument ignores the cumulative effect of physical activity—which is no less than the key to the entire national overfatness dilemma. While it may indeed take six hours of handball to burn off one pound of fat, you certainly don't need to play six *consecutive* hours of the game in order to do so. You could, instead, play an hour a day for 6 days. Or a half-hour a day for 12 days. Or a half-hour a day every other day for 24 days. At that rate, you'd burn off 15 to 36 pounds in a year. But why get hung up on handball, unless it's a game you enjoy? If you took three 15-minute walks a day, you'd lose a pound in 15 days, and that's 24 pounds a year!

Another often-stated argument against physical activity as a good way to lose weight has it that most activities don't burn off enough calories to make any significant difference. But if you took a look at the caloric requirement tables issued by the World Health Organization of the United Nations and the United States National Research Council, you'll see that a "sedentary" man requires approximately 2,400 calories a day to maintain his weight, while a "very active man" needs about 4,500. Laborers, soldiers, and athletes may have to consume, 6,000 or more calories per day in order to keep from burning away to nothing.

It's obvious that activity *does* make a difference. If intense physical activity results in a need in one person for almost twice as many calories as a less active person, then activity certainly is a major factor in determining whether weight will be gained, maintained, or lost.

Activity burns calories and calories count, though not necessarily in quite the same way so many people think they do. If you're concerned about weight, the number of calories you burn off is more important than the number you take in.

Why "A Few Extra Calories" Are Important

Physical activity is anything that gets you moving, using your muscles, burning off calories. Your fat-loss plan might be based on walking half an hour a day. Or dancing. Or stretch-and-bend calisthenics, if you like that sort of thing. Or on making a few simple switches in your daily life—like running up a few flights of steps instead of using the elevator and standing instead of sitting whenever you can (while you're ironing, for example, or when you talk on the telephone). Anything, in short, that burns off even *a few extra calories.*

A few extra calories doesn't sound like much, I know. And it isn't. But the difference between maintaining your ideal weight and gaining—or losing—pounds over the months and years is usually a matter of just a "few extra calories" a day.

To illustrate, suppose you eat 2,400 calories worth of food during a 24-hour period and your level of activity is such that you burn off exactly 2,400 calories as you work, sleep, and play your way through the day. Supply and demand are equal. Your body neither calls on reserves to make up a deficit, nor does it deposit extra calories in the form of fat. You're maintaining your weight.

But, if you take in 2,500 calories and burn off only 2,400 of them, your body will "store" those 100 unnecessary calories in its fat cells until such time as they're needed for energy.

One pound of fat is the equivalent of 3,500 unnecessary calories. It makes no difference whether those calories come from peanuts or pastry. With this in mind, we can see that if you eat 100 calories more than you burn off through physical activity, at the end of 35 days you'll have gained a pound. And if you continue on at the same rate, you'll be ten pounds heavier at the end of the year.

Well, most people don't gain weight at a steady ten-pound-a-year rate. If they did, we'd be a nation of 400-pounders. But as we've seen, even those who do are out of caloric balance by a mere 100 calories a day.

Most obesity problems are the result of being just a few calories per day out of balance. If you had some way of determining just how many calories out of balance you are, you could immediately stop gaining weight by finding an activity that could put you back into balance by burning off those few extra calories. And if you could find some *pleasant* way of burning off those calories, you could say goodbye to dieting—forever. That's what this book is all about.

If you're still in doubt about the significance of "a few extra calories," let me explain. The National Research Council periodically publishes a booklet detailing the recommended daily allowance of various nutrients for the different sexes, ages, and health states of Americans. Included in this book are the number of calories a person needs to eat to *maintain* his or her body weight. They have determined the number of calories a person uses through sleeping, working, etc., throughout the day.

Several decades ago when the book was first released the Council indicated that the average sedentary man needed to eat 3,000 calories a day to maintain his body weight. The average woman needed 2,400 calories a day. By the 1970's times had changed. Today, according to the Council, the average man uses 2,200 calories a day while the average woman uses about 1,600. In thirty years, 800 calories of activity were eliminated due to labor-saving devices.

One or two labor-saving devices would not be a problem. But put all 987 of them together and we've got significant problems. We have an extension phone which probably adds two pounds of body fat a year. We use electric typewriters rather than manual typewriters. That's another 6 or 7 pounds a year. The automatic dishwasher amounts to about two pounds a year. Ranch type homes save another 5 to 10 pounds of fat a home. We have two or more automobiles which amount to a good 10 pounds a year or more. Labor-saving devices are super, but not when it comes to burning calories.

Fat.* No one likes it. Yet until we understand just how that fat gets on our bodies, we'll never get rid of it. From now on, I want you to stop thinking about food and begin thinking about moving. The easiest, safest, and most effective way to lose fat is to begin a plan that is based on physical activity. You'll find that plan in the next chapter.

*See Appendix A—The Physiology of Fatness for an indepth discussion of fat.

2

The Inches Off
No-Diet Plan

People just don't get fat overnight. The fat doesn't appear in massive chunks here and there. Instead, getting fat is a relentlessly slow, steady process. My travels around the country as an author, consultant, and lecturer on matters of fitness and weight control have introduced me to many people whose lives confirm this.

Wade Oplinger was an accomplished athlete in high school and college. During the early years of his marriage he kept active in local recreational athletic leagues playing basketball, softball, and soccer. He was a real bon vivant. He didn't climb stairs, he bounded up them. He thought nothing of pushing the lawn mower for an hour, weeding his garden, and playing basketball after dinner. He enjoyed outdoor activities and often took his family to the beach on Saturdays. In the winter he hunted, played hockey on an outdoor pond, and often took his family sledding where he would pull his two boys up the hill over and over again. He really enjoyed life.

The years passed. He received a few nice promotions at work. The added responsibilities took more of his time and energy, but he took these in stride. He also didn't mind when his church asked him to chair the finance committee. And since his kids were now attending the local school, he felt he should join the Parent Teacher Organization. He was promptly assigned to a committee. These activities combined to crowd out the time he normally spent enjoying outdoor activities. Consequently, he started to put on weight. It was nothing drastic at first. A pound here, a couple of pounds there. Occasionally some of his old cronies would chide him about getting a little pudgy around the middle, but he laughed it off and attributed to his wife's good cooking. He promised himself that someday he'd get "back into shape."

Within a couple of years his lifestyle changed dramatically. Now he does little more than drag himself off to work in the morning, haul himself back home, and dawdle around waiting until it's time for bed. He's always too tired for golf, tennis, or basketball—things he enjoyed doing in his earlier years. When he was married he was a slim 170 pounds. Now he's huge. Over 240 pounds. On top of it, he seems to be uptight. His job no longer challenges him and he seems to catch every bug that comes around. He just isn't that happy, jovial picture of vitality he once was.

"I admit it," he shrugged in a conversation with me. "I don't like the way I look."

Only one man's problem? Hardly. Picture this: Anita was a real knockout in her college days. Perfect measurements and facial features—5'7" and 128 pounds. But ten years of married life, three children, Italian cooking, and virtually no real physical activity changed her svelte figure into 192 pounds of softness and obesity. Today, she is afraid to leave her home—afraid a classmate might recognize her and be shocked. Anita is depressed with herself, her family, and her lot in life.

Tragic. Yet millions are just like Wade and Anita. Fat people are not the robust, jovial people we think they are. And because they don't like the way they look, they are willing to try anything to slim down. Anything, that is, but exercise.

Let's look at Wade again. He has tried every diet, every gadget, and every device, all to no avail. Once he ate nothing but carrot sticks and celery for a week. By the end of the week he was ecstatic. He was also very weak. While he had lost 9 pounds in seven days, he had also practically starved himself to death. Naturally, he didn't stick with it very long. He celebrated his loss of weight with a small food binge. It felt so good to eat what he wanted that he did it again. Soon he was back to his old eating habits. When he finally got enough courage to get back on the scales, he was shocked to find he was almost back up to 240 pounds. That made him feel guilty. So he returned once again to eating because it made him feel better, and in a short time he was well over 240 pounds.

He was very unhappy about this, so he bought something called a "sauna suit." The ad said he could lose over four pounds by just playing basketball in it for an hour or so. And he did. I watched him pour the perspiration out of the suit after the game. Sure enough, he lost four pounds. Of water. Not fat, but water. Soon his body requested a replacement and after several glasses to abate his thirst, he regained the lost weight. And got upset with his suit, never to wear it again. (Which probably prolonged his life—they're dangerous.)

Some of the saner diets Wade tried worked. For a while. Once he shed 20 pounds and kept them off for over six months. He looked pretty good too, though he still had that annoying paunch. But as soon as he went off the diet, his weight climbed again. Currently he weighs 245 pounds.

The most distressing part of Wade's story is that he has never really been on top of things since he started putting on weight. Not even when he's losing weight successfully. The old zip has disappeared. A simple cold lays him up for two weeks. He's tired all the time, yet he gets 7 to 8 hours of sleep each night. And he sometimes falls asleep in front of the television after dinner. If he were a car, I'd say he was running on 3½ cylinders with partially deflated tires and a worn out transmission. And he's only 42 years old.

Anita is no different. She has tried pills, candy diet aids, every diet you can think of, and even hypnosis. She has tried exercising with people on TV and has joined every new health spa in town. All to no avail. She is still fat. I met her at a lecture. She asked me what new exercise equipment I could recommend to help her lose weight. When I told her "none," she was shocked. Flabbergasted. She argued with me about how the health club down the street had shiny new rollers that were *guaranteed* to remove her flab. When I told her the best thing she could do for herself right now was walk, she looked at me incredulously. "Walk? I walk all the time. I chase after my kids all day and do housework. Kuntzleman, you're crazy. I'm too tired to move my body any more."

Anita has yet another problem to deal with. Ironically, popular culture prizes a shapely female figure and yet perpetuates the myth that exercise is unfeminine when exercise would, in fact, help women maintain an attractive figure. It is an absurd situation—one that makes it extremely difficult for women to do anything about the way they look.

Although it has been reported that, on the average, women have a slightly lower fitness level than men in all areas except flexibility, research clearly points out that this is due to cultural patterns rather than biological factors. Until recently, women were not supposed to sweat. Strenuous physical activity was unbecoming to a prim and proper female. The "rough stuff" was strictly the men's private domain.

This deplorable way of thinking is ridiculous. The fitness needs of women are the same as those of men. Consequently, the guidelines set forth in this book apply to both men and women.

Life has developed into a disaster for both Wade and Anita. They are full of guilt, depression, lethargy, fear of food, and lousy self-concepts. They are exploited by authors, food manufacturers, physicians, and coaches. They are discriminated against by employers, colleges, insurance companies, and clothing manufacturers. It's time to put an end to those fraudulent practices, opinions, and concepts.

Losing weight is not easy. But it is possible. Losing weight takes a commitment. I hold no false promises. But the plan I have outlined will make you feel better and you will enjoy life more. Obviously though, I can't lose your weight for you. That's your job. I can only show you the way. You must put into practice the plan I have outlined.

At times, what I have to say may make you wince. I will force you to take a good hard look at yourself. You will need to be honest. But I think I can help you. I want you to get out of the guilt trap that surrounds dieting. I want you to realize that dieting is an outright fraud and that eating is okay. I'm not so concerned about whether you eat fish, carrots, bread, or yogurt. Eat them all. My concern is that you feel good about the way you look and that you have enough energy to enjoy this gift of life.

One note of caution: if I were packaging this, I would add this note to the box: CAUTION: THE AUTHOR HAS DE-TERMINED THAT THE CONTENTS OF THIS PACKAGE MAY SIGNIFICANTLY ALTER YOUR LIFESTYLE. If you follow this plan carefully, your life will be different. Sources of entertainment may change. Attitudes toward food will be altered. Even new feelings about your body will develop.

But I think you'll find the changes worth the risk. You'll welcome the new you with open (and better looking) arms. Over and over again I've seen people change. Both in appearance and attitude. The comments I hear go something like this: "I feel great, I sleep better, No more depression, I'm sexier, I'm eating what I like, I have more energy, I'm enjoying life."

The funny thing is that no one mentions losing weight, even though that's why they signed up for the program in the first place. Of course, they all lose weight. But the weight loss is no longer *the* objective. What keeps them going and sticking to the program is their good feelings and increased energy. They had forgotten how much fun life could be and were ecstatic with their rediscovery of the pleasant aspects of an active and healthy life. Remember, no gimmicks, gadgets, or tricks. There's nothing mysterious about this plan. In a nut shell, here it is:

THE THREE STEP INCHES OFF NO-DIET PLAN

1. Admit Your Problem
2. Plan The Attack
3. Stick With It

With this three step plan there are no magic bullets. Just some new (and old) ideas on losing fat. Let's look at the components of this plan briefly.

. Admit Your Problem

Believe it or not, this is perhaps one of the most difficult steps to the plan. It's easy to look at someone else and say they're fat. We have become extremely adept at pointing out other people's faults, while at the same time we have become very insensitive to our own. That's just human nature.

Unless you admit you have a problem, you will never solve it. I want you to take a good look at yourself and decide whether or not you think you are fat. In another chapter, I will offer some tests that will help you make your decision. Some are simple, some are exotic. I hope you take the time at least to stand in front of a full length mirror with little or no clothing on and evaluate what you see. You don't have to tell anyone else. They already know. You are the one who needs to be convinced that you have a problem.

A woman friend of mine used the mirror test. One morning after the kids had left for school she got undressed in front of a full length mirror. Her first reaction was: "Who's that?"

She actually did not recognize her body. She thought someone else much larger had somehow slipped into her skin.

Upset with herself she immediately starting doing sit-ups,

side leg raises, and swimming. Over the months she was doing 250 sit-ups and side leg raises, and 70 laps in the pool—daily.

Now her stomach is flat. Her hips thin. Her legs lean. She looks great! She rates a 10.

I'm not advocating swimming miles in a pool, doing 250 sit-ups or running marathons to lose weight. I've simply told her story to prove a point. You must *admit* that you are too fat before you can be successful in any fat or weight loss program. Saying you're a little pudgy or too big boned is not admitting to anything. To be successful you must "fess up." Can you honestly say you look as good as you want to? Are you as thin, firm, and taut as you were as a teenager? If you are, you're a rare specimen in our society.

No one had to tell Ginny Murling she was fat. Ginny knew it. I mean, when you weigh 345 pounds and stand just a shade over 5 feet tall, you *know* you're fat. Yet Ginny accepted it as her lot in life. Her albatross. She resigned herself into thinking she was just one of those fat ones who could never be skinny. Then one day *she decided* she'd had enough of the fat life. She walked into the Rome, New York YMCA and enrolled in an exercise class. She made a conscious decision to do something about the way she looked. Now Ginny has her weight problem under control. Last time I spoke to her she weighed 170. It took a lot of discipline and it took a lot of hard work. But before all that, it took a decision.

How many times have you heard one of your smoking friends declare, "One of these days I've got to quit smoking these things."? That's the way we think when it comes to doing something about our extra fat. The truth is, many of us know that we need to lose extra pounds. Yet we placate ourselves by thinking all we need to do is go on a crash diet and we'll get back to our slim and trim youthful years. And you know, it just doesn't happen that way. You need to make a conscious decision that you want to do something about the way you look.

If you think you are too fat, and want to lose it now, turn to the very last blank page of this book. Write the following: "I have decided I don't like the way I look. I am going to take an active role to change my appearance." Then sign your name and write in the date. When you get up out of bed tomorrow morning, turn to that page and read it to yourself. Do it again for a week. It may sound silly, but it may also be just what you need to convince yourself you're serious about changing.

One of my major complaints with the diet books is that they look at only one side of the weight loss equation. They tell you to stop eating this, limit your intake of that, and load up on something else. And yet, if you examine your eating habits in the past several years, you will probably find that you are eating no more than what you ate when you were thin.

Recently the government has pointed out that over the past several decades the number of calories the average American eats per day has declined. Interestingly, during that same period our weight has increased. The average weight of a woman under 30, today, is up to seven pounds heavier than her counterpart in 1959. Men are even worse off. Every age group shows an average gain. The only logical conclusion is that Americans are using fewer calories—they are less active than their parents and grandparents. Mark Hegsted, Ph.D., Administrator of the United States Human Nutrition Center, Science and Education Administration, has said that today the average American must increase his physical expenditure if he wants to get adequate nutrition. In other words, we have come to the point in our existence where we need so few calories each day that it is probably impossible to get enough calories to insure a proper balance of proteins, carbohydrates, fats, vitamins, and minerals.

The bottom line in all this discussion is this: you are too fat because you don't move your body enough. I know you are busy. I know you are active in your social, occupation, and family life. But let's face it. You are not active *physically*. Your activities are not the calorie burning kind.

Take some time to look over your daily routine. How much

time is spent sitting? How far do you walk? How many labor-saving devices do you use? Do you climb stairs instead of riding the elevator? Do you do anything during the day that causes you to huff and puff for 20 to 30 minutes? This self-evaluation can be as simple as answering the above questions or as advanced as the inventory in Chapter #6. The key to this plan is taking a look at your current lifestyle to see if there are ways you can program more activity into it. Once you know how many calories you are using compared to the number of calories you are eating, you can plan ways to lose weight through activity.

2. Plan The Attack

This is the *fun* part. After going through the first step, you will know exactly how much more activity you need to program into your life in order to lose the amount of weight you want to lose. I underscore the word fun. Losing weight doesn't have to be a drag. It doesn't have to be a process of self-denial. Losing weight can be one of the most enjoyable parts of your day. Just choose an activity you enjoy. Then treat yourself to it every day. Not only will you lose weight, but you will find yourself looking forward to the time of day you have set aside for the activity.

I'm going to give you guidelines on the "best" exercises for you. Some may surprise you. You may find that your favorite activity may not be a super fat burning exercise. But don't despair. There are plenty of good exercises which will help you keep your weight permanently under control. (See Chapter #7)

As you plan your attack against fat, forget all your excuses. Save them for something you really don't want to do. I've heard lots of excuses for not exercising in my years of working with people at Ys, schools, universities, corporations, and weight loss clinics. I suppose I could fill a book with them. It's too hot. It's too cold. I'm too fat. I'm too weak. I don't have the time. And so on. Yet as far as I'm concerned, there is only *one* valid excuse for not exercising: "I *choose* not to."

For many years I've talked about having a garden. Every year I made the excuse that I didn't have the time. Last year I finally put a garden in. I cultivated it once. At the end of the summer it was the biggest mess you ever saw. Weeds all over the place. My wife said she was going to take a picture of it and send it as a joke to *Organic Gardening and Farming*. At the end of the summer I realized that I really didn't want a garden. Once that decision was made I felt a lot better—no more anxiety or guilt. Take a tip from me. You make time to do the things you really want to do.

When we strip away all the rationalizations, we uncover the real reason people do not exercise. If you really want to do something, you will find a way to do it. In short, you choose to do it. Approach exercise in the same way.

You've heard all the adages. "There's no time like the present." "Don't wait for tomorrow for tomorrow may never come." "Don't put off until tomorrow what you can do today." They may all sound corny, but it's the best advice I can give. The sooner you get started, the sooner you will start seeing the results. Maybe you need to turn back to your declaration against fat on the last page of this book. But whatever you do, don't wait to begin your war on weight.

3. Stick With It

There are lots of reasons why people become weight control dropouts. Some of the reasons even appear to be good ones. I've known some who have started jogging but developed sore muscles and decided to quit. I've known others who tried walking but didn't dress properly for cooler weather and so they never really enjoyed it. I have a hunch that even you may have begun an exercise program once and then dropped it for what you thought was some very legitimate reason. But you can avoid being an exercise dropout. The knowledge of a few key preventive measures and extra hints (found in Chapter #10) will help you stick with the program until it becomes a regular part of your day.

So read on and enjoy. Come along on a journey to a new you. Try this new way to lose fat. It *works*. It works so well you will be amazed at the results. And once you have the figure or physique you want, you'll have a plan for staying there. What have you got to lose?

Part 1
ADMIT YOUR PROBLEM

3

A Not So Soft Look At Fat ... And How People Get That Way

Many people make the mistake of thinking that the overfat like being too heavy. Nothing could be further from the truth. Very few people want to be fat. Fat causes social, psychological, and physical problems. Problems that can ruin your enjoyment and zest for life. A key to losing weight without dieting is understanding just how people get fat. It certainly isn't by choice. Who would choose a condition that would lead to these problems:

- Fat high school women appear to have less chance of being admitted to the *college of their choice* than their thinner contemporaries—despite the fact that they have identical grades and college board scores.
- Young men and women who have completed college and want to teach are unable to get positions in certain communities if they are 25% or more overweight as defined by the standard height/weight charts. The same is true of firemen and policemen.
- Corporations, large and small, have indicated a definite bias in favor of fit, athletic looking people in filling upper echelon vacancies. A study ten years ago showed that only 10% of

the executives earning over $25,000 annually are overweight, while 35% of those earning $10,000 to $20,000 are more than 10 pounds overweight.

- The fat woman has fewer marital options, a fact that can affect her social and economic status.
- Insurance companies charge higher insurance premiums for fat people.
- The overfat are usually forced to pay more for their clothing.
- The overfat are ofttimes the brunt of jokes of poor taste. The statement "Everyone loves a fat man" is a lie.
- The fat person often demonstrates the personality characteristics of one who has been discriminated against. A "thin" society provides guilt trips by telling the overfat their condition is reversible, while skin color and natural origins are not.
- Ofttimes the overfat person has a low self-esteem which can aggravate depression, anxiety, and even psychotic states such as paranoia.
- Well-meaning physicians, relatives, and "friends" hassle the overfat for what they take to be "laziness" or "lack of willpower" or "lack of concern" for personal appearance. The myth of the "jolly fat man" dies hard.

The problems of overfatness, extend beyond your social and physiological being. Overfatness is dangerous. If allowed to progress without treatment, it can kill you. Being fat in itself is not fatal. But being too fat leads to numerous other life-shortening conditions and diseases that may do you in.

- Medical science has found that too much fat puts stress on your body's systems which can lead to heart disease, vascular problems, diabetes, kidney afflictions, digestive disorders, cancer, arteriosclerosis, high blood pressure, and arthritis.
- Surgery is more complicated with the fat person than with a person of normal body fat. In fact, the obese have less likelihood of surviving surgery.
- Extra fat makes you move more slowly. Result: because of fatigue, the overfat person cannot enjoy life to the fullest.

If fat is so hazardous and undesirable, why don't people lose it? Or, why don't they keep it off? These are the $64,000 questions. Or perhaps we should say $10 billion question. That's the amount Americans spend every year trying to lose weight. And 95% of those who do lose it gain it right back. Getting rid of fat is not as easy as some people like to make it seem.

One of my students is a perfect example. When Sam graduated from college he was six feet tall and weighed 180 pounds. In college he played basketball and baseball. He water skied in the summer. In short, he was a physical being. He had a super physique. After graduation, he assumed a job and became very sedentary—other than golf twice a week.

Over the years Sam's weight increased. By the year of his 10th college reunion, he had ballooned to 210 pounds. Upset with himself and fearing ridicule by classmates, Sam decided to lose some weight. Being a rational person, he first consulted his doctor. The doctor suggested a 1,200 calorie balanced diet. At first, Sam was angry. Twelve hundred calories was really Spartan. But he was willing to do anything to look better. He followed the plan faithfully over the weeks. His weight dropped. By June, Sam was down to 180 pounds. Ready to face his college classmates. In a swimsuit he was a little baggy and saggy, but in his Brooks Brothers suit, no one knew. He looked like good old Sam, the basketball man.

A month after the reunion, Sam went on vacation. He blew his diet. (He figured it wouldn't be any problem since he'd go back on it after his three week stay in Europe.) But two days after his vacation there was a company clambake, and still later two birthday parties. In a few weeks Labor Day rolled around, and Sam was back to his old eating habits. His weight was skyrocketing. By the end of the year he was back to 210 pounds. When he reached 215 pounds in March he decided something had to be done.

The current best seller told him calories didn't count. Carbohydrates were the bugaboo. So he followed the regimen of high protein, high fat, and low carbohydrate. During the first week he lost seven pounds. Excited, he stuck to the program. He lost a total of 20 pounds during the next six weeks. But soon his weight plateaued. In fact, it started to inch back up. He also felt tired all the time. He went to see his doctor for a checkup. An examination by the doctor showed that Sam not only had fatigue but also high blood pressure. The doctor ran a check on his cholesterol and triglycerides and found them severely elevated. Suspicious, the doctor inquired about Sam's eating habits. When the doctor heard what Sam was doing he hit high C. He quickly explained that a high fat, high protein diet can increase your chances of heart disease. And to make matters worse, he explained that most of the weight that Sam had lost was water and not fat.

Sam went home disillusioned. In the next few weeks the fat slid right back on and Sam soon weighed 220. Over the next five years Sam tried every diet best seller, drug, and weight loss plan known to man. But the pattern was always the same— weight loss, weight gain, weight loss, weight gain, etc. He was in the classic yo-yo syndrome. He was in the weight gain-weight loss cycle that Dr. Jean Mayer has called "the rhythm method of girth control." Tragically, Sam's blood has never been right since then. He's been continually plagued with cholesterol and triglyceride levels that are too high.

Unfortunately, there are too many Sams around. It has been estimated that only 5% of all the obese people who try to lose weight are successful in keeping their weight off. Another study has indicated that the average dieter goes on 2.3 diets per year. *Anyone can lose weight. But the real issue is: How do you keep the weight off?* Let's be rational. If any one of the best sellers which have appeared over the years had truly been successful, there would have been no reason for a new book to be written—or a new best seller to appear on the list.

The problem is that all dieting plans attack the symptoms and not the basic cause. Diets emphasize the food side of the

equation and completely ignore the physical activity side. Dieting is not successful in permanent weight or fat loss because it
is beset with physiological roadblocks, psychological hangups,
and cultural obstructions.

The Physiological Need For Food

Perhaps the best way to understand how people get fat is to first
understand what makes people eat. Physically, we must eat in
order to stay alive. It is that simple. Our bodies demand food,
and appears to demand it at regular intervals throughout the day.
That helps explain why dieting is usually unsuccessful. When
someone has abandoned a diet, the most popular reason for
giving up is summed up in a few words: "I was hungry all the
time." And they are probably right.

Hunger is perhaps one of the most misunderstood words in
the human vocabulary. Hunger is the craving for food usually
associated with stomach contractions, often called hunger pains.
The contractions produce a gnawing sensation that you experience when you skip breakfast and lunchtime approaches. (Most
of us, fortunately, have never known the severe pain of acute
hunger suffered by millions of starving people around the world.
Therefore, most of us do not understand true hunger.)

The term appetite is often confused with hunger. Appetite is a
desire for a specific type of food, such as strawberries, cookies,
milk, cake, soda, etc. Your appetite determines the kind of food
that you want to eat.

Satiety is the opposite of both hunger and appetite. It means
complete fulfillment—the absence of both hunger and appetite—
even though food may be available.

All of these terms—hunger, appetite, and satiety—refer to
complex sensations that determine your eating habits.

Surprisingly, the stomach does not control hunger. Your
brain does. Even people who have had part of their stomach
removed continue to experience hunger just as before. Hunger is
really a response to the level of blood sugar in the brain.

Scientists sometimes call this phenomenon the "glucostatic regulation of food intake." Although there are still missing links in this theory, it goes something like this:

The part of the brain that regulates your food intake is the hypothalamus—commonly known as the appestat. The appestat has special receptors that tell your body when you are hungry. When your blood sugar concentration falls too low, one part of the appestat is stimulated. Immediately, this part of your appestat sends out an alert to another part of your brain. This alert triggers a host of responses, two of which are:

1. An impulse to your stomach where contractions and a feeling of hunger begins.
2. A signal to your liver which starts to mobilize stored energy—a rather slow process.

What is not known with this theory is what determines the size of the meal eaten and the immediate sense of fullness after a meal. Some experts feel that in the stomach and intestines there may be special kinds of receptors that let the brain and the appestat know that you're full.

Most experts feel that bulk has very little to do with satisfying hunger for any period of time. You may have noticed this, since low calorie foods do not seem to "stick to your ribs." The reason is that calories (found in proteins, fats, and carbohydrates) are essential to satisfy hunger for any period of time. Proteins, fats, and carbohydrates provide the calories which in turn provide the blood sugar.

This phenomenon of calories, blood sugar, and the appestat demonstrate the futility of dietetic foods. People who use diet sodas, fruits, and crackers to lose weight and fat are just kidding themselves. They may lose weight in the initial stages of the diet, but their hunger will continue because of low sugar levels (not enough carbohydrates, proteins, and fats).

Scientific experiments illustrate this phenomenon. In one classic experiment, rats were given a certain amount of food over a period of time. Activity and diet were maintained at a constant level, and the rats were able to hold a steady diet. The researchers then changed 10% of their diet to materials that contained no calories—food very similar to that used by people who are dieting. They found that when the new food contained 10% inert materials, the rats ate approximately 10% more food. When the researchers raised the non-caloric portion to 20%, the animals ate 20% more food. That trend continued as the proportion of non-caloric food was increased. Finally, the animals literally ate themselves to death, attempting to satisfy their appetite with low calorie, high bulk foods.

So, calories are a necessary part of this theory. It's quite simple. If you don't get enough calories to raise your blood sugar level sufficiently, you are going to be hungry.

You may wonder why at certain times you are terribly hungry and then an hour or so later your hunger disappears. Earlier I told you that your brain signals both your stomach and liver when your blood sugar drops in your appestat. The signals to your stomach produce stomach contractions and a feeling of hunger. This response is immediate. So you start to look for food. When the liver is stimulated, however, it prepares to release sugar or glycogen. The activation of the liver, the actual release of the sugar, and the signal back to the appestat takes at least an hour. Therefore, your liver can only reduce your hunger about an hour after being stimulated if no food is eaten.

Unfortunately, we live in the "now generation." People don't want to wait that long. They spend 50¢ or a dollar on candy, sweet rolls, or a beverage.

Now you know why some foods satisfy hunger and others don't. But what's still not clear is why some people crave more food than others. That is, why do some people seem to be hungry all the time and others not?

Scientists think it's possible that the appestat or center of regulation may be "set" a little higher in some people than in others. A person whose appestat has a higher setting is usually the one who experiences greater difficulty in controlling weight. Although experiencing both hunger and satiety, the person with the high setting needs a little more food (glucose, to which proteins, carbohydrates, and fats are eventually converted) to satisfy the satiety center or appestat. Exactly why the appestat is set higher is not clear, but many scientists feel that the concept of the appestat is one which fits into human survival.

At one time humans had to hunt for their food or grow it themselves. We were extremely active during that period of history. In that primitive environment, game had to be stalked great distances, physically subdued, skinned, and prepared for eating. Those who planted crops had to spend long hours in the field. High appestat people were at an advantage in this environment. They felt hungrier sooner than others and thus went about the business of hunting much more avidly. They ate more food and stored more fat. And since they were physically active they also carried a lot more lean body tissue—that is bone, muscle, and organ tissue. When game was scarce, they could survive by living off their stored fat and lean body tissue. Clearly, having a high set appestat was an advantage in those days.

In modern Western society, the situation is reversed. No one needs to exert much effort to get food. A trip to the refrigerator does it. Or if the refrigerator happens to be empty, a quick drive (almost never a walk) to the supermarket. So the person with the high appestat setting is at a disadvantage. He or she still quietly harbors the ancient desire—instinct actually—to eat more in order to survive a food crisis—which almost certainly will never come. The appestat—indeed most of the systems and organs of the human body—is centuries behind the times.

A high appestat setting coupled with a sedentary lifestyle almost always leads to a weight problem. One can, of course, attempt to compensate by restricting caloric intake. You know what that means: bucking a continual gnawing desire for food.

So unless the will is truly Spartan, any diet is doomed to be an exercise in frustration, at least in the long run.

Suppose that by some magic you and your next door neighbor jumped back 5,000 years or more. In this magical world, you have a high set appestat and your friend has a low one. You, of course, are always hungry. Your appestat is always screaming for calories. So you are constantly on the prowl for food and eating whenever possible. The additional amount of food causes you to be heavier than your friend. Fortunately, since you are active most of your weight is in the form of bone, muscle, or organ tissue. Not fat. Your friend, on the other hand, is not very hungry, and very lean. His appestat does not demand a great amount of food.

At this time thousands of years ago, chances for a famine are pretty good. A famine that might last one, two, or more years. During the famine your neighbor does not survive. He simply does not have enough tissue (fat, bone, muscle, and organ tissue). But you do. You are emaciated, but you do survive for another period of plenty.

Thousands of years ago, you see, there was a very good reason to have extra tissue. It helped you get through those rough spots.

Now let's suppose by the same magic you and your neighbor jump ahead to today. As before, you both have appestats. Again, your appestat is set higher than your neighbor's, and you are hungrier than your counterpart. Unfortunately, you're not very active in gathering your food. You do not walk miles or till the soil. You simply walk to the refrigerator for your food or beverage. Your appestat calls for a lot of calories. But you do not burn many off. Certainly not enough to approach your appestat's demands. So you're fat. You are plagued with a constant battle of the bulge. When you try to diet your pounds off, your appestat screams for more food. Ultimately, your desire for food overwhelms you and your good intentions. So you eat. Your drive for food and calories is a lot stronger than your desire to have a slimmer figure or listening to your doctor's orders. Meanwhile, your neighbor with the low set appestat remains lean because he is rarely hungry.

When high appestat people diet, they are literally fighting their own instincts for more food. It's one thing to live with constant hunger when food is not available, but when it's all around you—sitting there in the refrigerator, displayed in the stores, staring out in glorious four-color detail from the pages of magazines, being eaten and gloated over on TV—well . . . that's tough to resist.

With activity, however, body and mind—instinct and reason— are not at cross-purposes. The body's instinctive desire for food does not subvert the rational decision to lose fat or weight. You eat as much as your appestat demands. But you burn off enough calories to match your appestat's requests.

Of course, there are other factors which influence the appestat other than the blood sugar level. But these factors do not predominate. These factors vary considerably from person to person but they are important and worthy of your consideration. They are:

- A higher body weight.
- A higher body fat.
- A greater number of fat cells.
- A lack of exercise.
- A hot environment or an increase in skin and blood temperature.
- An increase in stress or emotional pressure.
- The smell, taste, or thought of food.
- An increased amount of blood sugar released by the liver.
- An amino acid (protein) imbalance.
- A decreased amount of glucagon (a protein that elevates blood glucose levels).
- A large stomach size.

All of these may play a role in causing your appestat to demand more food.

Interestingly, exercise plays a role in the first five and possibly the first eight factors listed. Exercise, therefore, is important in your physiological need for food.

You can readily see how dieting causes problems. Your appestat may demand 2,500 calories a day. Yet your doctor's advice is 1,200 calories. It becomes a futile battle, since your desire for food ultimately overwhelms you.

Given the physiological explanation for eating, it's difficult to imagine anyone successfully warding off the urge to eat. And yet, that is only one reason why people eat. It may be the most obvious, but it may not be the strongest reason. The next chapter deals with a couple of very subtle yet powerful reasons why people continue to eat the way they do.

4

Eating When You Really Don't Want To

The appestat theory explains why diets are a lost cause. Physically, you need food to survive. Therefore, cutting food out of your daily diet doesn't make much sense, unless you eat for psychological rather than for physiological reasons. You see, food is often used as a devastating psychological tool. It begins in infancy and leads to a condition where stress, pressure, and boredom trigger people to eat excessive amounts of food.

The Psychological Theory

Vast numbers of children are encouraged to overeat (or at least to eat when they really don't have the desire to eat) in order to avoid negative consequences: "If you don't finish your dinner, dear, there will be no TV tonight." Or to get what they want: "If you finish your peas, I'll take you to the park after lunch." Or to win adult love and approval: "Such a good girl; you ate all your spinach."

All this is bad enough. But in addition, children are often rewarded with food when they've been "good" or submissive (think of the doctors who hand out lollipops to young patients when they don't cry). We also soothe and comfort children with food. I've seen parents give their kids cookies to divert attention from a badly scraped knee. I've been tempted to do it myself.

36

We seem to think there is love in a chocolate chip cookie or an apple pie.

When adults use food as a means of psychological manipulation, is it any wonder that their children invest eating with emotional connotations? Very often a child's first exposure to "force feeding" occurs within the first couple months of life. Many times a baby cries because he wants cuddling, companionship, a change of diapers, or a change of scene. But the new mother has a tendency to interpret any kind of crying as a demand for food, and if she is "modern," she will immediately attempt to gratify the child with breast or bottle. Thus, very early in life, the child learns to associate gratification of all emotional and physical needs with eating. Placating the baby with food when it is attention or stimulation it wants may also discourage the child's budding interest in actively exploring the outside world.

As the child becomes older the problem is compounded. Perhaps when the child was about two years of age, he fell and hurt himself. He ran into the house crying. Quickly, mother held him on her lap and said, "That's okay, son. Here's a lollipop." Soon everything was beautiful. A few days later he was outside playing with his best friend, when Whamo! He was hit right on the nose. Soon he was comforted with a lap, cookie, and love. Still later, he was supposed to go to the doctor. But he didn't want to go and told his mother, who said that if he didn't put up a fuss, they would go to the ice cream shop afterwards.

Established in babyhood and strengthened in childhood, the pattern of eating to relieve tension and frustration carries over into adulthood. Adults have job, domestic, and social pressures. They may even be bored. Because of this, they overeat. They are reacting to a behavior they learned years before. With this overeating there's a weight gain. The weight gain begets less activity (being heavier, we move less, become depressed at our figure, and tend to sleep even more). Because of this lessened activity, there is no natural outlet for the stress. Consequently, we eat even more.

It's a vicious circle: the more stress, the stronger the craving for food, the less active the person becomes—and the more weight is gained. In time, anxiety over obesity reaches a point where the obesity itself causes stress, and then the circle is complete.

Increased physical activity is the simplest means of breaking the obesity/stress/obesity syndrome. To understand why, we must once again go back in time.

For many thousands of years, human beings were engaged in a life-and-death struggle with the environment. Their bodies were ever-prepared for action. One didn't reason with wild animals and the forces of nature. In a dangerous situation, it was either fight or flight.

Today, the average person is underactive but overstimulated. Actual physical danger is rare, but we continue to be confronted by stressful, anxiety-producing situations, and the body's natural biological response to them is still to mobilize for action. Ordinarily, we must repress this response. We're civilized. In most instances, either to fight or to run away is equally inappropriate.

So the natural physical response gets bottled up, and this very bottling up causes more tension which, if not relieved, can lead to emotional or physical illness. Diseases resulting from, or aggravated by, stress include various metabolic ailments such as becoming overweight, endocrine malfunctions, gastrointestinal upsets and malfunctions, and musculoskeletal dysfunction. Emotional disorders include neurosis, depression, anxiety, and various compulsions. Each of these ailments—physical and emotional—can cause more tension. And so the cycle whirls and widens.

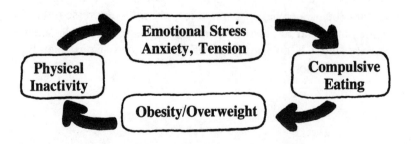

Dieting—cutting down on calories—isn't much help here, and many times it produces more stress. But activity is helpful. With regular physical activity, the natural biological response to anxiety—the impulse to *use one's body*—is directed into constructive channels and stress is relieved. With the reduction in stress and tension comes a reduction in the desire to overeat (at least for those people who have been conditioned to use food as a tension-relieving device). Then follows an increased capacity for more activity, which results in the burning of more calories and loss of weight. *The syndrome is reversed.*

Most people who come to my classes follow the typical pattern all too common in North America. Boredom, marital discord, family conflict, and the "empty-nest" syndrome all cause stress. As a result, they overeat. In fact, they "binge" eat—downing copious amounts of food and beverage at or between meals. When they are told to diet, many favorite "binge" foods are eliminated. They know these foods are especially fattening. They try to avoid them, but soon they become obsessed with the food they are told they cannot eat. This obsession causes more stress and a desire for even greater amounts of these foods. In fact, many of them prepare elaborate meals in an effort just to be near this good food.

Then when they eat these foods they feel guilty—they feel they are unable to control their lives. As a result, their self-esteem drops. They feel unfulfilled, inadequate, and incapable. They become depressed. They despise their figure and their self. More stress is created. The stress produces a desire for more food. The guilt produces depression and more sleep. The stress-eating-less activity cycle, therefore, is compounded into a Catch-22 syndrome. Tragically, candy-coated children become candy-coated adults.

Exercise seems to have a pervasive effect on reducing stress. Hans Selye, M.D., Ph.D., a world famous endocrinologist, says, "A voluntary change of activity is as good or even better than rest . . . for example, when either fatigue or forced interruption prevents us from finishing a mathematical problem it is better to go for a swim than to simply sit around. . . . Stress on one system helps to relax another.''

Reducing tension with exercise has been measured in the laboratory. Herbert deVries, Ph.D., an exercise physiologist at the University of Southern California, examined a group of men 50 years of age and over. All had a history of migraine headaches. He found that after a few weeks of regular physical activity, the headaches disappeared—without medication. (As you may know, the accepted theory about migraines is that they are somehow caused by tension.) In a second study, deVries discovered that a 15-minute walk reduced neuromuscular tension more effectively than the standard dosage of tranquilizers. deVries concluded that exercise can be more effective than medication.

Anxiety has also been reduced via exercise. Richard Driscoll, Ph.D., a psychologist at Eastern State Psychiatric Hospital in Knoxville, Tennessee, conducted a study where he had people exercise and think pleasant thoughts. Driscoll's report stated that exercising with pleasant thoughts substantially reduced anxiety. He had some theories about why physical activity helped to reduce this anxiety. First, he felt that activity and anxiety both triggered responses in the sympathetic nervous system that prepared the body for vigorous activity. That has long been known as the body's response to danger. These physical changes are also known to be the body's way of preparing for exercise. When the heightened physical state is a prelude to exercise, we may use up the tension and stimulation. When you feel tense because you are anxious, exercise can provide a vent for your anxiety.

Driscoll offered two additional explanations on why exercise helps to lower anxiety. First, physical exertion is intentional. It requires attention, effort, and motivation. That usually inspires a feeling of commitment and accomplishment. These constructive feelings relieve anxiety by making use of some of the bottled-up tension. Second, for many persons, physical exertion is associated with excitement, assertiveness, and friendship. These positive feelings may also help to relieve anxious feelings.

Exercise also seems to help relieve depression. The term depression is a catch-all which may include everything from the blahs to psychosis. Depression is a serious problem in our society. Doctors tell us that over 10% of the population will score in the "depressed" range on what is known as a depression questionnaire. Some hospitals report that depression is a primary problem with over half the patients coming to their clinics.

Doctors are now excited by reports that seem to show that exercise can short circuit depression. Although most of the studies to date have been done on running, I believe that conclusions can be extended to other forms of exercise as well. Anything that is repetitive in nature, that allows people to relax and gives them a feeling of accomplishment, seems to be helpful in reducing depression. Here are several reasons why:

1. Exercise requires patience. A person learns through exercise that it takes time to make significant physical changes. An appreciation of the value of patience may reduce depression.
2. Exercisers learn, often dramatically, that they can change themselves for the better. They can see that they are sufficiently in control of their lives to be able to improve their health, appearance, and self-image.
3. Exercisers develop a feeling of accomplishment. Any time you experience a sense of success, you will probably be pulled out of depression.

There's an old comedy routine about a doctor who steps on the patient's foot to make the patient forget about his headache. Let's face it. Exercisers notice new and significant body sensations which distract them. People who exercise tend to focus on those little aches that reaffirm the fact that they're alive. For once, they feel something besides the dullness of depression. Consequently, they forget about their condition.

The Cultural Theory

I would like to include another theory that is based on psychological explanations. I call it the cultural theory. Basically, it suggests that your culture encourages you to eat. Perhaps even to overeat. In other words, due to your culture you are programmed to eat without even thinking about it.

America is a food-oriented society. Victorious Little League baseball, basketball, and football teams are rewarded with trips to ice cream shops. You celebrate anniversaries and holidays by going out to dinner. Halloween is a festive occasion which puts candy in children's pockets, pumpkins, bags, and mouths. Birthday parties focus on luscious cakes, ice cream, and candy. Social engagements focus on going out to dinner or on food. Furthermore, some people feel that the mark of a good homemaker is the ability to provide excellent and delicious meals.

Magazines, TV, and radio convince you that sugar-coated cereals, potato chips, candy bars, beer, and wine are necessary for good and zesty living. The money spent on these advertisements is exceeded only by that spent on advertising over-the-counter drugs.

The emphasis on food is even more subtle. When you spend a weekend with your spouse or another group of people, most of the discussion is centered on what, where, and how much you are going to eat.

When you invite guests over to watch the game of the week, you provide a worthy snack and beverage—never just a glass of water. At church meetings you experience the "greet, meet, and eat syndrome." You can't wait for the meeting to end so that you can try some of your neighbor's luscious desserts and delightful pastries.

Food is a focal point in our society. You're continually trying to con your kids into eating more than they need or want.

Furthermore, you reward them and yourselves with food. And to top it off, many ethnic groups and nationalities place a great deal of emphasis on food, the preparation of food, and elaborate meal planning. Finally, the males of America seem to think that a sign of manliness is the ability to eat an abundance of food or pour down liters of a beverage. To the American male, more is macho.

I am not suggesting a revolution in our society with respect to food-eating patterns. That would be naive. The purpose of this discussion is to show you that food plays a central theme in your life. And since you are a social being, you must understand this phenomenon. As you try to restrict your calories and carbohydrates in dieting, you're bombarded with social and cultural cues to eat. I have a friend who has attended several of my classes. He tells me that throughout the day he does an excellent job of watching the calories. But in the evening it's an altogether different story. His social obligations clobber him. Wherever he goes he finds food being shoved in his face. Unfortunately, he has a very difficult time saying no.

And why shouldn't he have a hard time? His appestat is screaming for food. He loves to eat. He is psychologically addicted to food. For him dieting is a losing battle, as it is for most people.

Exercise, of course, helps fight the cultural dependency on food. If you're sitting watching the boob tube it stands to reason that you will be reaching for the pretzels, potato chips, and favorite beverage. Psychologists call it oral food—that is, a desire to have something in your mouth all the time. Exercise gets you up and out of that easy chair. And everyone knows it's pretty hard to run, walk, swim, or bike with a pretzel or potato chip in your mouth and a soda in your hand.

This discussion brings up another interesting thing about culture. People tend to eat any place, anywhere, any time. Some give very little consideration to the total number of calories they eat because they "eat on the run." When I have people do self-assessments on their total number of calories eaten, they tend to list only those eaten at the table. They fail to realize that ⅓ to ½ of their calories may be consumed while driving in a car, watching TV, going out the front door, standing next to the kitchen table, or sitting on the beach. Your pattern of living tends to mask the total number of calories you eat. So does the relative ease of obtaining food—getting it out of a bag or box with little or no preparation time.

Exercise can help you burn off those extra calories you're going to eat because of your social commitments and fast paced society. A woman named Pamela is a perfect example. She used exercise to get out of the guilt trap. Last year she told my wife it was her first Thanksgiving and Christmas that she ate a full meal during the holidays without feeling guilty. The guilt was gone because she knew she could go out and burn off the meal with a several-mile walk. She had caught the right idea. You can still be a social being, enjoy the good life, and pay the rent by engaging in extra physical activity. Furthermore, she had broken the chain of feeling guilty. She had gotten away from the idea that every pound she eats is going to turn into pounds. She knew that if she ate too much one day she could make it up with additional exercise the next.

The appestat, psychological, and cultural theories are all valid when it comes to weight gain. Obesity usually results from a high appestat setting coupled with stress, which begets overeating and a decrease in physical activity. Regardless of which of the three theories you subscribe to, one fact is very clear: physical activity is the surest way to weight and fat control.

My-Glands-Are-Against-Me Theory

A small, very small, segment of the population (approximately 2%) gains weight because its bodies are unable to handle food properly. But a lot of people use ''glands'' as a cop-out. If their glands aren't working properly, they can sit back and relax—and accumulate more pounds—cozy with the idea that they were born to be fat and there's really not much they can do about it. Or else they, or their doctors, decide that thyroid medication is the answer to the problem.

A sluggish thyroid, you see, is most often named the culprit. Frequently, in an effort to help their obese patients lose weight, doctors who ought to know better prescribe thyroid pills to rev up production of that hormone.

I had one woman in an early fitness class in Emmaus, Pennsylvania, who was on thyroid medication, but I wasn't aware of it at first. When I discovered her resting pulse rate was 132 beats per minute (normal for women is 72-80), I really panicked. I asked her whether she'd seen a doctor recently and she told me yes, and that he had put her on thyroid pills for "weight control."

It is neither sound nor medically justifiable for a physician to prescribe thyroid hormones without having established through laboratory tests whether the patient does indeed produce an insufficient amount of thyroid. Unfortunately, many times such medication is given on the general assumption that most obese people have a sluggish metabolism, which is definitely not the case.

The use of thyroid pills to supplement the production of the hormone is self-defeating. When additional thyroid is taken in, the body's own thyroid secretion slacks off and the metabolism is slowed even more. As a result, greater amounts of thyroid must be administered in order to prevent a weight gain. The possible side effects of high doses of thyroid are rapid heart rate, nervousness, and insomnia. It's a syndrome to be avoided.

I would never assume that excess pounds are caused by an abnormal glandular condition. The odds are something like 98 to 1 that glands have nothing to do with it.

People give a lot of other excuses for being fat. They're real gems. While they may seem plausible, they are pure hocus-pocus. Here are a few:

1. I'm big boned—no one has bones *that* big. Besides, there are no bones in your stomach.
2. My spouse likes me that way—have you ever considered why? A man doesn't have to worry about other men looking at his wife if she's fat.
3. I'm not really fat, just pleasantly plump—is it really so pleasant to have zippers that won't zip shut, buttons that pop, and seams that split?
4. My friends never say I'm fat—of course not. At least, not to your face.
5. There's just no hope for me—I'll always be fat—you may *want* to believe that, but you don't, do you? Why did you buy this book?

Fat accumulates when you burn fewer calories than you take in. And the way to burn off calories is to use your body the way it was meant to be used. Be active.

Of course, you could cut down on calories to get rid of unwanted pounds. But stepped-up activity is not only more fun, but a healthier, safer, more natural way to lose weight than what Peter Wyden has called the "pain and suffering marathon"—dieting.

5

Why Diets Don't Work

If you think I'm down on diets, you're right. But I have my reasons. First, dieting implies going on something and then off without any real change in eating habits. Dieting is a temporary measure that is doomed to failure. When you go off your diet, old habits return and the pounds pile up. The only way weight and fat will stay off permanently is to change your habits of living—with activity and good nutrition.

Second, many diets do more harm than good. Although most overfat people want to lose weight "at any cost," I implore you to be rational and intelligent. Dieting holds false promises with temporary and often tragic results.

Third, dieting may cause a weight·loss, but does it help you lose fat—AND does dieting help you keep the pounds off? Let's face it. Try any diet and you will probably lose weight for a week. If you're lucky, maybe a month. Then you will plateau. Weight loss will be slow. Maybe nonexistent. In fact, you may start to gain weight back. The fact is, 95% of those who lose weight by dieting gain it back—and then some—in a matter of months.

Dieting does not work because it does not attack the basic cause of getting fat—a sedentary lifestyle. Dieting is "unnatural." It works against your body's own instincts and drives.

Eventually your appestat, liver, and stomach can no longer comply with your diet's demands. So you give up the Spartan, blah eating habits and return to your old way of living. Your drive for food is more basic than your drive for slimness.

Dieting is fraught with psychological stumbling blocks. In many people the desire for food is linked to emotional needs that are as compelling as actual hunger.

Here's an example. Maybe donuts are your "forbidden food." You don't touch one for a week. On your way home from a tough day at the office you approach your favorite donut shop. The thought crosses your mind that a donut might taste good. In fact, you think: "Today I earned a donut." So you stop and order a box. On the way home you think: "I worked so hard I deserve at least one donut." Soon this degenerates into: "Gosh, I went off my diet so I might as well eat another." After two donuts you say: "What the heck. I might as well finish the whole box." Soon after you feel awful. Guilty. Then it hits you. "Why in the world did I ever eat all those donuts? You ding-a-ling!" You start to feel bad about yourself. Your self-esteem is reduced, which in turn produces an even greater amount of stress. Frustrated, you eat more because you are in the cycle of stress eating or binge eating.

Let's face it. Dieting is a counter-cultural phonemenon. In our society, food is plentiful. We are blessed with the richest agricultural assets in the world. Food is also big business. Food advertisers know how to play to our cravings in a way that only the strongest can resist. The TV and billboards wave delicious looking snacks and drinks in front of our eyes with deliberate emphasis on pleasure.

Frederick J. Stare, M.D., former professor and head of nutrition at Harvard University, has said that each time an individual quickly loses and then retains 10 pounds or more, he or she is subjecting him or herself to a period when blood vessel damage, possibly leading to atherosclerosis, may be accelerated. From a health point of view, this on-and-off approach may be more damaging than being fat and staying fat.

Fad diets are potentially dangerous for another reason: most of them drastically limit daily food intake or else certain food groups are emphasized to the near total exclusion of others. But the body always suffers when it does not get sufficient amounts of all the nutrients necessary for building and repairing new tissue and for regulating the various physiological processes crucial to life itself. I don't think I'm overstating the case when I say that you do yourself more harm by going on any diet— regardless of how widely acclaimed or well publicized—that does not include all the essential nutrients in proper proportions. Most of them don't.

One more very important point. No matter which diet book you buy, the authors tell you their approach is a new magic formula—a unique ingredient that will melt the fat and pounds right off your body to give you the shape you want. But the fact is, unless the diet takes into consideration calories expended, it won't work. The important rule in weight control is caloric balance. And all the hoopla, gimmicks, products, and "case histories" are not going to prove a thing unless the author recognizes that a calorie, is a calorie, is a calorie. Our body does not know the difference between calories in sirloin steak, ice cream, or raw carrots. If you ate 2,000 calories of bean sprouts, but only used 1,900 calories, you would still gain weight (and get sick of bean sprouts).

Let's look at some of the types of diets currently being promoted for weight loss.

Low Carbohydrate Diets

The Fat Pilot Diet, The Air Force Diet, The Mayo Clinic Diet, as well as The Drinking Man's Diet, The Calories Don't Count Diet, The Doctor's Quick Weight Loss Diet, Dr. Atkin's Diet Revolution, and Dr. Atkin's High Calorie Way To Stay Slim Forever Diet all have one thing in common: they stress keeping the carbohydrate intake at extremely low levels and then allow you to eat whatever else you want.

Because carbohydrates are among the easiest nutrients to digest and use, they are sometimes called the "body's most preferred foods." Carbohydrates are either immediately converted into energy or stored for later use. If used immediately, it will be as glucose, a simple sugar. If used later, they will be stored as glycogen or fat and converted into glucose as needed.

As mentioned previously, food is composed of carbohydrates, fats, proteins, water, vitamins, and minerals. Carbohydrates retain three times their weight in water—much like salt. If you eat less than 60 grams (a little over two ounces of carbohydrates) a day, you will lose weight, but only water weight. Of course, the scales will still show it as weight. In fact, in one week's time you may lose four to seven pounds of water. Obviously, this rapid loss turns people on to the diet and motivates them to "stick to it."

Naturally, the water weight comes back on when you eat more than 60 grams of carbohydrates or your body keeps from being dehydrated by holding onto any and all amounts of water. This phenomenon was dramatically illustrated by Theodore D. Van Itallie, Ph.D., director of the Obesity Research Center at St. Lukes Hospital in New York City, and several of his co-workers.

Dr. Van Itallie studied three groups of dieters. One group fasted, a second group went on an 800 calorie, balanced diet, and a third group ate 800 calories without carbohydrates. His findings: all three groups lost weight. The low carbohydrate group lost the most weight. But it was all in water weight. Over the long haul, it was the fasting group that lost the most weight. Hence, calories really count more than types of food that make up those calories.

Of course, some people often continue to lose weight after the first week on a diet of bacon, eggs, sirloin steak, ice cream, sour cream, cheese cake, and butter. The question is, how come? Some of the loss may still be due to water loss. In the body, carbohydrates bind with water. So when a small amount of carbohydrate is eaten, the body loses quite a bit of water. Unfortunately, the water loss is temporary. And no fat is lost. A second reason is that you may actually be eating fewer calories than before. It's an old trick with diet doctors to exclude one particular food group. When you do that, you tend to eat fewer calories because you find there are fewer foods that you can eat. So you lose weight. And again, calories are the key. Of course, Atkins, Stillman, and Company never tell you that. They imply that you can eat all you want (except carbohydrates) and still lose weight. Humbug! Your body just doesn't work that way.

Nutritionists have been outspoken in their criticism of low carbohydrate diets, and yet the concept continues to exert an appeal strong enough to rocket diet book after diet book to the top of the best-seller list. A report in the *Journal of the American Medical Association* states that "no evidence is advanced that controlled studies were ever carried out to evaluate the observation that weight can be lost by sedentary subjects who consume a carbohydrate-poor diet providing 5,000 kcal/day." The report, containing more than 40 references to research studies, questioned the body's ability to convert fat (of which the low-carb diets allow large quantities) into carbohydrates, noting that the concept is "biologically incorrect." Furthermore, The Medical Society of the County of New York warned at a press conference that extreme low carbohydrate diets can contribute to kidney disease and result in excess uric acid in the blood, disturbance in heart rhythm, loss of calcium, weakness, fainting, *and excess fat.*

To this I'd like to add:
1. A very low carbohydrate intake (60 grams or less) leads to an unhealthy buildup of ketones (ketosis) and can reach a point where the dieter's metabolism begins to resemble that of a diabetic. And while you are not diabetic, it is possible to have too many ketones released. When that happens, the blood pH is changed, and the fatal condition—ketoacidosis—

can occur. Some authors claim that "controlled" ketosis is possible, don't believe it! They are wrong.

2. When carbohydrates are severely restricted, so are some of the body's best sources of energy. Severe fatigue is a possible consequence.

3. Complex carbohydrates are rich sources of certain vitamins and minerals. By avoiding carbohydrates, one is also "avoiding" many of these essential nutrients.

4. One of the big drawbacks of the low carbohydrate diets is the rapidity with which weight is regained once the diet is abandoned. In other words, go off this kind of diet and you're back where you started from—twice as fast.

5. Any diet that is low in carbohydrates but supplies one with more fat and protein calories than are burned off through physical activity is going to result in a weight *gain.* Calories—not just carbohydrates—are what count.

6. Low-carb diets place no restrictions on fat intake. That's dangerous and crazy. Fats have been implicated in raising the level of cholesterol in the blood. (See Chapter #16) And although this is an area of raging controversy, many physicians believe that high cholesterol levels are a prime cause of atherosclerosis. Permitting unrestricted fat intake is ridiculous and irresponsible advice in light of what is now known about heart disease.

Fructose Diets

Basically the fructose type diets are low in carbohydrates and high in protein. Additionally, the fructose advocates tell the dieter to replace traditional carbohydrates (table sugar) with fructose (another sugar).

Fructose is a fruit sugar. It is a simple carbohydrate. The diet experts who espouse this type of diet recommend that you use fructose to sweeten your coffee, tea, drinks, salad dressings, desserts, and candy. Many soda manufacturers now use fructose as one of their sweeteners.

Often, diabetics are told to eat fructose in small amounts since the metabolism of fructose is not as much dependent upon insulin as that of sucrose. Studies seem to indicate that the hypoglycemic effect of sucrose in diabetes is not higher than that of starches. These same diet experts also recommend that whenever you are tired, anxious, or edgy you are to eat fructose.

The basic argument is that it may take longer for fructose to be absorbed by the bloodstream than regular simple carbohydrates such as table sugar. It is also postulated that insulin is not needed for entry into the liver.

While all this sounds good, the question still remains. Does fructose help you lose weight? No! Remember, your weight problem is due to a sedentary lifestyle. While fructose may be a "better" sugar, the key to weight control is balancing the number of calories you eat with the number of calories you use. And the idea of fructose being a healthier form of sugar is not without suspicion. Stan Winters, Ph.D., a chemist and nutritionist, has suggested that fructose is changed to glucose in the liver so eventually insulin is needed after all.

Low Protein Diets

The High Carbohydrate Diet, the Doctor's Quick Inches Off Diet, the Banana and Skim Milk Diet, and the Rice Diet are all based on the premise that large amounts of protein are unnecessary because the human body is capable of "recycling" its own internal protein supply.

Excess protein, say the supporters of this theory, is either wasted or deposited as fat. True. It is also claimed that a low protein intake is instrumental in reducing muscle mass. That is also true. But to restrict protein intake to the extent recommended by these diets is the equivalent to committing nutritional suicide.

In most of these diets, protein is limited to around 20 grams a day, which is far below the National Academy of Sciences-National Research Council's recommended 44-gram intake for women and 56-gram intake for men. (One exception is the Doctor's Quick Inches Off Diet, which permits the NAS-NCR suggested daily requirements.)

Proteins, the main constituents of muscles, nerves, glands, and many hormones, are present in all living tissue. They are used primarily to build and repair tissues, though in an emergency, they can be burned (oxidized) for energy. But protein can be diverted from its main use for only a limited time because the body requires it for building and repairing, and nothing else—neither fats nor carbohydrates—will do those jobs. When protein intake is drastically reduced, as it is apt to be when one follows a low protein diet, the body must draw on itself—utilize the protein already present in its own tissues. The result is a state nutritionists call "negative nitrogen balance." Tissues become depleted of protein and the body actually begins to waste away.

Consequently, I can think of four very good reasons *not* to go on a low protein diet:

1. A diet too low in protein has a definite detrimental effect on growth, development, and cell regeneration. Right now, as you are reading this page, millions of cells in your body are in the process of being destroyed, which is only natural and nothing to be alarmed about. With sufficient protein your body automatically repairs and replaces these cells. But, if you're on a very low protein diet (or are otherwise, for whatever reason, not getting enough of the stuff), you're in trouble.

2. Low protein advocates assert that a reduced protein intake reduces the muscle mass and in the process converts fat cells into muscle fiber cells. A low protein intake will indeed reduce muscle mass, but there is not one reputable physiologist in the world who would go along with the idea that a reduction in protein consumption converts fat cells into muscle-fiber cells. Fat cells and muscle-fiber cells are like

apples and oranges—distinctly different. They cannot be transformed from one to the other.

3. Many high protein foods are extremely valuable sources of vitamins and minerals. To go without these foods is almost certainly to diminish your intake of these nutrients—in effect, you're setting yourself up for nutritional deficiency diseases.

4. As I pointed out previously, a calorie is a calorie. No matter what nutritional group is emphasized in a diet—proteins, carbohydrates, or fats—if you don't burn off at least as many calories as you take in, you're going to gain weight. On the other hand, you can eat as much as you like of *anything* and not put on an ounce, if your body burns off as many calories as you consume.

Liquid Protein

In 1978 the hottest selling diet item was liquid protein. It was based on the concept that a few diet doctors were using on an experimental basis during the 70's. Their concept was called "The Protein-Sparing Modified Fast." The basic idea of the fast was to provide 70 grams of protein a day. This approach supposedly preserved muscle tissue while taking off fat. Along with this plan doctors provided vitamin and mineral supplements, recommended lean meat and some low-calorie bulk foods. And, of course, all were under close medical supervision.

The original idea was to use this Protein-Sparing Modified Fast with the hopelessly obese and to look at the changes in selected patients under experimental conditions.

But as with most things, greed entered the picture. An osteopath from the Philadelphia area wrote a book called *The Last Chance Diet*. In this book he claimed that he discovered a formula which he called Prolinn. "A formula comprised of all the amino acids needed to form a protein molecule." His book and Prolinn were an instant success. Unfortunately, (or fortunately, depending upon how you look at it) his diet was not.

Here are some of the problems associated with this diet:

1. Experts estimated that 58 people died as a result of this diet. Most deaths were probably due to cardiac arrhythmias.
2. In the book the doctor says, "The formula is protein extracted from beef hides." But later he modified his statement and said it came from sow underbellies as well, which may have implications for certain religious groups. Furthermore, the United States Food and Drug Administration found contaminated inventories, which implied sloppy extracting procedures of the drug company in obtaining the protein source.
3. Surprisingly, a liquid formula that the doctor was advocating was deficient in one very important amino acid, thereby making the whole formula incomplete and useless.
4. The approach of using the liquid supplement to treat obesity is only a temporary measure.
5. Many patients reported disturbances of their metabolism.
6. Doctors reported an increase in kidney and liver disease among users.
7. The same doctors reported a worsening of gallstones.

Of course, there were other modifications of this plan, some of which still exist. But my opinion is the same for all. Stay away from any weight loss plan that talks about protein-sparing unless you are prepared to court with death, severe disease states, and outright fraud.

Fasting

One of the new "old" methods of weight loss is fasting. At one time fasting was used solely for religious and meditation purposes. The practice of fasting began years ago in the Middle East or Eastern cultures. Then there were no antibiotics or really effective ways of treating infection of the intestinal tract or food poisoning. Under these circumstances, it is possible to see how fasting was beneficial. Today, it has been billed as a means of giving you a healthier body, i.e., "gives the vital organs a complete rest," "restores youthful condition of the cells," and "clears and strengthens the mind."

Here I do not plan to address these issues. Rather I'll only look at the implications of fasting to weight loss. My attitude toward fasting is, if you want to lose weight fast—fast. If you want to gain the weight back and then some—fast.

When you fast, your body doesn't know whether you are fasting or starving. So it responds in the primitive way. It responds biochemically.

If you fast for a day or two (for religious reasons), you are not likely to have any problems. But if you go longer you're probably headed for trouble. Experts note that while you lose weight (most of which is water and lean body tissue), your heart rate and metabolic rate slow down. This has severe implications for weight gain later on. Furthermore, for every 10% of your body weight that you lose there is an appreciable decrease in physiological performance. This would include the ability to do daily tasks such as walking and cleaning. This "slowdown" is due to a decrease in muscle strength and coordination as well as a decrease in heart function.

Surprisingly, most of the fat that is lost as a result of fasting occurs in the area of the intestines rather than the fat under the skin. Furthermore, you not only lose fat in the intestines, you also lose protein from your muscles, liver, heart, kidneys, and brain.

Besides all these grotesque things, you will experience many of the problems of the low carbohydrate and protein diets. Starvation or fasting over a long period of time should only be used by tyrannical rulers as a method of cruel torture.

I have to admit that starvation and crash diets for ultra-quick weight loss have a certain appeal. Everyone likes the quick and easy scheme for anything. But let me warn you, weight loss may be quick, but there's nothing "easy" about it.

The near equivalent of fasting, crash dieting, was probably spawned by the practice of some physicians to "starve" their very obese patients. Often overlooked is the fact that these people were hospitalized and/or under constant medical supervision during the fast.

Men and women who stay on a starvation diet for more than a couple days almost always experience faintness and dizziness, a feeling of fatigue, and general weakness and hunger pangs bordering on the painful. And here's another thing to consider: if you're a person with a job to do—any kind of job—forget it. People who fast have difficulty performing even the most routine tasks. The nutritional consequences of fasting are obvious: you simply don't get enough of anything for your body's needs.

Moreover, there are two other problems associated with starvation diets. First, research has shown that when these people go back to normal eating patterns—even if they are in caloric balance—they gain weight. Physiologists are unable to explain this phenomenon. Some theorize that it may be due to the body's desire to perserve normalcy. There may be some biological mechanism telling the body to maintain or get back to normal weight. Psychologists have even noted that people who follow these diets develop personality patterns similar to those of a starved person. Second, research has indicated that people on a rigid calorie restricted diet have a reduced metabolic rate—perhaps as much as 15%. Therefore, their weight loss does not equal the expected loss based on their caloric intake.

Even the most liberal doctors now hesitate to recommend a diet of less than, 1,200 calories a day. Consuming fewer calories than this results in a quicker weight loss. But is it worth it? I, for one, am not willing to pay the price.

Some of my class members point out that many people in the Middle East or Eastern countries who fast are thin. That's true, but it is not due to their occasional fasting. People from those nations don't have as many cars, televisions, and other conveniences that lead to a sedentary lifestyle.

Vegetarianism

I have a 17 year old daughter who wants to be a vegetarian. I have no quarrel with that. I tell her she can switch to vegetarianism any time that she understands and can apply the basic principle regarding the balance of essential amino acids daily and perhaps at each meal. If you want to switch to vegetarianism for healthy eating reasons, fine. *Just make sure you know what you're doing.* Becoming a vegetarian for the sake of losing weight is not wise. I've known many fat vegetarians. They're the ones who sit all day.

There are three basic kinds of vegetarian diets.

1. Vegetarian—Some people call these strict or pure vegetarians. The only foods that they are permitted to eat are plant origin, including seeds, grains, nuts, fruits, and vegetables.
2. Lacto-vegetarian—The lacto-vegetarians are allowed to eat foods of plant origin, plus foods made of milk such as yogurt, cream, and cheese.
3. Lacto-ovo-vegetarian—These persons can eat all foods of plant origin, plus dairy foods and eggs.

Occasionally some vegetarians may vary their theme, but they do not eat fish or land animals.

The biggest danger in vegetarianism is that most people do not get enough of the B vitamins, especially B_{12}. Generally, if people eat plenty of dairy products, there is no danger. But if they go the pure vegetarian route (no dairy products), then they will probably have to take a vitamin B_{12} supplement.

I'm not opposed to vegetarianism as a means of healthful living. But as a means of weight control, you must remember you still have an appestat and must live with that. And if your appestat is calling for 2,500 calories but you're only eating 2,000, you're still going to be hungry.

Second, if you have a psychological dependency on food, vegetarianism is not going to solve that problem nor is vegetarianism going to solve your cultural dependency on food.

If you still persist in following vegetarianism, I would suggest you get one of the following books: 1) *Diet For A Small Planet,* 2) *Recipies For A Small Planet,* or 3) *The Alternative Diet.*

Pritikin Diet

The Pritikin Diet is not vegetarian, but it's the closest thing to it. There are two modes to the Pritikin Program: the first relating to diet and the second to exercise. The diet aspect is low in fat, cholesterol, protein, and highly refined carbohydrates such as sugars. It is, however, high in starches. Most of the starches are unrefined carbohydrates and are basically "foods as grown," eaten raw or cooked. Pritikin asks you to keep your salt, fat, and sugar intake at extremely low levels. He suggests keeping fat at about 5 to 10% of your daily calories, 0 grams of sugar and honey, 1 to 2 grams of salt, 2 to 5 mg. caffeine, and less than 100 mg. of cholesterol. Additionally, he asks that you exercise vigorously and on a regular basis with things such as walking and jogging.

While many nutrition experts have problems with the Pritikin Program, I do not. I like it, not for weight loss, but for good eating. His dietary regimen is sound. Unfortunately, I think it's difficult for most people to follow and rather expensive. But frankly, if my back was to the wall with cardiovascular disease, it would be a diet that I would follow.

The other thing Pritikin advocates is exercise. He asks that you exercise vigorously and on a regular basis with things such as walking and jogging. And he's not just talking about a mile a day. He's advocating covering 5 to 6 miles a day on a regular basis. That burns a good 500 to 600 calories a day.

United States Senate Guidelines

These dietary guidelines for America were presented by the United States Senate Select Committee on Nutrition and Human Needs. And while it is not a diet, per se, it does provide excellent recommendations for good eating. It is a more moderate position than Pritikin's, and one you should follow for healthful living. Almost every industry including meat, dairy, salt, and sugar industries have attacked this diet. So has the American Medical Association. Interestingly, it has been staunchly defended by the American Heart Association and several other people in the scientific nutrition community. Basically the dietary goals are as follows:

1. Lose weight and keep it off.
2. Increase the consumption of complex carbohydrates (starches) and "naturally occurring sugars" (in fruits) from 28% of total daily calories to 48%.
3. At the same time, reduce the amount of refined sugar you eat every day from 18% of daily calories to 10%.
4. Eat less fat (from 40% of daily calories to 30%) or balance the kinds of fats you eat so that 10% of the daily calories are saturated (butter); 10% unsaturated fats (chicken, turkey, and nuts); and 10% polyunsaturated fats (safflower and corn oil).
5. Hold daily cholesterol consumption to 300 mg. a day (slightly more than the amount in one egg yolk).
6. Eat no more than 5 grams of table salt a day.

Again, I have no problem with this diet. Like Pritikin, I think it's good nutrition. It's a more moderate position than Pritikin takes and it might be your first step. But don't consider it just a way of losing weight. Remember, your basic problem is a sedentary lifestyle.

High Fiber Diet

Although high fiber diets have been around for years, it wasn't very popular until Dr. Ruben's publication in 1975, *The Save Your Life Diet*. Dr. Ruben has proposed that we correct our dietary lack of natural fiber. Fiber is basically cellulose, plus a few other constituents. The fiber in cereals differs from that found in fruits and vegetables, but they all have the same effect: they stimulate the intestines and pass the waste material through the digestive system in a more rapid fashion. In fact, in a nut shell, that is what the diet is all about.

The basic argument is that the natural fiber in the diet will speed up the passage of semi-digested and digested food through the intestinal tract. While this speed up of passage may contribute to the health of the organs of digestion, the notion that anyone can lose weight because it reduces the time food spends in the intestinal tract is questionable. A calorie is still a calorie is a calorie. And how quickly the intestines work to absorb the calorie matters little in the day's total caloric income.

My suggestion is that you eat plenty of fiber for the health of your gastrointestinal tract and not for weight loss AND make sure you burn calories to counteract your sedentary lifestyle—the real cause of your weight gain.

The Pill Treatment

In our society, where more and more Americans are turning to pills to solve their problems, it's not surprising that so many fat Americans turn to diet pills to solve their weight problems. It does sound tempting. No more calorie counting . . . no more meager meals . . . no more exercise. Just pop a pill. Instant thin.

But as you know, the pill treatment is dangerous. Many injuries and hundreds of deaths have been linked to diet pills. Perhaps you remember reading about the Philadelphia college student who died fighting a desperate battle to overcome narcotic addiction which began, innocently enough, with diet pills. Overweight at the age of 12, a physician put her on a weight control program and gave her the pills. Her mother paid for them. By the time she was 14, the girl had discovered that these same pills helped to ward off boredom and depression. A year later, she turned to more powerful drugs and—finally—to heroin. And death.

Not everyone who uses diet pills meets with the same end, of course. But the "rainbow" pills prepared for weight control are always a witch's brew of potential trouble. They contain amphetamines to suppress the appetite; barbiturates to counter the nervousness brought on by the amphetamines; digitalis, a heart stimulant; a diuretic to remove fluid; thyroid to step up metabolism; and laxatives.

Thyroid and amphetamines (now banned for use in weight control) are known to have a taxing effect on the heart. With diuretics, essential chemicals as well as water are flushed out of the body, occasionally resulting in poisoning, spasms, even death.

Don't take a chance. The pill treatment is dangerous and, like every "quick loss" plan, ignores the real source of your weight problem; inactivity.

HCG—The Sex Hormone

Back in 1965, a prominent Chicago endocrinologist hailed the discovery of the most promising reducing regimen he'd ever come across. The new treatment employed HCG (human chorionic gonadotrophin), a hormone produced by the placenta during pregnancy. HCG was used for many years to treat young boys with undescended testicles.

In the 1950s, A. T. W. Simeons, M.D., a British physician, began to think of HCG as a possible anti-obesity drug. He had been using it to treat boys afflicted with Froelich's Disease—an illness characterized by sexual underdevelopment and extreme obesity—and had found that the hormone not only corrected the sexual deficiency, but also reduced accumulations of fat around his patients' hips and mid-sections. When his young patients ate normally, they lost no weight; the fat was simply redistributed. But when the boys were put on a 500-calorie-a-day diet, they lost a pound a day and suffered no hunger pangs whatsoever.

Dr. Simeons, now at Rome's Salvador Mundi International Hospital, operates a clinic devoted solely to HCG anti-obesity therapy, treating more than 1,000 patients a year.

It sounds like Simeons has the ultimate fat cure, right? Unfortunately, no. HCG happens to be one of the hormones included in the fertility drug that has caused multiple births in previously infertile women. The dosage prescribed for reducing purposes is smaller. But who can say what may be triggered by this tampering with the hormonal balance of the human body?

More recent studies have cast considerable doubt on one value of this drug. Several studies have indicated that HCG is not any more valuable in helping an obese person lose weight than a placebo.

At present, HCG is the subject of a lot of controversy. We don't know how safe or unsafe it will prove to be, but for the moment it is considered "potentially" dangerous, and that's enough to scare *me* off.

Again, I certainly understand and sympathize with the impulse to lose weight in order to *look* better. I know from experience that many men and women want to get slim mainly to improve their personal appearance. That's fine. But let's not forget that we're dealing with our bodies here, our most precious asset: health.

And there is one other thing. Drugs apparently have no lasting value in the treatment of obesity because of increasing tolerance. Many people have the feeling that drugs are of value at the beginning of a weight loss regimen to encourage a person to lose some weight. Unfortunately, when a person first starts an exercise program, restricts calories, or sees a physician on what to do concerning his weight, he is more strongly motivated. If he can't lose weight at this time without medication, he certainly will not be able to lose weight several months later when the medication becomes less effective.

Magic pills and miracle drugs would certainly make things a whole lot easier for the overweight society. But these things don't exist. Or at least not in any safe version. Maybe someday someone will come up with a remedy that not only works, but is also guaranteed not to wreak havoc with the human body. But until it happens, I'm going to keep advocating physical activity as the best and safest way to lose weight.

6
How Fat Is Your Fat?

Fat is your problem, not weight. If your tummy is too big, if you have saddlebags, and if you have a double chin, the problem is fat. If you are worried about your chances of having a heart attack or developing diabetes, the problem is fat. If you don't like what you see in the mirror, the problem is fat. And if your clothes no longer fit you, the problem is fat.

Most people think that overfatness is the same as overweight. That's incorrect. While it is possible to be overfat and overweight at the same time, it is also possible to be overweight but not overfat. I've even known people who were *underweight* but overfat. This all sounds like double talk, but it's not. Let me explain this strange set of affairs.

Suzanne W. was a 41-year-old real estate agent who was enrolled in one of my fitness classes. Her case was all too typical of most overfat Americans.

A former cheerleader and fashion model, Suzanne told me at the start of the class that her real goal was "to get rid of her fat abdomen." She also mentioned she was perplexed. "I weigh less than I did when I was 25, but my figure doesn't look as good. I'm very careful about what I eat. But my bust is smaller and my waist is larger. Why?" Suzanne was 5'6" and weighed 121. According to the height/weight tables, she was "right on."

She was not overweight, but in her leotard she appeared to be fatter than she should have been around her waist and middle.

Quite frankly, Suzanne was too fat.

But I felt a test was in order before springing the ego-shattering facts on her.

Every class that I conduct involves some testing. The first test I performed on Suzanne was a simple measurement of her body fat. Testing showed that 30% of her body weight was fat. Well over the recommended 19% for women. I told her that 36 of her 121 pounds were fat! Suzanne got a little huffy and said, "What do you mean I have 11% too much fat? And that I carry 36 pounds of fat? I'm not overweight. If I was, my doctor would have told me."

"Hold on," I told Suzanne. "You must understand the difference between overweight and overfat. Overfat refers to too much fat on your body. Overweight is when you weigh more than your doctor and insurance company's height/weight charts. And there's a big difference between the two. You can have two men who are 6'2" and weigh 235 pounds. One man plays halfback for the Los Angeles Rams and the other is a typical male citizen of the United States. According to the height/weight charts, both are overweight since they aren't supposed to exceed 198 pounds. However, when you tell both men to take off their shirts, there's an obvious difference between the two. The professional football player has minimal body fat. He looks very good. The weight is in the form of chest and arm muscle. The other gentleman carries a large amount of fat. He doesn't look so good. The weight is in the form of a flabby tummy. In short, a low amount of fat makes our bodies more attractive."

After listening to this discussion, Suzanne got moving. She bought the idea and started on the road to repair by increasing her physical activity. Soon things were rearranged. Her chest got bigger, her waist got smaller, she dropped a whole dress size (two in some fashions). Surprisingly, however, her weight stayed the same. But Suzanne didn't care about the weight anymore. Her body looked great and that was what she was after.

Suzanne was unique. I usually have difficulty explaining this concept of body fat and weight to women. Women panic at the sight of unwanted pounds. They are slaves to the scales. More so than men. To women, pounds are the issue. When exercise is mentioned, they think of muscles, and the last thing they want is to look "horsy" with bulging biceps and thick calves. But just remember, behind every attractive curve in the female form is a well conditioned muscle. Some of the most attractive women in America exercise daily. It doesn't matter what you weigh if you like your figure and what you see in the mirror. Don't let the scales be your master. They're deceiving.

Closely allied with the body fat concept is that of lean body tissue. Your lean body tissue is the bone, organ, and muscle tissue of your body. Your body is composed of two types of tissue—fat and lean tissue. A person in good physical condition has a lot of lean body tissue and a low amount of fat. On the other hand, an unfit person is just the opposite. For example, let's assume that you weigh 100 pounds and have 10% body fat. That would mean that 90 of your pounds would be lean body tissue. The remaining 10 pounds would be fat. By the way, if you only have 10% body fat you will have a very good looking body. On the other hand, if you have 30% body fat and weighed 100 pounds, you would have 70 pounds of lean body tissue and 30 pounds of body fat. Unfortunately, in this case your body would not be very attractive.

As you get older, your lean body weight decreases and your percentage of body fat goes up. An unfortunate but common occurance. Former President Ford is a perfect example. Early in his presidency he claimed he weighed only four pounds more than when he played football at the University of Michigan. That doesn't sound too bad, except for the fact that his waist measurement jumped from 32 to 38 inches. What happened was that his lean body tissue decreased while his percentage of body fat went up.

So, an overfat person may not be overweight according to the height/weight tables. It's possible to weigh just what you ought to weigh—again according to the tables—but have a total percentage of body fat several points over what is desirable and healthy.

If you're interested in losing weight, a diet will do. But if you're interested in losing fat, exercise is the best way. Besides, going on a diet is temporary but exercise is permanent. It has been estimated that for every three pounds lost due to dieting only one pound lost is fat and the other two pounds are lean body tissue. And when you lose lean body tissue, you're losing what makes you attractive. That is why many women get discouraged with diets. They lose the lean body tissue that holds their breasts firm and erect, while they keep the body fat that has accumulated around their waistlines. The result is an okay weight on the scale and a lousy looking figure in the mirror. To look good your body has to be firm and well toned. Exercise is the only way to get results. Remember, it's fat you want to lose, not lean body tissue.

That was the case with Suzanne. She weighed 125 pounds in her senior year in college. As time went on, though, she became more and more sedentary. The muscle tone of her body became less dense and thus less heavy. All things being equal, she should have lost weight. However, there was a corresponding enlargement of her fat cells, which accounted for a gain in fat weight. In short, her body's lean-to-fat ratio had changed, and she became overfat but not overweight.

I've even known people who were underweight. And looked it. Yet they were overfat. I remember telling one woman she was overfat, after she complained she was underweight. She got so mad she didn't speak to me for a week.

Skinny, yet fat? Sounds impossible. Yet a study done by Ancel Keyes, Ph.D., at the University of Minnesota supports this contention. He ran a series of tests on adult males and found that 20% of his subjects fell into the "underweight but too fat" category. I think you've seen people like that. Very thin yet they had a "soft appearance." That is, a protruding abdomen, sagging chest muscles, and flabby arms. They were underweight but probably overfat.

Keyes' study had another interesting finding. Somewhere between 20 and 30% of the men were overweight, but within the normal range of fat distribution. Many were, in fact, extremely lean. They were similar to the 6'2", 235 pound football player.

From this same study came another interesting finding: the men who were both overfat and underweight led very sedentary lives, while the men who were overweight but not fat engaged in heavy labor.

Professional athletic coaches now know this. At one time they told their athletes to report back to camp weighing a certain weight. Since size is important in this sport, their weights were often set quite high. It got to be a joke. Players would lie around and eat all summer and report back with the additional 20-30 pounds. But they looked like blimps. All those pounds were fat, which doesn't do a very good job of opening holes in the defensive line. What they needed was 20-30 pounds of extra muscle. Today, these athletes are told to report back weighing a certain weight, and under a certain percentage of body fat. Sure, they are still overweight, but they are not fat. They must gain lean body tissue—muscle—not fat.

The Keyes study and athletic emphasis buttresses everything said so far. Fat is the problem, not weight. Which is not to suggest that you hire yourself out as a ditch digger or an athlete. Rather, to lose fat and keep it off, you have to use your body. Sitting around is what makes you fat. Even dieting and sitting around can result in being fat. You may achieve a certain weight, but your body could still have that sagging, bulging look.

In view of all this, the height/weight tables should always be taken as something less than the last word. At best, they are just a rough guide. Don't be misled. And don't be one of the many Americans who uses the tables to put one over on himself. It's so easy to do!

One woman told me that when she was 20 she weighed 116 pounds. She was 5'6" tall, and way back then she classified herself as having a "small frame." Over the years, she put on weight. In her late 20's she was hovering around the 135 pound mark. She really didn't look fat, she says, and since all the height/weight tables indicated that 135 pounds was not a bad weight for a 5'6" woman of "medium frame" she relaxed and decided that a "medium frame" is what she had been after all. In her mid 30's, the same woman weighed around 143. The height/weight tables say this is an okay weight for a woman her height with a "large frame." She re-evaluated the situation and considered that, yes, she'd been a "large framed" person all along. It was only when she hit 150 and ran out of frame categories that she finally faced up to the fact that she had a fat problem.

Men tend to manipulate the tables a little differently. Instead of reclassifying themselves by frame, they add inches to their height. One man "grew" 1½ inches over the years: at 20 his height was measured with his shoes off; at 30 or so he had himself remeasured wearing shoes with one inch heels and straining to stand as tall as possible. By reclassifying himself by height, he was able to justify an accumulation of 19 pounds of fat.

I have a difficult time understanding why people continue to use these charts when fat is the issue in a good looking figure and shape. But the concept of weight is ingrained in us from a very early age. Young girls are told to pay close attention to the height/weight charts. Women's magazines espouse old cliches that the skinny-looking model is best. It's all ridiculous. In the United States, the height/weight charts exercise a kind of tyranny not seen in other countries. It's a cultural phenomenon and a rather curious one. In Scandinavia, for example, a fit and attractive body is emphasized; pounds are just numbers on a scale and relatively unimportant. It's how you look that counts, not what you weigh. In the United States and Canada, however, I've known people who have a fanatical desire to weigh what the tables say they ought to—unaware, for the most part, that the indicated "ideal" weights may not be at all ideal for the structure and composition of their individual bodies.

Just how much fat is too much? Nutritionists and physiologists have determined that there are desirable and healthful percentages of body fat. Currently, experts feel that children— boys and girls—should not exceed 12%. When it comes to adults, men should be 15% body fat or less and females should be 19% or less. (The 4% difference between male and female is attributed to fat in the breasts.) Of course, adults and children can have lower percentages of body fat, but it's not necessary from a health and fitness point of view.

As you would expect, the lowest percentages of body fat have been recorded by athletes. Kyle Heffner, the third place marathoner for the 1980 U.S. Olympic team, has a recorded percentage of body fat of .8%. Nadia Comaneci and Olga Korbut, the fantastic gymnasts, when they were in their prime had 1.5% body fat. These are extremes. But you will find that most long distance runners (men and women) have 5 to 9% body fat, most football halfbacks have 9 to 11%, and most interior linemen have 15%. If you stay close to the 15% for men and the 19% for women, you will look great. Regardless of your weight.

How much body fat is too much? As you would expect, experts have recommendations here too. Generally, it is felt that if a child exceeds 20% body fat, he is considered overfat. If a man exceeds 20% and a woman 30%, he or she is considered overfat. And overfatness is a cause for real concern. Not only is your appearance and fitness level poor, you're also set up for a host of diseases including heart disease, high, blood pressure, osteoarthritis, and diabetes.

Not surprisingly, quite a few people are considered overfat. It has been estimated that 19 to 25% of all children between 7 and 12 years of age are overfat. Furthermore, 25 to 30% of all adult males are overfat, and 30 to 50% of all adult females are overfat. Clinical observations that I have made indicate that these percentages are rather low. I suspect that in the United States almost 40% of all men and almost 60% of all women are obese or overfat.

Of course, knowing your percentage of body fat goes beyond disease implications. It can be used to determine your ideal weight regardless of your age, sex, height, and body type. Let me explain. Let's assume you are a woman who weighs 150 pounds and has 31% body fat. That means you have 12% too much body fat (remember, 19% is ideal for women). Consequently, you should lose 12% of your 150 pounds or approximately 18 pounds. Therefore, your ideal weight would be 132 pounds—regardless of what the height/weight charts say. On the other hand, if you weigh 130 pounds and have 15% body fat, you would already be at your ideal weight and no fat loss would be necessary.

Occasionally, some people protest after finding out that their percentage of body fat is okay. They state, "But I still look fat." Invariably, those who are critical of their figures are those whose percentage of body fat at one time was rather low. Most are former athletes, cheerleaders, and fashion models. They continually compare their current percentage of body fat to what it was when they were in fantastic shape.

When I talk about ideal weight, I'm talking about what is the best weight for you from a fitness and wellness point of view. Naturally, you can go lower if you wish as long as you don't get down to the extreme levels of 4% or less. And for those of you who are somewhere between ideal weight and overfatness, it's probably best for you to think about reducing your percentage of fat. Because as you get older the battle of the bulge becomes more difficult.

How Do I Measure My Fat?

All this discussion has been leading you through the first step in the Inches Off No-Diet Plan. In Chapters #3–6, I tried to show you that you gain weight and fat because of a sedentary lifestyle. You must own up to this fact. Unless you do, the plan will not work.

As part of this first step, you must also admit that your problem is fat—not weight. For many that is a difficult admission. Fat has a lot more negative implications than weight. It smacks of slovenliness. But the truth is that fat is your problem—as the following tests indicate. The first few are quite simple, homespun measures; yet they give a good indication of the extent of your problem.

CHEST/WAIST TEST

Here's one way to tell if you're too fat. Stand with your shoulders pulled back and *maximum chest expansion*. Measure the circumference of your chest just below the arm pits. Be certain your tape measure is flat and level. Then measure your waist (at the navel), with your stomach in a relaxed position—not sucked in or forced out. For men, the chest should be five inches greater in circumference than the waist; for women, the difference should be ten inches. If your chest/waist difference is *less* than the five or ten inch criteria, you can conclude that you are too fat.

THE WEIGHT GAIN TEST

Another test is to simply recall what you weighed when you were 18 if you are a woman, or 21 if you are a man. If memory fails, you can dig out old medical records. You can assume that each pound gained since that time represents an accumulation of fat.

THE MIRROR TEST

The quickest, easiest way to find out if you are too fat

is to get undressed and stand in front of a full length mirror. Be critical. Do you like what you see? Have your body contours changed? If you look fat, you can reasonably conclude that you are fat. If you sag where you don't want to sag, if your waist protrudes, you're probably moving into the obese range or are already there.

Ask yourself these questions:

		YES	NO
1.	Does your stomach protrude?	_____	_____
2.	Are your hips too big?	_____	_____
3.	Do you have saddlebags on the tops of your thighs?	_____	_____
4.	Do your breasts or chest muscles sag?	_____	_____
5.	Do you have handle bars above your hips?	_____	_____
6.	Do the back of your arms seem flabby?	_____	_____
7.	Do your legs seem to have the cottage cheese look?	_____	_____
8.	Are your ankles too big?	_____	_____

If you answer yes to any of these questions, you are probably carrying too much fat.

When you do the Mirror Test, don't be too hard on yourself. Younger women, especially, are apt to want to measure up to a fashion model's ideal figure which, unless one is built along long, lean, ectomorphic lines, is probably not possible or even desirable.

THE JIGGLE TEST

If the mirror test doesn't tell you too much, you might try running in place. If parts of your body jiggle and they're not supposed to, you can conclude that what you see jiggling is fat. And should be lost.

THE PINCH TEST

This test can be taken to measure whether the things you see with the Chest/Waist, Weight Gain, Mirror, and Jiggle Tests are really an indication of atrophied muscles or too much body fat. Using only your thumb and forefinger, try to grasp the skin and fat anywhere on your waist, midriff, abdomen, back of arm, thigh, or hip. If the skin you pinch measures more than three-quarters of an inch (men) or one inch (women) between your thumb and finger, your problem is due to too much body fat.

THE BEST WEIGHT TEST

All the previous tests only tell you if you are too fat. None tell you your best weight. I've found that most people can tell me their best weight (if they are honest). My clinical studies have shown that there is a high relationship between ideal weight based on body fat and a person's perceived best weight. Therefore, simply state what you think is your best weight (perhaps your weight at 21 for men and 18 for women). Record. I think my best weight is _____ .

Of course, there are much more sophisticated techniques that can be used to determine your body fat. Here are two.

HYDROSTATIC WEIGHING

By far the most accurate method yet devised to estimate your body fat and lean tissue is hydrostatic weighing. For this, the subject is immersed and the amount of water displaced is determined. Other measurements—residual lung volume, body weight in and out of water, etc.,—are made. From these measurements, the proportion of body fat can be calculated and ideal weight established. Hydrostatic weighing requires elaborate and expensive equipment and is obviously not a do-it-yourself project—unless you have a very large bath tub and some pretty fancy equipment.

MEASURING SKINFOLD THICKNESS

A more practical method is the measurement of skinfold thicknesses. The National Center of Health Statistics in Washington points out that "skinfolds permit a closer estimate of body fat than do the tables of relative weight . . . skinfolds are becoming established as the easiest and most direct measure of body fat available in the doctor's office, the clinic, or in a large scale population survey."

In most people under the age of 50, at least half of the body fat is stored directly beneath the skin. By measuring the thickness of the fold produced when the skin and tissue just under it are firmly grasped, it is possible to get an idea of how much fat is present. Accurate measurements can be made with a caliper. Some of the most common locations at which this measurement is taken include the back of the upper arm, the middle of the back at the shoulder blades, the abdomen/waistline, under the armpit, and chest. Once your percentage of body fat is determined, it is possible to establish your best weight. To do this, just determine how much you are over the 15% and 19% limit, then multiply that amount by your percent weight. Roughly, the product will be the number of pounds you need to lose. Here's an example:

Current weight: 180 pounds

Excess body fat	10%
Current weight	x 180
Excess fat weight	18 pounds

Percent body fat	25%
Desirable body fat	− 15%
Excess body fat	10%

In other words, this man needs to trim 18 pounds of body fat and get down to 162 pounds, regardless of what the height/weight charts say.*

*See Appendix B for a more detailed explanation.

Now that you have some methods of determining whether you're too fat, are you ready to face the facts? I suggest you try two or three of these methods. If they all seem to suggest the old guy or gal has too much fat, swallow your pride and say, "I'm too fat." If you can say that, you're on your way. Good. Don't be embarrassed. You have a lot of company. Don't be discouraged. Just face it. You can lose it. Help is on the way.

PART #2
PLAN THE ATTACK

7
Activities To Reduce Your Fat—The Big 4 Plus

It should be obvious by now that dieting is a lost cause. Everything is working against you. But even if dieting were fun—even if you could go without food and suffer no ill effects—it still wouldn't be the best way to look and feel better. You need something more—something to lose fat, flatten your stomach, and shape your hips. What you need is a physical activity that you really enjoy.

William Zuti, Ph.D., and Lawrence Golding, Ph.D., set out to compare the effects of several different methods of weight reduction on body weight, body composition, and selected blood measurements. The twenty-five women participating in the study were all between the ages of 25 and 40 and were 20 to 40 pounds overweight. Three groups were formed: (1) eight women were on a diet, reducing their caloric intake by 500 calories per day, but holding their physical activity constant; (2) nine continued to eat as usual, but increased physical activity to burn off 500 extra calories a day; and (3) eight reduced caloric intake by 250 calories a day and increased physical activity to burn off 250 calories per day. Before and after the sixteen-week period, the subjects were tested for body weight, body density, skinfold and girth measurements, and selected blood lipids (fats).

The results indicated that there was no significant difference between the groups in the amount of weight lost. The average individual weight loss in all three groups was 11.4 pounds. All of the methods were extremely effective in controlling weight. However, the significant finding of the study was that there was a difference between the groups with regard to body composition. Those in the exercise group and in the combination exercise/diet group lost body fat. The diet group lost body fat *and* muscle tissue. The members of the exercise group also had more stamina than the others. Their circulatory systems were much better able to withstand the rigors of exercise. The report concluded that the use of exercise in a weight-reduction program is far superior to dieting alone in its effect on body composition and physical fitness.

When people lose weight by dieting they often remain flabby. But if you exercise while you diet or use exercise as a means of losing weight, your muscles will be much firmer. Therefore, you will look and feel better after losing weight through exercising.

I think people are starting to see this. There has been a revival of activity lately. It seems that everyone has a flashy double knit warm-up suit. Yet we are getting fatter. That's because of the types of activities people are turning to. I was talking to a college student who was overfat. He questioned the value of exercise for weight control. He complained: "I play intramural basketball four times a week and I still don't lose any weight."

While I'm glad to see people enjoying tennis, golf, basketball, racquetball, and other recreational sports, I know they won't lose much fat that way. While increased activity is good, some activities are better than others for fat loss. In short, the best ones are those that make most or all of your body move without a lot of pauses for free throws, retrieving tennis balls, time outs, and waiting for your partner to putt.

The activities which qualify as big calorie burners are walking, running, bicycling, and swimming. These are the big four.

The plus activities are cross country skiing, running in place, stair climbing, rope jumping, and aerobic dancing. Let's take a quick look at some of them.

Walking

Advantages: An excellent fat burning activity for practically everyone. Can easily be built into your daily routine with a minimum of hassle. It is pleasurable and can be done with the entire family.

Disadvantages: It takes more time than most other fat burning exercises for changes to occur.

Calories Expended: 250 to 350 calories per hour.

Running

Advantages: Running is the best activity for reducing body fat. It takes the least amount of time. According to Dr. Kenneth Cooper, running is the best of the big four.

Disadvantages: Running's not for everyone. Running may shorten the muscles in the back of the leg, thereby reducing flexibility and making you more prone to injury and leg pain. The overfat may find it too hard on the legs, knees, and ankles.

Calories Expended: Running burns anywhere from 600 to 700+ calories per hour depending upon your speed.

Swimming

Advantages: An extremely effective activity for the obese. Causes very little problems to the joints, and the water helps to support you. Consequently, there are fewer problems for ankles, knees, and hips.

Disadvantages: You need a pool and the ability to swim. You may also find it difficult to keep going for an extended period of time. When you become an extremely efficient swimmer, you may find it difficult to burn enough calories.

Calories Expended: 400 to 800 calories per hour.

Bicycling

Advantages: Bicycling is an excellent fat control activity for practically all ages. It can provide you with a vigorous workout. It not only strengthens the leg and back muscles, it subjects the body to very little wear and tear.

Disadvantages: The biggest problem is that most people pedal too slowly to derive full fat burning benefit. Cycling at 8 mph will not, as a rule, burn a significant number of calories. If you're going to rely on bicycling as a primary fat burning exercise, you have to pedal fast, ride up hills, and use a gear that offers substantial resistance.

Calories Expended: Around 350 to 500 calories per hour for the average person.

Cross Country Skiing

Advantages: It burns more calories than any other fat burning exercise.

Disadvantages: You can't ski all year around, and in some parts of the country, you can't ski at all.

Calories Expended: 600 to 900 calories per hour.

Aerobic Dancing

Advantages: A fun activity for all ages and sexes.

Disadvantages: It's difficult to measure progress. There's no way of knowing if you improve from week to week other than a subjective feeling.

Calories Expended: 250 to 600 per hour.

Running In Place & Rope Jumping

These two activities are combined since they have similar criticisms and advantages.

Advantages: They're a good rainy day replacement for other kinds of outdoor activities.

Disadvantages: Most people who rope skip or run in place find that motivation is the basic problem. They also tend to be subjected to a lot of knee and ankle pain. Both make it difficult to measure progress.

Calories Expended: Anywhere from 300 to 1,000 calories per hour. In the initial stages of learning you can burn 700 to 1,000 calories per hour. But once you have learned the skill, you expend only 300 to 500 calories per hour.

Stair Climbing

Advantages: This activity burns a lot of calories.

Disadvantages: Extremely boring. May be too demanding for most people. Would suggest only as a supplement to one of the big four.

Calories Expended: 700 to 1,200 per hour.

Stationary Bicycling

Advantages: Similar to those stated for bicycling.

Disadvantages: Can be an extremely boring activity.

Calories Expended: Burns 300 to 500 calories per hour.

Why Are These "Best" Exercises?

There's a good reason why these exercises are the champion fat burners. During these exercises your heart beats faster, your breathing becomes deeper, and your blood vessels expand and open up to carry oxygen and blood to your working muscles. In short, these activities place a greater demand on your heart, blood vessels, lungs, and muscles. They force you to take in, transport, and use extra amounts of oxygen. In other words, a lot of calories are used. Experts refer to these kinds of exercise as "aerobic" or "with air." I refer to them as fat-burning exercises.

Fat-burning exercises are to be continuous. This permits enough oxygen to get to the exercising muscles for as long as the exercise is continued. Any rhythmic, repetitive and dynamic activity which can be performed for three or more minutes without huffing and puffing qualifies. The jogger, swimmer, and bicyclist is engaging in a "pay as you go" type of exercise. In other words, enough oxygen is taken in to meet the demands of the exercise (aerobic). These are real fat-burners. A person sprinting, however, is not involved in a consistent fat-burning activity. The sprinter cannot keep up that pace without getting winded. This type of activity is called anaerobic exercise.

Another exercise that does not permit sustained activity is weight lifting. Weight lifting may be vigorous and do wonders for your arm and leg muscles, but it does very little to burn calories because the activity is not sustained. When lifting, the body is exercising vigorously, but you must rest after each intense effort. The drawback here is the intermittent pattern of lifting.

A popular activity which does not burn many calories is bowling. Here, too, the action is not sustained. When you deliver the ball, the effort is somewhat intense, but then you return to your seat and rest until it is your turn again. So bowling is not much of a calorie burner.

Golf also fails as a high fat-burner. Too often the game is played too slowly—about a one mile per hour pace—or from a cart. Consequently, its contribution to weight control is negligible— unless you play it the way former Michigan Governor George Romney does—running from hole to hole.

Even calisthenics may be insufficient in calorie burning. Most calisthenic programs tell you to do push-ups, rest, do sit-ups, rest, etc. The "rest" is the problem. For calisthenics to be effective in burning calories, you must keep moving.

Fortunately, some calisthenics programs can be adapted for use in calorie burning exercise. The idea is to keep moving from one exercise to another, smoothly and without pause. You might try doing your running in place in the kitchen, your knee bends in the living room, your push-ups in the bedroom. The point is to move and keep moving, but more on this later.

The key words, then, in describing a type of exercise to be selected for fat burning are "continual," "rhythmic," and "whole-bodied." Exercises that consist of erratic stopping and starting are indeed exercises and may serve other purposes, but they do little to burn calories.

Oxygen, Calories, And Heart Rate

To understand why certain activities qualify as fat burners and others do not, we need to look at what happens inside your body. Everything you do in life requires oxygen—sleeping, eating, studying, walking, running, swimming, and mountain climbing. Without oxygen your body could not survive. The nature of the activity dictates the amount of oxygen you will use for a given period of time. For example, when sleeping the average person uses about ⅕th to ¼th of a liter (a liter is slightly less than a quart) of oxygen per minute. When walking, one liter of oxygen is used and when running, two to three liters are used. The reason you use more oxygen while running and walking compared to sleeping or resting is that you use more muscles. And when more muscles are used, your body demands greater amounts of oxygen to keep working.

Oxygen supplies your body with energy. Without oxygen your heart wouldn't beat, your muscles wouldn't contract, your body simply wouldn't function. You need a minimum amount of oxygen each minute just to stay alive.

Surprisingly, the amount of oxygen used varies significantly from person to person for the same activities. The amount of oxygen your body requires just to keep going may be quite a bit more, or less, than what some other person's body needs to keep from grinding to a halt.

The difference has to do with individual basal metabolic rates. Roughly defined, the basal metabolic rate is the rate of oxygen necessary (measured when the subject is sleeping or at rest) to sustain all your body's vital processes.

Basal metabolic rate, in turn, has a lot to do with your size. For example, most men are bigger than most women. Men use about ¼th of a liter of oxygen per minute while resting or about

15 liters per hour. Women, on the other hand, usually use only about ⅛th of a liter per minute or about 12 liters per hour.

In the same way, different people use significantly different amounts of oxygen during activity. Variations occur depending upon age, level of fitness, sex, skill, nutrition, environmental conditions, and most importantly—body size. For instance, during an hour of walking a 200 pounder will use about 95 liters of oxygen, while a person weighing 100 pounds uses only 45 liters of oxygen. (Much as a big luxury car uses more gas than a little economy model to go the same distance.)

The following chart gives you an idea of how body size and the type of activity influences the amount of oxygen used.

Table 1
LITERS OF OXYGEN USED PER MINUTE

Activity	Weight			
	100	140	180	220
Sleeping	.17	.21	.26	.28
Watching TV	.22	.29	.34	.38
Driving a Car	.24	.31	.36	.40
Washing Dishes	.33	.43	.52	.55
Walking 2 mph	.47	.60	.71	.78
Playing Tennis	1.07	1.40	1.62	1.79
Running at 8 mph	1.76	2.28	2.68	2.93

But there's more to oxygen than meets the eye. Physiologists and nutritionists use the amount of oxygen consumed by your body to tell them how many calories you use for a particular activity. Generally, one liter of oxygen is the equivalent of 5 calories (4.825 actually). Therefore, if a half a liter of oxygen is used during a particular activity, slightly less than 2½ calories are used. If two liters of oxygen are used, then almost 10 calories per minute are used.

So Table #1 can be changed into the following. The answers given on this chart are the figures listed above and multiplied by 4.825.

Table 2
NUMBER OF CALORIES USED PER MINUTE

Activity	100	140	180	220
Sleeping	.83	1.00	1.25	1.33
Watching TV	1.08	1.41	1.66	1.83
Driving a Car	1.16	1.50	1.75	1.91
Washing Dishes	1.58	2.08	2.50	2.66
Walking 2 mph	2.25	2.91	3.41	3.75
Playing Tennis	5.16	6.75	7.83	8.66
Running 8 mph	8.50	11.00	12.91	14.16

As you can see, there is nothing mystical about calories. The more oxygen you use, the more calories you will burn. Consequently, the deeper you breathe *because of exercise*, the more calories you are using.

Now that you understand the best kinds of physical activity for fat control and the relationship between oxygen and calories, it's time to bring everything together.

Here I want to show you how hard, how long, and how often you must engage in fat-burning exercise to do you the most good.

How Hard?

Over the years physiologists have established that the best way to determine how hard you should exercise is to measure how much oxygen your body can use when exercising. To do this, doctors have you ride a specialized bicycle or walk and/or run on a treadmill. While you ride the bike or walk on the treadmill, and you give it an all out effort, the doctor can then measure your maximum aerobic capacity or your maximum oxygen consumption. Based on this information he can then give you a prescription on how hard you should exercise.

Unfortunately, most of us don't have access to such testing. And if we did, the cost might be prohibitive.

Fortunately, there is an alternative—and that alternative is your heart rate. In other words, the harder you breathe when exercising the faster your heart beats. A faster heart beat is the primary way you get more oxygen circulating through your body. Because of this parallel increase, you can use your heart rate as a worthy replacement for all the sophisticated testing described earlier. It's an indirect way, but it still works. While you can't always hop on a treadmill and monitor your oxygen consumption, you *can* reach for your wrist or neck and count your heart beat. Then you just make sure you work at a level that keeps your heart beating at the proper rate. That rate will be different for different people.

Everyone has what is called a "maximum heart rate." Your maximum heart rate is the number of beats your heart makes per minute when you are running as far, as fast, and as long as possible. (Another term for this is maximum aerobic power level.) Although it varies from person to person, your maximum heart rate is roughly 220 minus your age. If you're 20 years old, your maximum heart rate is about 200; if you're 40, it's about 180.

There is no need for you to exercise at your maximum heart rate level. That could be dangerous for the untrained. Physiologists have figured out a safe heart range for most people. They call this your target heart rate. Your target heart rate, as it is called in cardiovascular exercise programs, is considered about 70 to 85% of your maximum heart rate. That is your optimum level of exercise. That doesn't mean you can't improve your fitness if your heart rate is above or below this range. It's just that the 70 to 85% range is the safest, most efficient range.

Table #3 shows the maximum heart rate, target heart rate range, and the target heart rate for ages 20 to 70 in five year increments. You may calculate your own rate and range from this chart if your age falls between the ages listed. To use the chart, you must be able to take your pulse.

Table 3
YOUR TARGET HEART RATE AND HEART RATE RANGE

Age	Your Maximum Heart Rate (Beats per min.)	Your Target Heart Rate (75% of the Maximum in beats per min.)	Your Target Heart Rate Range (Between 70 and 85% of the Maximum in beats per min.)
20	200	150	140 to 170
25	195	146	137 to 166
30	190	142	133 to 162
35	185	139	130 to 157
40	180	135	126 to 153
45	175	131	123 to 149
50	170	127	119 to 145
55	165	124	116 to 140
60	160	120	112 to 136
65	155	116	109 to 132
70	150	112	105 to 128

There are three ways to take your pulse: at the radial artery on your wrist, the temperol artery on your forehead, and the carotid artery on your neck. To take your pulse at your wrist, use the second, third, and fourth fingers of your hand to feel for the pulse along the thumb side of your wrist. When you find your pulse (a thump or push), count it for 6 seconds and multiply the number of beats by 10. The number you get is your pulse per minute. If you want to take your pulse at your forehead, simply place your third and fourth fingers on your forehead and press. The counting is the same as for the wrist pulse.

If you can't find your pulse at your wrist or at the forehead, use the neck pulse. But if you do this, be careful and press lightly. Physicians frown upon taking a pulse this way. When people place their fingers at their neck and press hard, they may develop heart arrthymias (irregular heart beats), which for some could be serious. Their pulse rates also may slow down and give a false reading. So if you take your pulse this way, be sure to press lightly.

Figure 1. **Taking your pulse**

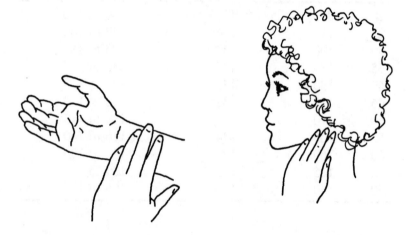

Once you have determined your target heart rate range based on the above chart, the next step is learning how to keep your heart rate in the proper range when exercising. The only way you can do this is by going out and exercising. Choose one of the fat-burning exercises, (walking, running, bicycling, etc.) and give it a try. Stop occasionally and count your pulse. If it's lower than your target range, you need to work a little harder. If it's higher, slow down. At first, you will have to experiment a little. But after a while you will be able to tell whether you are in the range simply by the way you feel.

If you tire quickly and noticeably when you exercise within your target heart rate range, reassess your range and lower it. That will most likely happen if you've been inactive for several years. Slow down until you are still working hard but not overexerting yourself. If, on the other hand, you do not feel the effect of your exercise, you may have to exercise at a faster rate.

Here's a pleasant thought to consider when you are exercising: when you are working at your target heart rate range, you're burning somewhere between 8 to 12 calories per minute depending upon your body size. And you're probably enjoying yourself. Isn't that a lot better than self-denial and hunger pain?

How Long?

When trying to burn calories and fat, the longer you work out, the better. At rest, your energy comes from glycogen and glucose (carbohydrates). When you sprint or do other types of anaerobic exercise, most of your energy will also be coming from carbohydrates. But when you perform aerobic exercise, there is a shift in your metabolism. During the first few minutes of exercise most of your energy comes from carbohydrates and very little, if any, comes from fat. But as you continue to exercise aerobically, the energy shift continues toward using more fat. After about 30 minutes, about half your energy comes from carbohydrates and the other half from fats.

That's why activities like basketball, tennis, weight lifting, and softball are not as effective as the Big 4 in burning fat. They may be enjoyable supplements to your regular aerobic activity, but you should not build a fat-burning program on these activities. There is too much time spent standing or sitting around. While you may achieve target heart rate, it is not sustained for any length of time. Let's take softball for example. When you step up to the plate and swing the bat a couple of times, your heart begins to speed up a little. If you get a hit, you take off toward first base at top speed. Within a very short time, you have reached target heart rate. Let's say it's a good hit and you round first, then head into second. Your heart is really cooking now. You reach second base safely, and then you stop. After all, you don't want to get thrown out at third. Now your heart starts to slow down a bit. By the time the next batter is up, your heart is beating much slower than target heart rate. If the next batter strikes out or walks, you're still left standing on second base. And your heart rate is back to normal. Finally, the inning is over, and you trot out to your position in left field, where you must stand for perhaps the whole inning, waiting for action. So in that inning of perhaps 10 minutes, you received approximately 30 seconds of target heart rate exercise. The same could be said for many other team sports. They do not offer enough sustained aerobic activity to burn substantial amounts of fat.

The longer you exercise aerobically, the more the shift is toward using fat. If you would exercise for about two hours, most of your energy would come from fat and just a small percentage from carbohydrates. So you can see it is very important that you choose an activity you can sustain for at least 30 minutes.

To determine the minimum amount of time you ought to spend exercising aerobically each day, you must first estimate your caloric imbalance. A quick way to do this is to find out how many pounds you gain (or seem to struggle with) each year. If five pounds is your problem, you can guesstimate that you are out of caloric balance by about 50 calories a day. If ten pounds is your problem, 100 calories a day is what you are out of balance. Fifteen pounds is 150 calories. And so on. You simply add a zero to the number of pounds you struggle with each year. That will give you the approximate number of calories that you are out of balance daily. Once you know that, you can then apply the next principle. Which is: for every 100 calories you are out of balance—that is every 10 pounds you want to lose or keep under control yearly—you need 8 to 12 minutes of exercise per day at target heart rate level. For most people, 30 minutes of target heart rate exercise causes a nice drop in body fat and weight. Additionally, the drop is fast enough to keep most people motivated to stay on the program because they see rapid results.

Table 4
SAMPLE WEIGHT LOSS CHART

Number of pounds you want to lose in a year. Average number of minutes of target heart rate exercise needed *daily* to lose weight.

Number of pounds you want to lose in a year.	Weight				
	100	125	150	175	200
5	6	5½	5	4½	4
10	12	11	10	9	8
15	18	16½	15	13½	12
20	24	22	20	18	16

How Often?

Now that you know how long and how hard, the next question is how often should you exercise? I recommend that you exercise a minimum of four times a week. Studies show that exercising two to three times a week may not be enough to make fast enough changes in body fat. So it becomes frustrating. Michael Pollock, Ph.D., Director of Cardiac Rehabilitation Laboratory at Mount Sinai Hospital in Milwaukee, has found that exercising four days a week is more effective for body composition than two days. This observation was supported by some of my own research showing that four-day-a-week exercise is superior to two-day-a-week exercise in altering body composition.

Interestingly, all the activities classified at the end of this chapter as moderate high, high, and very high are those which probably will produce target heart rate levels, or very close to target-heart-rate levels, depending upon your physical condition. So next time you engage in one of those exercises, check your pulse to find out for sure.*

The activities listed as moderate high, high, and very high are also the big calorie burners. They burn approximately 8 to 12 calories per minute for the average person.

If your heart rate does not get up to target heart rate levels, especially in those exercises listed as moderate, you can still use them in your weight control program. Simply double the length of time you do the exercise. If you want to do 30 minutes of target heart rate exercise but find the moderate activity doesn't get your heart rate up that high, exercise at a lower heart rate level for 60 minutes. You'll get the same fat-burning benefits.

The following tables indicate the number of calories you use when participating in various activities for one hour. A more detailed explanation of the Moderate, Moderate-High, High, and Very High exercise levels can be found in Appendix D.

---

*See Appendix C—Pulse Rate & Calories for an explanation of how you can use your heart rate to estimate the number of calories you use when exercising.

Table 5
CALORIES USED FOR MODERATE LEVEL ACTIVITIES
Per Hour
Weight in Pounds

Activity	71 or less	72–82	83–93	94–104	105–115	116–126	127–137	133–138	149–159	160–170	171–181	182–192	193 or more
Calisthenic Program													
a. Medium	250	275	300	325	350	370	395	420	445	470	490	515	540
Archery	180	195	210	230	245	260	280	295	315	330	345	365	380
Badminton													
a. singles recreational	200	220	235	255	275	295	310	330	350	370	385	405	425
b. doubles recreational	170	185	205	220	235	250	270	285	300	315	335	350	365
c. competitive (doubles)	260	290	310	335	360	385	410	435	460	485	510	535	560
Baseball													
a. pitcher only	220	245	265	285	305	325	350	370	390	410	435	455	475
b. catcher only	195	215	235	255	270	295	310	330	350	365	385	405	420
Bicycling													
a. 10mph	235	260	280	300	325	350	370	395	415	440	460	475	505
Calisthenics (general)	170	185	200	220	235	250	270	285	300	315	335	350	365
Canadian XBX													
a. Level 12	170	185	205	220	235	250	270	285	300	315	335	350	365
Canoeing													
a. 2mph	170	185	200	220	235	250	270	285	300	315	335	350	365
Carpentry work													
a. heavy	190	220	240	260	280	300	315	335	355	375	395	415	430
Carrying trays, dishes, etc.													
a. busboy	170	185	205	220	235	250	270	285	300	315	335	350	365
Chopping wood													
a. hand	255	280	305	330	355	375	400	425	450	475	500	525	550

Table 5
CALORIES USED FOR MODERATE LEVEL ACTIVITIES
Per Hour
Weight in Pounds

Activity	71 or less	72–82	83–93	94–104	105–115	116–126	127–137	138–148	149–159	160–170	171–181	182–192	193 or more
Dancing													
a. Aerobic (medium)	250	275	300	325	350	370	395	420	445	470	490	515	540
b. rumba	170	185	205	220	235	250	270	285	300	315	335	350	365
c. square	240	260	285	305	330	350	375	400	420	445	465	480	510
Farming													
a. haying & plowing with horse	225	250	270	290	315	335	355	380	400	420	445	465	485
Fencing													
a. recreational	170	185	205	220	235	250	270	285	300	315	355	350	365
Fishing													
a. stream (wading)	170	185	205	220	235	250	270	285	300	315	355	350	365
Fitness Finders Workout													
a. low	180	195	215	230	215	265	280	300	315	330	350	365	385
Gardening (weeding, hoeing, digging, etc.)	220	240	260	285	305	325	345	365	390	410	430	450	470
Gas station attendant													
a. fix flats—wrecker work	190	220	240	260	280	300	315	335	355	375	395	415	430
Golf													
a. two some 9 holes in 1½ hrs., (carrying clubs)	215	235	255	275	295	320	340	360	380	400	420	440	460
b. two some 9 holes in 1½ hrs., (pull clubs)	190	205	225	245	260	280	295	315	335	350	370	385	405
Gymnastics													
a. light	170	185	205	220	235	250	270	285	300	315	335	350	365

	71 or less	72–82	83–93	94–104	105–115	116–126	127–137	138–148	149–159	160–170	171–181	182–192	193 or more
Hiking													
a. 20 lb. pack, 2 mph	170	185	205	220	235	250	270	285	300	315	335	350	365
b. 20 lb. pack, 3½ mph	220	235	255	280	300	320	340	360	380	400	420	440	465
c. 20 lb. pack, 4 mph	255	280	305	330	355	375	400	425	450	475	500	525	550
Horseback riding													
a. trot	235	260	280	300	325	350	370	395	415	440	460	475	505
Hunting (not sitting)	255	280	305	330	355	375	400	425	450	475	500	525	550
Jackhammer (pneumatic tools)	25	280	305	330	355	375	400	425	450	475	500	525	550
Lawn mowing													
a. push	260	285	310	335	360	385	410	435	460	485	510	535	560
Motorcycling													
a. racing	170	185	205	220	235	250	270	285	300	315	335	350	365
Pick & shovel work (continuous)	225	250	270	290	315	335	355	380	400	420	445	465	490
Rowing													
a. pleasure 2 mph	170	185	205	220	235	250	270	285	300	315	335	350	365
Rowing machine													
a. easy	170	185	205	200	235	250	270	285	300	315	335	350	365
Sawing													
a. hand	220	245	265	285	305	325	350	370	390	410	435	455	475
Scuba diving	255	280	305	330	355	375	400	425	450	475	500	525	550
Sex													
a. intercourse (aggressor)	170	185	205	220	235	250	270	285	300	315	335	350	365
Skating (leisure)													
a. ice	200	215	235	255	275	295	310	330	350	370	385	405	425
b. roller	200	215	235	255	275	295	310	330	350	370	385	405	425
Skin diving	255	280	305	330	355	375	400	425	450	475	500	525	550
Sledding	240	265	290	310	335	355	380	405	425	450	470	495	520

Table 5
CALORIES USED FOR MODERATE LEVEL ACTIVITIES
Per Hour
Weight in Pounds

Activity	71 or less	72–82	83–93	94–104	105–115	116–126	127–137	138–148	149–159	160–170	171–181	182–192	193 or more
Snowshoeing 2.2 mph	215	235	255	280	300	320	340	360	380	400	420	440	465
Stacking lumber	215	235	255	280	300	320	340	360	380	400	420	440	465
Stationary bicycle—resistance sufficient to get pulse rate to 130													
a. 10 mph	240	260	285	305	330	355	375	400	420	445	465	490	515
Stone masonry	215	235	255	280	300	320	340	360	380	400	420	440	465
Swimming (crawl)													
a. 20 yards per minute	170	185	205	220	235	250	270	285	300	315	335	350	365
b. 30 yards per minute	240	260	285	305	330	350	375	400	420	445	465	480	510
Table tennis													
a. recreational	170	185	205	220	235	250	270	285	300	315	335	350	365
b. vigorous	255	280	305	330	355	375	400	425	450	475	500	525	550
Tennis (singles)													
a. recreational	240	265	290	310	335	355	380	405	425	450	470	495	520
Tennis (doubles)													
a. recreational	170	185	205	220	235	250	270	285	300	315	335	350	365
b. competitive	240	265	290	310	335	355	380	405	425	450	470	495	520
Treadmill													
a. 3 mph	170	185	205	220	235	250	270	285	300	315	335	350	365
b. 4 mph	195	215	235	255	270	290	310	330	345	365	385	405	520
Volleyball													
a. recreational	200	215	235	255	275	295	310	330	350	370	385	405	425

	71 or less	72–82	83–93	94–104	105–115	116–126	127–137	138–148	149–159	160–170	171–181	182–192	
Walking													
a. 2 mph	105	115	125	135	145	155	165	175	185	195	205	215	225
b. 2½ mph	145	160	175	185	200	215	230	240	255	270	285	300	310
c. 3 mph	170	185	205	220	235	250	270	285	300	315	335	350	365
d. 3½ mph	180	195	215	230	245	265	280	300	315	330	350	365	385
e. 4 mph	195	215	235	255	270	290	310	330	345	365	385	405	420
f. 4½ mph	255	280	305	330	355	375	400	425	450	475	500	525	550
g. upstairs (normal pace)	255	280	305	330	355	375	400	425	450	475	500	525	550
h. downstairs (normal pace)	255	280	305	330	355	375	400	425	450	475	500	525	550
Weight training (does not include super sets)	170	185	205	220	235	250	270	285	300	315	335	350	365
Weeding	170	185	205	220	235	250	270	285	300	315	335	350	365

Table 6
CALORIES USED FOR MODERATE HIGH LEVEL ACTIVITIES
Per Hour

Activity	71 or less	72–82	83–93	94–104	105–115	116–126	127–137	138–148	149–159	160–170	171–181	182–192	193 or more
Calisthenic Program													
a. High	315	345	375	405	435	465	495	525	555	585	615	645	675
Badminton													
a. competitive (vigorous) singles	345	380	410	445	480	510	545	575	610	645	675	710	740
Basketball													
a. nongame, ½ court, ect.	315	345	375	405	435	465	495	525	555	585	615	645	675
b. officiating	315	345	375	405	435	465	495	525	555	585	615	645	675
Beach stepping—30 steps per minute													
a. 7"	345	380	415	455	480	510	545	575	610	645	675	710	745
Boxing (sparring only)	310	340	370	400	430	460	490	520	550	580	610	640	670
Canadian 5Bx													
a. Chart 1A	290	315	345	375	400	430	455	485	510	540	565	595	620
Canadian XBX													
a. Level 24	290	315	345	375	400	430	455	485	510	440	565	595	620
Canoeing													
a. 4 mph	355	390	425	450	490	525	560	595	625	660	695	730	765
Dancing													
a. polka	305	335	365	395	425	455	480	510	540	570	600	630	655
Digging	285	310	340	365	390	420	445	475	500	525	555	580	610
Fencing													
a. competitive (vigorous)	345	380	415	445	480	510	545	575	610	645	675	710	745

Weight in Pounds

	71 or less	72–82	83–93	94–104	105–115	116–126	127–137	138–148	149–159	160–170	171–181	182–192	193 or more
Fitness Finder Workout													
a. medium	275	300	325	350	375	405	430	455	480	505	535	560	585
b. high	340	375	415	435	470	500	535	565	600	630	665	695	730
Football													
a. playground (touch)	340	375	405	435	470	500	535	565	600	630	665	685	730
b. officiating	315	345	375	405	435	465	495	525	555	585	615	645	675
Gymnastics													
a. medium	290	316	345	375	400	430	455	485	510	540	565	595	620
Handball													
a. cut throat	340	375	405	435	470	500	535	565	600	630	665	695	730
b. 4	290	315	345	375	400	430	455	485	510	540	565	595	620
Hill climbing	340	375	405	435	470	500	535	565	600	630	665	695	730
Horseback riding													
a. gallop	340	375	405	435	470	500	535	565	600	630	665	695	730
Mountain climbing	340	375	405	435	470	500	535	565	600	630	665	695	730
Orienteering	340	375	405	435	470	500	535	565	600	630	665	695	730
Ropeskipping													
a. 50–60 skips left foot only (per min.)	290	315	345	375	400	430	455	485	510	540	565	595	620
b. 80–80 skips left foot only (per min.)	315	345	375	405	435	465	495	525	555	585	615	645	675
Run in place													
a. 50–60 steps per min. (left foot only)	290	315	345	375	400	430	455	485	510	540	565	595	620

Table 6
CALORIES USED FOR MODERATE HIGH LEVEL ACTIVITIES
Per Hour

Weight in Pounds

Activity	71 or less	72–82	83–93	94–104	105–115	116–126	127–137	138–148	149–159	160–170	171–181	182–192	193 or more
b. 70–80 steps per min. (left foot only)	315	345	375	405	435	465	495	525	555	585	615	645	675
Running													
a. 5.5 mph	370	405	445	480	515	550	585	620	655	690	725	760	795
b. 6.0 mph	375	415	455	490	525	760	595	630	670	705	740	775	810
c. 6.5 mph	385	425	465	500	535	570	610	645	685	720	755	790	830
d. 7.0 mph	395	435	475	510	550	585	625	660	700	735	775	810	850
e. 7.5 mph	425	465	510	545	585	625	670	710	750	790	830	870	910
Skating (vigorous)													
a. ice	355	385	420	455	485	520	555	590	620	655	690	720	755
b. roller	355	385	420	455	485	520	555	590	620	655	690	720	755
Skiing													
a. downhill (continuous riding & lifts not inluded)	355	370	400	435	465	500	530	560	595	625	660	690	720
Snowshoveling													
a. light	345	380	415	455	475	510	545	575	610	645	675	710	745
Soccer	340	375	405	435	470	500	535	565	600	630	665	695	730
Swimming (crawl)													
a. 35 yards per minute	305	335	365	395	425	455	480	510	540	570	600	630	655
b. 40 yards per minute	340	375	405	435	470	500	535	560	600	630	665	695	730
Tennis (singles)													
a. competitive	340	375	405	435	470	500	535	565	600	630	665	695	730

	71 or less	72–82	83–93	94–104	105–115	116–126	127–137	138–148	149–159	160–170	171–181	182–192	193 or more
Volleyball													
a. competitive	340	375	405	435	470	500	535	565	600	630	665	695	730
Walking													
a. 5 mph	315	345	375	405	435	465	495	525	555	585	615	645	675
Winter skiing	275	300	325	350	375	405	430	455	480	505	535	560	585

Table 7
CALORIES USED FOR HIGH LEVEL ACTIVITIES
Per Hour
Weight in Pounds

Activity	71 or less	72–82	83–93	94–104	105–115	116–126	127–137	138–148	149–159	160–170	171–181	182–192	193 or more
Basketball													
a. game (full court, countinuous)	425	465	505	545	585	630	670	710	750	790	830	870	910
Bicycling													
a. 13 mph	370	410	445	480	515	550	585	620	655	690	725	760	780
Canadian 5Bx													
a. Chart 2A	365	400	435	470	505	540	575	610	645	680	715	750	785
Canadian XBX													
a. Level 36	370	410	445	480	515	550	585	620	655	690	725	760	780
b. Level 48	450	490	535	575	620	660	705	750	790	835	875	920	960
Dancing													
a. Aerobic (high)	370	405	445	480	515	550	585	620	655	690	725	760	795
Gymnastics													
a. hard	405	440	480	520	555	595	635	670	710	750	785	810	865
Handball													
a. 2	440	485	525	565	610	650	695	735	775	820	860	905	945
Jogging (5.5 mph)	370	405	445	480	515	550	585	620	655	690	725	760	795
Jduo	450	490	535	575	620	660	705	750	790	835	875	920	960
Karate	450	490	535	575	620	660	705	750	790	835	875	920	960
Martial arts	450	490	535	575	620	660	705	750	790	835	875	920	960
Ropeskipping													
a. 90–100 skips left foot only (per min.)	370	405	445	480	515	550	585	620	655	690	725	760	795

	71 or less	72–82	83–93	94–104	105–115	116–126	127–137	138–148	149–159	160–170	171–181	182–192	193 or more
Rowing													
a. vigorous 4 mph	370	405	445	480	515	550	585	620	655	690	725	750	795
Rowing machine													
a. vigorous	370	405	445	480	515	550	585	620	655	690	725	750	795
Run in place													
a. 90–100 steps per min. (left foot only)	370	405	445	480	515	550	585	620	655	690	725	750	795
Running													
a. 8.0 mph	455	495	540	585	625	670	715	755	800	845	885	930	975
b. 8.5 mph	490	530	580	630	670	720	770	810	860	905	950	1000	1045
c. 9.0 mph	525	570	620	675	720	770	825	865	920	970	1020	1070	1120
d. 9.5 mph	560	605	660	720	765	820	880	920	980	1030	1085	1140	1190
Skiing													
a. cross country—5 mph	395	435	475	510	550	585	625	660	700	735	775	800	850
Stationary bicycle—resistance sufficient to get pulse rate to 130													
a. 15 mph	370	405	445	480	515	550	585	620	655	690	725	760	795
Swimming (crawl)													
a. 45 yards per minute	390	430	465	500	540	575	615	650	690	725	765	800	835
Trampolining	450	490	535	575	620	660	705	750	790	835	875	920	960
Walking													
a. 5½ mph	370	405	445	480	515	550	585	620	655	690	725	760	795

Table 8
CALORIES USED FOR VERY HIGH LEVEL ACTIVITIES
Per Hour
Weight in Pounds

Activity	71 or less	72–82	83–93	94–104	105–115	116–126	127–137	138–148	149–159	160–170	171–181	182–192	193 or more
Bench stepping—30 steps per minute													
a. 12"	455	495	540	585	625	670	715	755	800	840	885	930	970
b. 16"	630	690	750	810	870	930	990	1050	1100	1170	1230	1290	1350
c. 18"	795	870	945	1020	1095	1170	1245	1325	1400	1475	1550	1625	1700
Canadian 5Bx													
a. Charts 3A & 4A	545	600	650	700	755	805	910	960	960	1010	1065	1115	1170
b. Charts 5A & 6A	550	600	655	705	760	810	865	915	970	1020	1075	1125	1180
Football													
a. tackle	475	520	565	610	660	705	750	795	835	885	930	975	1020
Hockey													
a. ice	510	560	610	655	705	755	805	850	900	950	1000	1045	1095
b. field	510	560	610	655	705	755	805	850	900	950	1000	1045	1095
Lacrosse	510	560	610	655	705	755	805	850	900	950	1000	1045	1095
Ropeskipping													
a. 110–120 skips left foot only (per min.)	510	560	610	655	705	755	805	850	900	950	1000	1045	1095
b. 130–140 skips left foot only (per min.)	680	745	810	875	940	1005	1070	1135	1200	1265	1330	1395	1460
Run in place													
a. 110–120 steps per min. (left foot only)	510	560	610	655	705	755	805	850	900	950	1000	1045	1095
b. 130–140 steps per min. (left foot only)	680	745	810	875	940	1005	1070	1135	1200	1265	1330	1395	1460

	71 or less	72–82	83–93	94–104	105–115	116–126	127–137	138–148	149–159	160–170	171–181	182–192	193 or more
Running													
a. 10.0 mph	590	645	705	760	815	875	930	980	1040	1095	1155	1210	1265
b. 10.5 mph	625	680	745	805	860	925	980	1040	1100	1155	1220	1280	1335
c. 11.0 mph	660	720	785	850	910	975	1035	1095	1160	1220	1290	1350	1410
d. 11.5 mph	695	760	825	890	955	1025	1090	1155	1220	1285	1355	1420	1485
e. 12.0 mph	790	865	940	1015	1090	1165	1240	1315	1390	1465	1540	1615	1690
f. 12.5 mph	880	965	1050	1135	1220	1300	1385	1470	1555	1640	1720	1805	1890
Sprinting	1385	1520	1650	1780	1915	2045	2180	2310	2440	2575	2705	2840	2970
Skiing													
a. cross country—9 mph	565	620	675	730	785	835	890	945	1000	1055	1105	1160	1215
Snowshoveling													
a. heavy	600	655	710	770	825	885	940	995	1055	1110	1170	1225	1280
Stationary bicycle—resistance sufficient to get pulse rate to 130													
a. 20 mph	505	550	600	650	700	745	795	840	885	935	985	1030	1080
Swimming (crawl)													
a. 55 yards per minute	475	520	565	610	660	705	750	795	835	885	930	975	1020
Walking													
a. upstairs, 2 at a time, rapidly	565	620	675	730	785	835	890	945	1000	1055	1105	1160	1215

8

An Extra Dose—The Little Things That Count

So far, I've talked about big muscle activities that will help you lose weight. Without dieting. Choose your activity, check your pulse, and stick with it. You'll see the results soon. For a bonus, I also recommend some changes in your lifestyle to help keep the pounds off. Program a little more activity into your life. You can't go back to the good old days of no frills hard labor, but you can find ways to "move to lose."

Just as you might take a vitamin or mineral supplement to augment your regular diet, you can add some of these bonus activities to supplement your normal daily activity. These mini-activities are not major fat-burners, but they do boost your caloric expenditure, and the results add up nicely. Mainly, these activities involve doing things the "hard way." This doesn't necessarily mean that the activities are difficult. They just help you use a little more energy than the minimum that's required when you do things the "easy way."

Here's an example of a mini-activity at its most basic: when you sit, you burn more calories than when you lie down flat. Not many more, mind you. In fact, the difference amounts only to two calories an hour. But if you watch an average five hours of TV daily, and you are in the habit of reclining on the sofa to do it, sit up instead. By doing this, in a year's time you will burn the equivalent of one pound of fat.

So what? Well, a single pound of fat in a year isn't going to have much of an effect on your appearance, your health, or your dress size. But by programming many different mini-activities into your life, the total pound difference at year's end will make you glad you did.

Here are a few "slow-burners" that are worth keeping in mind:

1. Never lie down when you can sit up.
2. Never sit when you can stand. The caloric difference per hour is 10 calories, more or less depending upon your present weight—not much, perhaps, but enough to have a discernable effect over the months.
3. Get into the habit of "pacing." Instead of dropping into a chair to mull over a problem, get up and move around. (Some of the world's best thinkers are habitual floor pacers!)
4. As a general rule, never sit more than an hour and a half without standing, stretching, and walking (or pacing) for 5 minutes or so. Not only will this burn extra calories, but you go back refreshed to whatever you were doing, and you'll be more efficient at it.
5. Run in place whenever you can, even if it's only for 30 seconds or so. "Waiting time" is a natural for this. You can run in place as you wait for your toast to pop up or the tea water to boil. A friend of mine always runs in place for a minute or two when he visits the bathroom.

The next recommendation is so important that it deserves capital letters and a whole section of its own. In today's gimmic- and gadget-oriented society, it becomes very easy to sit back and watch machines do the work that we should be doing. NEVER USE A MACHINE WHEN YOU CAN USE BODY POWER INSTEAD. In other words:

Don't use the escalator or elevator if there are stairs.
Don't drive if you can get there by bicycle or foot.
Don't use an electric mixer or blender if you can do the job by hand.
Don't use a power saw if a hand saw will do the job.
Don't use a dryer if you have a clothes line out in the yard to help you bend and stretch.

I'm sure you can think of dozens of instances where body power can be substituted for mechanical or electrical power without really causing much inconvenience; there's no need for me to list them all here. But let's take a brief look at a few selected activities and the comparative calorie consumption of using body power versus operating a machine.

The following examples were computed on a per-hour basis, using the average weight of a 120 pounder.

Table 9

BODY POWER VS. MACHINE POWER

Walking (3 mph)	250	vs	Riding in a car	65
			Driving a car	85
Bicycling 5.5mph	205	vs	Motorcycling	170
Bicycling 13mph	550			
Climbing stairs (1mph)	375	vs	Escalator or elevators	85
Hanging wash on the line	205	vs	Putting clothes in dryer	135
Washing dishes by hand	110	vs	Using dishwasher	95
Using manual typewriter	95	vs	Using electric typewriter	90
Beating cake batter by hand	140	vs	Using mixer	95
Using shovel for snow removal	885	vs	Using snow blower	210
Walking behind power mower	225	vs	Driving tractor-type mower	120

Obviously, the doing-things-the-hard-way concept can be carried to the point of absurdity (there's no point in rubbing two sticks together instead of using a match or cigarette lighter). You'll have to arrive at your own decision as to where to draw the line. But as you can see from the above examples, you might burn somewhere in the neighborhood of 15 extra calories by washing a large load of dishes by hand instead of running the dishwasher, and this could make a 1½ pound difference in your weight if you did it every night for a year. But it might also mean you'd have less time for a more important, high fat-burning activity that you enjoy. The point, of course, is to know that in the long run doing things the hard way can have a real impact on fat loss. Once you accept this philosophy, you can use the information in whatever ways make most sense for your time, energy, and personal preferences.

You may also discover a fun and interesting fringe benefit to doing things the hard way. Sometimes the "hard way" is the "fun way." Perhaps one reason many people find life so boring is that they have gradually allowed machines to rob them of all the fun involved in doing. Machines have changed us from active to passive people. While that has many positive implications, it can produce some negative ones too. Let me illustrate. A friend of mine has a fireplace. Every fall he orders a few cords of wood. Last fall, his supplier dropped off the customary three cords of wood. However, something was different. The wood hadn't been split. At first my friend was upset. When he cooled off, he decided that he would merely rent a hydraulic log splitter and do the job. When he saw the cost of renting the machine for an hour, he gave in and bought a large ax. Says he, "I'd forgotten how much fun it was to split wood. Now, it's a regular part of my day. And one that I look forward to!" To top it all off, he discovered purchasing wood that hadn't been split was cheaper.

Here's another example of the shape-up potential of doing things the hard way: Sid J. was a 48-year-old editor who carried about seven extra pounds of fat. His muscles, especially the ones around the middle, were slack and flabby from lack of exercise.

Sid went to a couple of my classes, became enthusiastic about the basic premise, but decided to drop out of the course and apply the principles his own way.

It seems that over the years he had collected an impressive array of power equipment including a tractor-type lawn mower, snow blower, power saw, electric hedge clippers, and other conveniences. These aided him in the upkeep and maintenance of his house, a sprawling ranch model set back on an acre of heavily-wooded land. He was struck by the possibilities of doing without all this elaborate equipment. So, in an effort to get his weight down and his body back into shape, he either loaned out or gave away most of his tools.

That winter found Sid hoisting the snow from his drive with a shovel. When the weather warmed, an old hand mower, retired to the garage for many years, was hauled out and reactivated for lawn duty. Shrubbery and hedge were clipped and pruned with hand clippers. When there was carpentry to be done, Sid sawed the wood by hand. And so on.

Sid started doing things the hard way in February. By September, he had dropped eight pounds and trimmed two inches from his waist, without dieting, and he had never felt or looked better.

You may not have a big house or an acre of lawn to take care of, but that needn't stop you from programming mini-activities into your life. You can boost the calorie consumption of almost anything you do by doing it the hard way—and thereby speed up the weight loss process.

Here's a good basic plan for supplementing regular activities with mini-activities. Start off with these; add more as you think of them.

1. Stand when dressing and undressing.
2. Park your car several blocks from your ultimate destination

and walk the final distance. (Be sure to walk vigorously. Al Melleby, co-founder of the National Y's Way to a Healthy Back Program, calls it "striding.")
3. Take a 10-minute walk at noon and a 15-minute walk in the evening.
4. Don't collapse into a chair immediately after dinner. Wait until 9:00 or so. Until then, pursue a hobby, do chores, or find some other way to be active.
5. Housework, yardwork, any kind of work should be done with brisk, vigorous movements. Bend, reach, stretch, move as much as possible.
6. If you're a parent, take time out for active play with your kids. Teach them how to do somersaults, log rolls, cartwheels. This kind of family fun not only helps you burn extra calories, it will encourage the children to be more active, and you can't teach them a better habit.
7. Save money and get a good workout too by washing and waxing the car yourself.
8. If you have a remote-control TV channel selector, be good to yourself and put it away in a closet. If you're going to spend a lot of time watching TV, the very least you can do is get up, stretch your legs, and walk over to the set to switch channels every once in a while.

Here are some examples of people I know:

—One woman with a large family walks to the store and buys only one gallon of milk at a time. The store is one half mile from home. That way she is forced to get one extra mile of walking in every day, since milk never lasts long around her place.
—Another woman I know puts the clothes hamper at the bottom of the basement stairs. This forces her to use the stairs more frequently.
—Many men and women who work in large office buildings

use the stairs instead of elevators. They are discovering first hand that you burn more calories per minute climbing stairs than running a marathon.

—A couple that lives just outside of town are building their own home. In addition to solar and wind energy, they are incorporating the use of their own energy. They have developed a water system that relies on gravity. A reservoir in the attic is filled regularly. How is it filled? They have rigged up a pump to a stationary bicycle. A few minutes of pedaling each day fills the reservoir and gives them a little extra exercise. Extreme, perhaps, but they enjoy it.

—Another housewife I know turns her record player on when it's time to do housework. Then she literally dances her way to a cleaner house. By the time she is finished, she has a clean house and a rapidly beating heart. And she says it makes housework a lot less tedious.

—A man I know refuses to use his car for a trip less than one mile. He has made it a standing rule for himself and his family. The only exception is terribly inclement weather. He discovered two things: he took fewer "necessary" trips to the neighbors, the party store, and the post office. He also discovered that making those trips on foot provided a pleasant relief from the rat race.

We all know people who could fit here. People who make a special effort to program activity into their lives. Now we need to do it for ourselves. We need to become the examples. Take a look at the things you do where you rely on a machine. Pick one of those things and resolve to do it by hand for a week. I think you will enjoy the results.

Family Plans

One of my favorite techniques for motivating people to exercise is to arrange a once a week family session—one that's organized around activities that allow everyone to burn off a few hundred extra calories. What better gift could you give your family? Not only will you be introducing your spouse and children to a helpful alternative to television and other sedentary habits, you will also be closer as a family. I know. I've done it, and I know other families that have done it too. They all mention the feeling of greater closeness that comes as a result of taking time out to play together.

Saturday and Sunday afternoons are probably the best times for these sessions, but during long daylight hours of the summer, an hour after supper always works fine. As for activities; cycling is good, so is swimming, jogging, walking, hiking, and such games as volleyball, softball, or touch football. The key word should be FUN. Avoid doing the same things day in and day out. Learning to do a new sport together as a family can be an enjoyable experience. Or, equip the backyard with a simple apparatus for chin-ups, rope climbing, or high jumping to help "induce labor." Why not set up a make-shift obstacle course and time everyone once a week, then chart everyone's improvement? There are endless possibilities here including old tires to run through, a two-by-four tight rope, bails of straw to hurdle, or a rope stretched between two trees to hand walk.

Your children may enjoy simple games as skipping rope and wheel barrels. Another fun activity for the little ones is imitating animals (kangaroo, crab, inch worm, bunny, etc.). Or why not just a little free form rough and tumble play? Toddlers love it and so do most grown ups once they shed their inhibitions. And don't forget about dancing. A friend of mine told me he'll always remember the rainy Saturday afternoon he and his wife taught their two teenage girls the Jitterbug while the kids reciprocated with instructions for disco dancing.

What about TV? Television has become the scapegoat for just about every conceivable ill that plagues society. I suppose I could add my voice of criticism by suggesting that children (and adults too for that matter) spend far too much time sitting around watching television and becoming sedentary. I choose to take a more positive approach. I think television may even be used as a motivator. In my family, we have a beat up black and white portable television. It is seldom used. That's because it's a pay TV. For every minute of TV watching, I ask my children to add an extra minute of physical activity into their lives. So, a half hour program means a half hour of jogging, cycling, swimming, or lawn mowing. Not a bad trade off. In addition, I monitor what they watch, and I have learned where the on/off button is. I believe that given a choice, most children would rather do something active rather than sit and watch television. Part of the problem is that we often provide very little opportunity for them to do anything but sit and watch the tube. Perhaps pursuing fitness as a family will help put television in proper perspective for you and your kids.

The rationale behind family fitness sessions is that you're far more likely to spend an extra hour or two on activity if you work out with a group—or even with just one other person—than if you try to do it alone. If you're single, get a few friends who want to stay in shape—or get back into shape—and institute a "friendly" fitness session.

These weekly sessions are a pleasant way to burn off an extra 400 calories or so without trying too hard. You'll have fun doing it, and by the end of the year you'll be at least five pounds ahead of the game.

Now it's time for you to take over. Be creative and put your mind to work. I've given you an idea of the types of activities I'm talking about when I refer to "bonus activities." The sneaky little ways to burn off fat without actually having to think about it. As you may have noticed, I never mentioned running 20 miles at a five-minute-per-mile pace or furiously pedaling a bicycle uphill all day. If you have been told that the only way to lose weight through activity is to run yourself to a frazzle, you have been sadly misinformed. I contend that losing weight through activity is not only effective but fun. More and more people who try it are discovering life is a lot more exciting when you put something into it.

Here are some activities which are low or mild in terms of calories expended, but they can make a significant difference when it comes to helping you lose fat. Don't neglect them.

The following tables indicate the number of calories you use when participating in various activities for one hour. A more detailed explanation of the Low and Mild exercise levels can be found in Appendix D.

Table 10
CALORIES USED FOR LOW LEVEL ACTIVITIES
Per Hour
Weight in Pounds

Activity	71 or less	72–82	83–93	94–104	105–115	116–126	127–137	138–148	149–159	160–170	171–181	182–192	193 or more
Baking													
a. using mixer	65	70	75	80	85	95	100	105	110	115	125	130	135
Bartending													
a. slow	75	85	90	95	105	110	120	125	135	140	150	155	160
Card playing	50	55	60	65	70	75	80	85	90	95	100	105	110
Checkout counter work	75	85	90	95	105	110	120	125	135	140	150	155	160
Chess	50	55	60	65	70	75	80	85	90	95	100	105	110
Class work (sitting)	50	55	60	65	70	75	80	85	90	95	100	105	110
Coffe klatch	55	60	65	70	75	80	85	90	95	100	105	110	115
Driving a car													
a. standard—heavy traffic	75	85	90	95	105	110	120	125	135	140	150	155	160
b. standard—light traffic	55	60	70	75	80	85	90	95	100	105	110	115	120
c. automatic—heavy traffic	55	60	70	75	80	85	90	95	100	105	110	115	120
d. automatic—light traffic	55	60	65	70	75	80	85	90	95	100	105	110	115
Driving a truck													
a. regular	80	90	95	105	115	120	130	135	145	150	160	170	175
Eating	50	55	60	65	70	75	80	85	90	95	100	105	110
Fishing													
a. boat	75	85	90	95	105	110	120	125	135	140	150	155	160
Kneeling	45	50	55	55	60	65	70	75	80	80	85	90	95
Lecturing													
a. standing	70	75	85	90	95	100	110	115	120	130	135	140	150
b. sitting	55	60	70	75	80	85	90	95	100	105	110	115	120

	71 or less	72–82	83–93	94–104	105–115	116–126	127–137	138–148	149–159	160–170	171–181	182–192	193 or more
Personal Toilet	70	75	85	90	95	100	110	115	120	130	135	140	150
Piano playing	70	75	85	90	95	100	110	115	120	130	135	140	150
Resting	45	45	50	55	60	65	65	70	75	80	85	90	90
Sex													
a. foreplay	55	60	70	75	80	85	90	95	100	105	110	115	120
b. submissor	75	85	90	95	105	110	120	125	135	140	150	155	160
Shining shoes	75	85	90	95	105	110	120	125	135	140	150	155	160
Sitting													
a. quietly	45	50	55	55	60	65	70	75	80	80	85	90	95
b. reading	50	55	60	65	70	75	80	85	90	95	100	105	110
c. hand work—knitting, crocheting, sewing	55	60	65	70	75	80	85	90	95	100	105	110	115
d. in truck or car	50	55	60	65	70	75	80	85	90	95	100	105	110
Sleeping	35	40	45	50	50	55	60	60	65	70	75	80	80
Standing													
a. light activity—dishwashing	75	85	90	95	105	110	120	125	135	140	150	155	160
b. normally	55	60	70	75	80	85	90	95	100	105	110	115	120
Studying	45	50	55	60	65	70	75	80	85	90	90	95	100
Telephone (talking)													
a. sitting	50	55	60	65	70	75	80	85	90	95	100	105	110
b. standing	65	70	75	80	85	95	100	105	110	115	125	130	135
TV watching	45	50	55	55	60	65	70	75	80	80	85	90	95
Typing													
a. electric	60	65	70	75	80	90	95	100	105	110	115	120	130
b. manual	65	70	80	85	90	95	105	110	115	125	130	135	0

Table 10
CALORIES USED FOR LOW LEVEL ACTIVITIES
Per Hour
Weight in Pounds

Activity	71 or less	72–82	83–93	94–104	105–115	116–126	127–137	138–148	149–159	160–170	171–181	182–192	193 or more
Washing dishes													
a. by hand	75	85	90	95	105	110	120	125	135	140	150	155	160
b. dishwasher	65	70	75	80	85	95	100	105	110	115	125	130	135
Writing	50	55	60	65	70	75	80	85	90	95	100	105	110

For an alphabetical listing of calories used per minute, see Appendix D,

Table 11
CALORIES USED FOR MILD LEVEL ACTIVITIES
Per Hour
Weight in Pounds

Activity	71 or less	72–82	83–93	94–104	105–115	116–126	127–137	138–148	149–159	160–170	171–181	182–192	193 or more
Calisthenic Program													
a. Low	155	170	185	200	215	230	245	260	285	290	305	320	335
Assembly & Assembly line work													
a. light/medium machine parts at own pace	125	140	150	160	175	185	200	210	220	235	245	260	270
b. light/medium machine parts at 500 times per day or more	150	160	175	190	205	220	235	245	260	275	290	305	315
c. working on assembly line where parts require lifting at about every 5 minutes or so lift is for a few seconds and weighs less than 45 lbs.	150	160	175	190	205	220	235	245	260	275	290	305	315
d. same as c. but objects weigh more than 45 lbs.	165	180	200	215	230	245	260	280	295	310	325	340	360
Baking													
a. beating cake batter by hand	95	105	115	120	130	140	150	155	165	180	185	195	205
Bartending													
a. busy	130	145	155	170	180	195	205	220	230	245	255	270	280
Baseball													
a. other than pitcher or catcher	160	175	190	205	220	235	250	265	280	295	310	325	340
Bicycling													
a. 5½ mph	135	150	165	175	190	205	215	230	245	255	270	280	295

Table 11
CALORIES USED FOR MILD LEVEL ACTIVITIES
Per Hour
Weight in Pounds

Activity	71 or less	72–82	83–93	94–104	105–115	116–126	127–137	138–148	149–159	160–170	171–181	182–192	193 or more
Bowling													
a. continuous	150	170	180	195	210	225	240	255	270	285	300	310	325
b. regular	105	115	125	140	150	160	170	180	190	200	210	220	230
Bricklaying	115	125	0	150	160	170	180	195	205	215	225	235	250
Carpentry work													
a. light	130	145	155	170	180	195	205	220	230	245	255	270	280
Carrying trays, dishes, etc.													
a. waitress	140	150	165	180	190	205	215	230	245	255	270	285	295
Chopping wood													
a. automatically (power saw)	125	140	150	160	175	185	200	210	220	235	245	260	270
Crane operator	130	145	155	170	180	195	205	220	235	245	255	270	280
Cranking up dollies, hitching, trailers, operating large levers, jacks, etc.	145	160	170	185	200	215	230	240	255	270	285	295	310
Dancing													
a. Aerobic (low)	155	170	185	200	215	230	245	260	275	290	305	320	335
b. fox trot	145	155	170	185	195	210	225	240	250	265	280	295	305
c. contemporary (rock)	145	155	170	185	195	210	225	240	250	265	280	295	305
d. waltz	145	155	170	185	195	210	225	240	250	265	280	295	305
Dinner preparation	75	85	90	95	105	110	120	125	135	140	150	155	160
Domestic work (cleaning windows, mopping, scrubbing floors—no pause)	145	155	170	185	195	210	225	240	250	265	280	295	305

	71 or less	72–82	83–93	94–104	105–115	116–126	127–137	138–148	149–159	160–170	171–181	182–192	193 or more
Driving a truck													
a. heavy rig—including getting on & off frequently, & some arm work	130	145	155	170	180	195	205	220	230	245	255	270	280
Electric work (rewiring home)	145	155	170	185	195	210	225	240	250	265	280	295	305
Farming													
a. modern equipment	130	145	155	170	180	195	205	220	230	245	255	270	280
Fishing													
a. ice	100	110	120	130	140	150	160	170	175	185	195	205	215
b. standing (little movement)	90	95	105	115	120	130	140	145	155	165	170	180	190
c. surf	100	110	120	130	140	150	160	170	175	185	195	205	215
Gas station attendent													
a. pump gas—wash windows	125	140	150	160	175	185	200	210	220	235	245	260	270
b. mechanic—car	130	145	155	170	180	195	205	220	230	245	255	270	280
c. wash cars	135	145	160	170	185	195	210	225	235	250	260	275	285
d. combination of above three	145	155	170	185	195	210	225	240	250	265	280	295	305
Golf													
a. 4-some 9 holes in 2 hrs. (carry clubs)	150	170	180	195	210	225	240	255	270	285	295	310	325
b. 4-some 9 holes in 2 hrs. (pull clubs)	145	155,	170	185	195	210	225	240	250	265	280	295	305
c. cart	125	140	150	160	175	185	200	210	220	235	245	260	270
d. driving	145	155	170	185	195	210	225	240	250	265	285	295	305
e. putting	90	95	105	115	120	130	140	145	155	165	170	180	190
Handtools—light assembly work—radio repair, etc.	80	90	95	105	115	120	130	135	145	150	160	170	175

Table 11
CALORIES USED FOR MILD LEVEL ACTIVITIES
Per Hour
Weight in Pounds

Activity	71 or less	72–82	83–93	94–104	105–115	116–126	127–137	138–148	149–159	160–170	171–181	182–192	193 or more
Horseback riding													
a. walk	95	105	115	120	130	140	150	155	165	175	185	195	205
Horseshoes	130	145	155	170	180	195	205	220	230	245	255	270	280
Housework (general) See also													
Dinner, Domestic, Telephone,													
Sitting, Standing, Washing													
Clothes, Shopping, Ironing	115	125	140	150	160	170	180	195	205	215	225	235	250
Isometrics	130	145	155	170	180	195	205	220	230	245	255	270	280
Lawn mowing													
a. power—must push	150	170	180	195	210	225	240	255	270	285	300	310	325
b. power	145	155	170	185	195	210	225	240	250	265	280	295	305
c. sitting	80	90	95	105	115	120	130	135	145	150	160	170	175
Making beds	120	130	140	150	165	175	185	195	210	220	230	245	255
Masonry (wall)	120	130	140	150	165	175	185	195	210	220	230	245	255
Mechanical work (truck, auto repair)	130	145	155	170	180	195	205	220	230	245	255	270	280
Metal work	120	130	140	150	165	175	185	195	210	220	230	245	255
Motorcycling													
a. regular	115	125	140	150	165	170	180	195	205	215	225	235	250
b. trail riding	130	145	155	170	180	195	205	220	230	245	255	270	280
Office work (secretary)	80	90	95	105	115	120	130	145	145	150	160	170	175
Painting house	120	130	140	150	165	175	185	195	210	220	230	245	255
Paperhanging	120	130	140	150	165	175	185	195	210	220	230	245	255

	71 or less	72–82	83–93	94–104	105–115	116–126	127–137	138–148	149–159	160–170	171–181	182–192	193 or more
Personal toilet (dressing, washing, showering, shaving, combing, etc.)	115	125	140	150	160	170	180	195	205	215	225	235	250
Pool	90	95	105	115	120	130	140	145	155	165	170	180	190
Raking leaves and dirt	125	140	150	160	175	185	200	210	220	235	245	260	270
Sanding floors (power)	130	145	155	170	180	195	205	220	230	245	255	270	280
Sailing													
a. calm water	90	95	105	115	120	130	140	145	155	165	170	180	190
b. rough water	105	115	125	135	145	155	165	175	185	195	205	215	225
Sawing													
a. power	130	145	165	170	180	195	205	220	230	245	255	270	280
Shopping	95	105	115	120	130	140	150	155	165	180	185	195	205
Shooting													
a. pistol	90	100	110	115	125	135	145	150	160	170	180	185	195
b. rifle	105	115	125	135	145	155	165	175	185	195	205	215	225
Snowshoveling													
a. snowblower	145	155	170	185	195	210	225	240	250	265	280	295	305
Snowmobiling	115	125	140	150	160	170	180	195	205	215	225	235	250
Stacking shelves (packing & unpacking small or medium packages—grocery shelves)	130	145	155	170	180	195	205	220	230	245	255	270	280
Steward & stewardess work (unless sitting)	130	145	155	170	180	195	205	220	230	245	255	270	280
Waitress work	140	150	165	180	190	205	215	230	240	255	270	285	295
Walking													
a. 2 mph	105	115	125	135	145	155	165	175	185	195	205	215	225
b. 2½ mph	145	160	175	185	200	215	230	240	255	270	285	300	310

Table 11
CALORIES USED FOR MILD LEVEL ACTIVITIES
Per Hour
Weight in Pounds

Activity	71 or less	72–82	83–93	94–104	105–115	116–126	127–137	138–148	149–159	160–170	171–181	182–192	193 or more
Washing cars & polishing	130	145	155	170	180	195	205	220	230	245	255	270	280
Washing clothes													
a. modern methods	90	100	110	120	125	135	145	155	160	170	180	190	195
b. scrub board	130	145	155	170	180	195	205	220	230	245	255	270	280
c. drying clothes—clothes dryer	90	100	110	120	125	135	145	155	160	170	180	190	195
hanging clothes on line	140	150	165	180	190	205	215	230	245	255	270	285	295
Welding (light)	90	100	110	115	125	135	145	150	160	170	180	190	195
Window cleaning	130	145	155	170	180	195	205	220	230	245	255	270	280
Yoga	130	145	155	170	180	195	205	220	230	245	255	270	280

9

Planning Your Program For Best Results

Now is the time to bring it all together. You have the theory. You know which exercises are best for burning calories and which ones are supplements. Now's the time to plan your program. Let's go.

The first part of your fat-burning plan requires a close look at the calories you take in and burn off. You must decide how many calories a day you are out of balance. There are two ways of determining your caloric imbalance. The easiest way is to establish the number of pounds you seem to struggle with each year. Once that's determined, simply add a zero to that number. If you struggle with five pounds annually, you are probably over your caloric balance by 50 calories a day. To stop gaining you need to burn off that extra 50 calories a day. A 10 minute walk will no doubt solve that problem. To begin losing fat you need to burn off even more calories.

The above method is a good estimate, but if you are fascinated by figures, record keeping, and balancing budgets, you may want to use a more accurate method (but you must be *thoroughly* honest). Here you use the activity and food calorie charts found in Appendices D and E respectively in this book. The charts and system are similar to balancing your check or bank book.

How To Determine Your Caloric Income

Our activity budget is no different from any other budget: you need to know your income in order to manage your outgo. To determine your income, simply make a list of everything you ate and drank yesterday (unless yesterday was Saturday or Sunday—weekend eating habits are not usually "typical"). If it is near bedtime, you might want to use today as a prototype. If you can't remember every single bite you took during the last 24 hours, plan to record what you eat, as you eat it, tomorrow. (For your convenience, there are additional forms at the end of this chapter which you can use to record your caloric income and caloric outgo.)

One word of caution: most people tend to underestimate the amount of calories they consume. You should list everything that you eat or drink, including that mid-morning coffee, evening potato chips and even the stick of chewing gum or piece of hard candy you had during the afternoon. I even suggest you include everything you put in your mouth—pencils, paper clips, hair pins, water. That way nothing will be missed—cake batter, nibbles, and cocktails. Keep in mind, though, that the idea is to get an idea of what is usual or normal for you. Do not modify your diet as you record it.

After you have listed all you have eaten on a typical day, enter the number of calories for each item. Then add up all the calories to find the total for the day. (Use the "Calorie Content of Food" in Appendix E to determine the number of calories for each item.)

Assuming you are neither on a diet now, nor just going off one, your total caloric income on a typical day is probably between 2,000 and 2,500 if you are a woman, and between 2,500 and 3,000 if you are a man. The truth is, the majority of people do not eat very much more—or less—than this. However, do not round off your figures when calculating your caloric income. Accuracy is what we need here.

Every once in a while, someone will protest that it is not

CALORIC INTAKE (Average Day)

SAMPLE:
BREAKFAST

Food	Calories
4 ounces Orange Juice	55
8 ounces of milk	165
1 ounce of cereal (Wheaties)	100
+ ½ cup of milk	80
1 piece of buttered toast	115
1 scrambled egg	150
TOTAL	665

YOUR
BREAKFAST

Food	Calories

Morning Snack and Drink

Coffee (cream and sugar)	65
TOTAL	65

Morning Snack and Drink

Lunch

Chicken Soup (cup)	100
Crackers	100
Hamburger	200
Roll	150
Coffee (cream and sugar)	65
TOTAL	615

Lunch

Food	Calories	Food	Calories
Dinner		Dinner	
Lettuce salad (French dressing)	100		
Steak (chopped)	350		
Potatoes (Baked with butter)	175		
Peas	110		
Coffee (cream and sugar)	65		
Layer Cake	350		
TOTAL	1,160		

Afternoon Snack and Drink		Afternoon Snack and Drink	
Coffee (cream and sugar)	65		
TOTAL	65		

Evening Snacks and Drinks		Evening Snacks and Drinks	
Bottle of beer	75		
TOTAL	75		

TOTAL FOR THE DAY 2,645

possible to determine average caloric consumption on the basis of one day's recording. Strange as it may seem, it actually is possible. That is because we are creatures of habit. Although there are exceptions (holidays, parties, and trips always mean additional calories), what we eat one day is usually not very different in quantity and substance from what we ate the day before. If you are unconvinced that one day's caloric income is representative of your everyday eating habits, keep score for a few days and average the results.

How To Determine Your Caloric Outgo

Now that you have a good idea of your daily caloric income, it is time to determine your present caloric outgo. To do this, make another list. This time, record everything you did in a 24-hour period. If you slept eight hours (or 10 or 6), start with that; then try to retrace your steps throughout the day. Be sure to include all activities and the approximate time you spent on each.

A word of caution: there is a tendency to overestimate not only the intensity but the duration of various kinds of physical activity. For example, George Burger, of the Central YMCA in Philadelphia, tells of a nurse who felt there was no need for her to jog. "Why should I? I walk at least ten miles a day on the job," she insisted. George was doubtful. She volunteered to wear a pedometer to prove she was right. The following day she reported to George that she had walked 1 ⅛ miles. "But it was a very slow day," she added. She wore the pedometer again the next day. It was a typical day; but to her utter amazement, she clocked only two miles!

Ask a man how much he walks, and the answer is practically always "a lot." He may go on to say that he is on his feet all day. Perhaps he is. However, most research shows that over-weight people rarely walk more than 2½ miles a day. (People who are lean tend to walk four to five miles a day.)

The day of an average office worker may be as follows. He

CALORIC OUTGO (Average Day)

Sample: 150 pound man			Your Own Schedule		
Activity	Length of Time	Calories	Activity	Length of Time	Calories
Morning			Morning		
Personal Toilet	½ hr.	103			
Walk	¼ hr.	46			
Eating	½ hr.	45			
Drive Car	½ hr.	67			
Sit at Desk	3 hrs.	270			
	TOTAL	531			
Afternoon			Afternoon		
Walk	¼ hr.	46			
Eating	¾ hr.	67			
Sit at Desk	4 hrs.	360			
Drive Car	½ hr.	67			
	TOTAL	540			
Evening			Evening		
Walk	½ hr.	92			
Eating	¾ hr.	67			
Read	2 hrs.	180			
Resting	½ hr.	37			
Watch TV	1½ hrs.	120			
	TOTAL	496			
Night			Night		
Personal Toilet	½ hr.	103			
Sleep	8 hrs.	520			
	TOTAL	623			
TOTAL FOR THE DAY		2190	TOTAL FOR THE DAY		

drives to work and parks the car as near to the office as he can. He always uses the elevator or escalator, never the stairs. Rather than walk a few yards for a face-to-face talk with a co-worker, he picks up the intercom. At midday, he takes his car to and from lunch. At 5:00 he drives home. He then eats dinner, collapses into a chair for a few hours of watching television, and then goes to bed.

Women, especially housewives, are just as likely to overestimate the amount of activity they engage in during the day. There is a tendency to automatically figure in eight hours of housework. Though a woman often is in the house for eight hours at a stretch, it is unlikely that the whole time is spent scrubbing floors, vacuuming, dusting, and the like. In fact, after learning what is actually meant by the term "housework," many women have to admit that they spend a total of only one hour a day on the part requiring heavy physical effort.

All of this simply indicates that most people are less active than they think they are. In order to counteract the tendency to overestimate physical activity, it is always a good idea to compensate by deliberately erring on the short side whenever you are not absolutely sure how much of any activity you did.

After you have listed all activities for a typical 24-hour period, calculate the number of calories expended on each. You can do this by referring to the Activity Charts in Appendix D. You may want to record your activities for several days and average the totals.

Regardless of the method you choose, you should now see your problem of fat gain. You are not *physically* active enough. I suspect you will also be surprised to discover you're just a few calories out of balance a day. Maybe only 50 to 100 calories. A handful of crackers or a bottle of beer. But you like your crackers and beer. Rather than give them up, find a way to burn an extra 50 to 100 calories each day through activity. Then burn a few extra calories to lose weight.

Planning Your Activity

I usually advise people who want to design their own fat loss program to start out by choosing two activities. The first activity is to get them back into caloric balance (make caloric output equal to income). I call this your caloric balancer. The second activity is to establish a deficit so that weight is actually lost rather than maintained—your fat burner activity.

Your Caloric Balancer

I recommend walking as your caloric balancer. I believe it is a key to sticking with the program and seeing the pleasant results of fat loss. Too many people try something more difficult. Like running. They want to get those pounds off fast so they head for the roads on the double. Such enthusiasm is commendable, but it will most likely be a discouraging experience. Especially if you have quite a bit of weight to lose. First, you run a good chance of hurting yourself, delaying your program, and causing unnecessary discomfort. Second, your cardiovascular system may not be ready to handle that level of exertion. You may find that running is no fun because your lungs ache, your head pounds, and your entire body rebels. Finally, it just isn't necessary to push yourself that hard. Remember, the main ingredient in your program should be FUN. Walking is a great calorie burner and may be a lot more fun for you than running. If you are 100 calories over your daily limit, you can walk for 20 minutes or run for 10. For starters, I think you'll enjoy the walking.

One more note on walking. I've found that young to middle-aged men turn their noses up at walking. At first, they think it's not tough enough. Or boring. Or silly. Given our cultural bias I can understand those feelings. At one point, I felt that way too. You know, men play football or baseball. The rough stuff. Something that involves a lot of competition and perhaps a bruise or two.

The best answer I have to this line of thought is to ask you to just give it a try for 3 to 4 weeks. Toss aside your notions about sports and approach your walk as an adventure in fat loss and health. One thing you will notice right away is that walking isn't a cream puff activity.

After all, if John Wooden, dean emeritus of college basketball, Woody Hayes, ex-football coach of Ohio State, and former President Harry Truman used walking as their exercise program, you can too.

If you walk at a brisk pace, you'll sense an increase in pulse rate and you'll be breathing as hard as you care to. As you walk, look around. Notice your surroundings. Breathe deeply and enjoy. If it's in the morning before work, mentally plan your day. If it's in the evening, walk away from the tension and stress of the day. You'll find walking as tough as you want it to be, as fun as you'd like it to be, and more successful than you dreamed it could be. And remember, real toughness is sticking to a project or exercise regimen, not jumping from pillar to post.

Fat Burner Activity

Now you're ready to build a solid fat control program. You will notice the remainder of this chapter has several charts. You should start on the first chart. This chart is the beginning of a program which will put your weight under control. It will also provide you with a breaking-in period for increased physical activity. After all, your body has probably been stagnating through long years of relative misuse and needs to be gradually prepared. Your feet, your legs, your back—your whole body, really—and your cardiovascular system in particular, are about to do things they haven't done for years. You want to make it as easy as possible for them.

Before skipping over the charts and deciding you don't need a reasonable approach to your exercise, please read the explanations preceeding each chart. For additional help, follow the directions in the next chapter and assess your fitness level. This will give you a good indication of what you can physically handle.

Caloric Balancer Program

Walk briskly and daily for the length of time specified on the chart. As you walk, stop a couple of times and check your pulse. You shouldn't exceed 70% of your maximum heart rate. You are to progress through the specified time steps as you feel capable of doing it. Whenever you feel comfortable moving from the 15-minute Step #1 to 18 minutes of Step #2, make the change.

If you feel daring and want to make a substantial jump ahead to a later step, you should bear in mind all the cautions I have raised about trying to do too much too soon. It is all too tempting for people to imagine themselves as being younger and more limber than they really are. It's fine to overestimate what you can do in some things. But in exercise, it's not a very good idea. Still, some of you will really be conditioned enough to move ahead quickly. Some, in fact, will find you are prepared to skim through the various steps. Don't do it, however, unless your physician tells you it's okay for you to begin at an advanced level.

Everyone should progress up to a minimum of Step #6 before going on to Level #2 (The Fat Burner Program). In the event you are out of caloric balance by 200 or more calories a day, I suggest working up to Step #10 before progressing to Level #2.

Level #1 Caloric Balancer Program

Level #1 is your introduction to the exciting new world of a better looking body. A program of brisk walking will get your body in shape for the time when you actually engage in target heart rate exercise. Walking is also beneficial to your cardiovascular system. It's mild enough for almost everyone to enjoy. As your physical condition improves, try more challenging walks: cover greater distances or walk faster. But remember, as you walk you don't want to exceed 70% of your target heart rate. (See p. 91)

After reaching Step #6 (Step #10 for those of you who are really out of caloric balance), progress to Level #2.

Table 12
CALORIC BALANCER PROGRAM

Level #1	Duration of Exercise	Frequency	Activity
Step 1	15–17 minutes	6–7 times per week	Walk
Step 2	18–20 minutes	6–7 times per week	Walk
Step 3	21–33 minutes	6–7 times per week	Walk
Step 4	24–26 minutes	6–7 times per week	Walk
Step 5	27–29 minutes	6–7 times per week	Walk
Step 6	30–33 minutes	6–7 times per week	Walk
Step 7	34–37 minutes	6–7 times per week	Walk
Step 8	38–41 minutes	6–7 times per week	Walk
Step 9	42–44 minutes	6–7 times per week	Walk
Step 10	45–50 minutes	6–7 times per week	Walk

Beginning Fat Burner Programs
After reaching Step #6 (Step #10 in a few instances) you are ready to really start losing weight. Remember, I have suggested two activities. The first—walking—is to help you achieve a balance in your caloric output/input. Though you may have already lost some pounds with this activity, the real weight loss will come with your second activity—the Fat Burner.

Level #2 Beginning Fat Burner Program
With the Beginning Fat Burner Program you have several options. You can run, bicycle, swim, cross country ski, aerobic dance, run in place, jump rope and, of course, continue walking. As you do these exercises, you are to push your heart rate up to about 70% of your maximum heart rate. That is the lower side of the range which is found on page 91. During the first several weeks, stay at the low level. As your fitness level continues to improve, you can move up to mid range. Remember, however, you are not to exceed 85% of your maximum heart rate.

To make the transition between Level #1 and Level #2

smoother and easier, a certain number of minutes should be devoted to walking before progressing to the target heart rate exercise. The chart provides the appropriate guidelines.

Table 13
BEGINNING FAT BURNER PROGRAM

Level #2	Caloric Balancer Walking	Fat Burning Target Heart Rate Exercise	Frequency
Step 11	30 minutes	10 minutes	4 times a week
Step 12	27 minutes	13 minutes	4 times a week
Step 13	25 minutes	15 minutes	4 times a week
Step 14	22 minutes	18 minutes	4 times a week
Step 15	20 minutes	20 minutes	4 times a week
Step 16	17 minutes	23 minutes	4 times a week
Step 17	15 minutes	25 minutes	4 times a week
Step 18	15 minutes	28 minutes	4 times a week

Start off with the specified amount of walking and then finish up with the target heart rate exercise. If you select walking, push yourself at a faster pace when you're doing the Fat Burning target heart rate exercise. If you choose running, simply run at a pace that you feel is comfortable. Just make sure it gets your heart rate up to the target zone. If you are unable to run for a sustained length of time (perhaps 10 minutes), you can try the old boy scout pace of walking a telephone pole, jogging a telephone pole, and walking a telephone pole, etc. If you're swimming, jump in and swim to one end, get out and walk back, swim another lap, walk back another lap, etc. Once you learn to listen to your body, you will see that it is quite easy to modify the program to meet your own needs and your own heart rate.

Level #3 Moderate Fat Burning Program

By the time you reach Level #3, you will be a veteran: one of those exercisers you used to admire. Level #3, Step #20 is the minimum goal of most people who are interested in reducing their body fat. Because at Step #20 you're getting 30 minutes of target heart rate exercise. Therefore, most people will find that they'll prefer to stay within Level #3 and go no further. There may be several reasons for this. Some people may not be able to spend the extra time required to go to Level #4. Or, they may not be interested in longer periods of target heart rate exercise. If you decide to stop at Level #3, Step #20, that's fine. You will continue to reap substantial fat-burning benefits if you are getting 30 minutes of target heart rate exercise a minimum of 4 times a week. Stick to that and I think you will be happy.

You may decide you want to move up beyond this point in the chart and try to lose a few extra pounds each month. That's up to you, but I suggest that you not lose more than one pound per week. And remember, 3,500 calories equals one pound of fat. Therefore, if you want to lose a pound a week you would have to go into caloric deficit of about 500 calories a day. Your minimal goal should be around Level #3, Step #20. If you want to lose more fat, simply refer to the caloric charts and determine how many minutes of exercise are necessary for you to lose a sufficient amount of fat to reach your goal.

At this level the Calorie Balancer Program of walking can be done any time. Just make sure you do it. Also, your calorie balancing may be larger. Your rule of thumb is that 20 minutes of walking is equivalent to about 100 calories. Or about five calories per minute.

Table 14
MODERATE FAT BURNER PROGRAM

Level #3	Caloric Balancer Walking	Fat Burning Target Heart Rate Exercise	Frequency
Step 19	15 minutes	28 minutes	4 times a week
Step 20	15 minutes	30 minutes	4 times a week
Step 21	15 minutes	33 minutes	4 times a week

(continued)

Table 14 (continued)
Caloric Balancer Fat Burning Target

Level #3	Walking	Heart Rate Exercise	Frequency
Step 22	15 minutes	35 minutes	4 times a week
Step 23	15 minutes	38 minutes	4 times a week
Step 24	15 minutes	40 minutes	4 times a week
Step 25	15 minutes	43 minutes	4 times a week

Level #4 Advanced Fat Burner Program

This level is really for the serious exerciser. If you are able to perform at this level, you are at an advanced stage of fitness. By now, however, you may have decided that there is nothing wrong with being a dedicated exerciser. Once you reach the last step here (a full hour of target heart rate exercise), you may consider yourself an expert. That is, you have conditioned your body to such an extent that you can exercise as long as you wish and as often as you wish. Just be careful. Keep your exercise in perspective. Remember, the main ingredient to a successful program is FUN. If you simply don't find it fun or enjoyable to exercise more than an hour a day, don't do it. The extra benefits may not offset the negative feelings you might begin to develop if you are pushing yourself too hard.

Table 15
ADVANCED FAT BURNER PROGRAM

Level #4	Walking	Heart Rate Exercise	Frequency
Step 26	15 minutes	45 minutes	4 times a week
Step 27	15 minutes	48 minutes	4 times a week
Step 28	15 minutes	50 minutes	4 times a week
Step 29	15 minutes	53 minutes	4 times a week
Step 30	15 minutes	55 minutes	4 times a week
Step 31	15 minutes	58 minutes	4 times a week
Step 32	15 minutes	60 minutes	4 times a week

Fat Burning Supplements

Regardless of the step and level you are working on, you may want to supplement your fat control program. Do this by building extra activities into your life. That includes many of the low and mild activities listed on pages 120 to 128. The word "activity", as I use it here, refers to anything that lets you move your muscles. It need not be "exercise" in the traditional sense of the word.

Housework—mopping, scrubbing floors, vacuuming, and dusting are activities. And pretty good ones for burning calories. So is lawn work. So are washing the car, painting the garage, chopping wood, and climbing stairs. However, with the exception of housework, which, as everyone knows only too well, never ends; you couldn't very well plan a whole program based on these activities (Who'd want to go out and paint the garage every day anyway?). Instead, it's best to regard these occasional muscle movers as "bonus" activities. Their real value is supplementary. Do them as often as you can to boost your total weekly caloric expenditure.

Here are a few of my all time bonus activities or supplements:

1. Family or "significant other" walks.
2. Walking to and from work or at lunch.
3. Taking the stairs rather than the elevator or escalator.
4. Family fitness sessions.
5. Dancing.
6. Learning a new sport.
7. Washing the car (yes, washing the car).
8. Mowing the yard (walking not riding).
9. Working in the garden.

Your Suggestions

10.
11.
12.

Before And After Target Heart Rate Exercise

There is more to target heart rate exercise than simply getting your heart rate up, keeping it there, and burning fat. You cannot simply jump into your shoes, set out at a brisk pace, and then relax. Every experienced exerciser knows the importance of warming up and cooling down.

Warm-Up

When you go to a track meet, you go to watch the main events. You keep your eyes on the competition. Few people pay attention to all the other activities going on around the perimeter of the field. Yet if you look around, you'll see a lot of people who are not competing at the time, but who are moving around quit a bit. The pole vaulter is doing 10 quick push-ups, several runners are jogging leisurely around the track, others are running in place. Some athletes are doing toe touches, others do body twists, and still others . . . well, the list is pretty long.

The scene is really a combination of mass calisthenics and jogging. It is not essential, or even particularly interesting, for us as spectators, but it certainly is crucial for the competitors who will run, jump, hurdle, and vault. They know they have to warm up to get their muscles loosened and limbered and their hearts and lungs pumping.

This is true for every sport. Football players, tennis players, volleyball players, even serious table tennis players go through various forms of warm-up exercises designed to work on all the specific muscles, ligaments, tendons, and joints that will absorb the stress of their particular activity.

Warming up is equally important for the exerciser who's interested in reducing body fat. You need to be concerned about preparing not only your muscular and skeletal systems, but your cardiovascular system as well. Your heart and lungs are going to be used and tested just like the muscles of your legs and joints of your feet and knees. It only takes 5 or 10 minutes to warm up for target heart rate exercise, but it is extremely important and should not be neglected.

It is tempting to skip the warm-up. After all, it is uninteresting. For us, target heart rate exercise is the main event. But if we skip this very important warm-up, we often pay.

It is estimated that as many as half the injuries caused by exercise could have been avoided if the person had warmed up properly. The muscles and the joints are simply not ready to handle serious target heart rate activities unless they are warmed up.

I'm not saying that this is the greatest cause of an exerciser's aches and pains—you're going to have some of them anyway. I'm referring to the strains and sprains that can be avoided—the injuries which plague us while we're exercising as well as those which may force us to curtail our exercising or even give it up entirely.

Every exerciser, no matter how long he or she has been working out, should warm up before beginning target heart rate exercise. Just because you have finally gotten into shape doesn't mean you can forego the warm-up. You know how your car reacts when it's been sitting idle for a while, especially in the dead of winter. Well, the human body reacts in much the same way. The body of a regular exerciser, of course, is much more used to the activity. But, even so, it has been at rest since the last exercise session, maybe a day or two before, and the muscles and joints have to be primed once again.

One complaint often heard from exercisers is that before they began their target heart rate exercise program, they could touch their toes, but after six months of exercise they can't. The reason is that target heart rate exercise causes the muscles in the back of the legs and arms and shoulders to contract. Repeated contractions shorten these muscles, tendons, and ligaments. To prevent this, begin doing some stretching exercises.

What kind of exercises are best? One of the foremost guides to physical fitness, *The Official YMCA Physical Fitness Handbook,* emphasizes the importance of flexibility exercises for warming up. The handbook recommends exercises that:

1. Stretch muscles and joints to their fullest extent without straining;
2. Are rhythmic in nature with one movement flowing naturally into the next;
3. Combine muscle stretching with increased cardiovascular activity;
4. Include all parts of the body; and
5. Gradually increase the intensity as the warm-up progresses.

I subscribe to those guidelines and urge you to do so as well. How you go about it, of course, is up to you. I caution you only to be sure that you do not overdo the warm-up. After all, the warm-up is simply to help you in your target heart rate exercise.

I feel it's best to select the warm-up activities that are most comfortable and enjoyable for you. You must, however, note the parts of the body that are affected by a particular exercise. Don't just use the ones you remember from the days when you were training with the high school basketball team. On the following pages is a series of exercises that you may want to use. They are stretching and mobility exercises.

After doing the stretching and flexibility exercises, do some fat burning exercises. These will prepare your heart and lungs for more demanding work. And the older and less fit you are, the more warm-up time your heart needs. Fortunately, the Caloric Balancer activity—walking—provides that warm-up time.

Cool-Down

At the same track meet where all those runners and jumpers were warming up, you would also have seen them cooling down after their event. They don't simply stop, walk over, pick up a medal if they win or amble off to the locker room if they lose. They continue either to run lightly, walk, or do some other kinds of exercises. Whatever it takes to properly cool-down from their vigorous experience.

Stopping abruptly after a target heart rate exercise session is not advisable. It can result in lightheadedness, dizziness, nausea, and even fainting. I strongly advise that you come out of your target heart rate exercise gradually and smoothly. Let your body return to its normal state at a moderate rate. Remember, the blood has been going to your muscles and now it is being diverted back to its normal circulation pattern, and you don't want that shift to be too abrupt. Without a cool-down period, blood will pool in the feet and lower extremities, ultimately depriving the brain of much needed oxygen. The cool-down also gives you an excellent opportunity to work on some stretching exercises to help compensate for all the ballistic movements you were doing while engaging in target heart rate exercise.

Approximately 5 to 10 minutes of cool-down are appropriate. At the end of the cool-down period, your pulse rate should be within 30 beats of what it is when you aren't exercising.

The way you cool-down, like almost everything else in this book, is a matter of personal preference. But some easy walking, mild calisthenics, and flexibility should be an integral part of your fat-burning program. An easy way to cool-down is to do the warm-up in reverse. Start with walking and then progress to the calisthenics and stretching.

Summary

What I'm saying here is simple. The fat-burning experience should be in a three part cycle: warm-up, target heart rate exercise, and cool-down. The first and the last of the three do not need to be long, drawn-out affairs. They should be short and effective, as natural as putting on and taking off your exercise gear.

Now for a quick review. In this chapter I have shown you four progressive levels in your fat reduction program. The charts have indicated the amount of time necessary to work gradually into your goal of 30 minutes of target heart rate activity. I hope you begin with Level #1, Step 1 and work through each step even if it seems slow going at first. My experience has shown that one of the main reasons people drop out of an exercise program is that they try to do too much too soon and then get discouraged. The charts are designed to bring you along at a pace that is comfortable and that will prevent you from overdoing it. In addition, I highly recommend a warm-up and cool-down to further prevent you from any unnecessary soreness or stiffness. So give this plan a try and follow it carefully as you might have followed all those diets you once tried. I think you'll enjoy it more and see better results.

1. Sitting Toe Touches—Sit with your legs extended in front of you. Feet together and legs on the floor. Reach for your toes with your hands, bringing your forehead as close to your knees as possible. Hold.*

2. Calf Tendon Stretcher— Stand about two to three feet from the wall. Lean forward, body straight. Place your palms against the wall at eye level. Step backward. Continue to support your weight with your hands. Remain flat footed until you feel your calf muscles stretching. Hold.

*On all these exercises the hold position refers to a 10 second hold. Over the weeks gradually increase to a 30 second hold.

3. Calf Stretch—Assume a stride position with the right leg forward. Place your hands on your hips. Lean your upper body forward. Simultaneously, bend your right leg at the knee to a 130° angle. Extend the left leg so that it is in line with the upper body. Your left foot should be flat on the floor. Hold. Return to the starting position. Repeat with the left foot forward.

4. Sprinter—Assume a squatting position, hands on the floor. Extend your right leg backward as far as possible. The left leg should be bent at your knee and kept under your chest. Hold. Then repeat with your left leg back and right leg forward.

5. Standing Leg Stretcher—Find a chair or table 2½ to 3 feet in height. Place your left foot on the table or chair. Keep this leg straight and parallel to the floor. Your right leg should be firmly planted on the floor. From this position slowly extend your fingertips toward your outstretched leg on the chair. Hold and return. Eventually you should attempt to get your

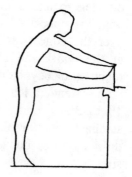

forehead to the knee. Repeat with the other leg.

6. Side Stretch—Stand with your feet shoulder-width apart, legs straight. Place one hand on your hip, and extend the other hand up and over your head. Bend to the side on which your hand is placed. Move slowly. Hold. Repeat on the other side.

7. Shoulder Stretch—With your arms over your head, hold the elbow of one arm with the hand of the other arm. Slowly pull the elbow behind the head. Do not force. Hold. Repeat on the other side.

8. Hamstring Bench Stretch— Sit on the edge of a table with one leg extended in front of you, the opposite leg hanging over the edge. Bend forward at the waist and attempt to touch on or beyond the toes of your extended leg. Hold for 10 to 30 seconds. Return to starting position. Make sure you do *not* bob or bounce as you stretch.

9. Roll-Overs—Lie down on the floor with your hands at your sides. Slowly lift your legs until they are perpendicular to the floor. Keeping your shoulders on the floor and legs straight, reach up and grab your legs as close to the ankles as possible. Gently pull your legs down toward your head until you feel a slight resistance. Hold. Return.

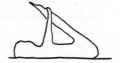

10. Single Leg Stretch—Sit on the floor with your legs spread apart. Bend your right leg at the knee so that the sole of your right foot rests against the inside of your left thigh. Reach forward with both hands and grab the ankle of your left leg. Lean forward until you feel a tug on the back of your extended leg. Hold and return. Repeat with the other leg.

CALORIC INTAKE (Average Day)

Breakfast   Calories

_____
_____
_____
_____
_____
_____
_____

                                                TOTAL_____

Morning Snack and Drink

_____
_____
_____

Lunch

_____
_____
_____
_____
_____

                                                TOTAL_____

Afternoon Snack and Drink

_____
_____
_____

Dinner

_____
_____
_____
_____
_____
_____
_____

                                                TOTAL_____

Evening Snacks and Drinks

_____
_____
_____

                                TOTAL FOR THE DAY_____

CALORIC INTAKE (Average Day)

Breakfast   Calories
_____
_____
_____
_____
_____
_____
_____
                                    TOTAL_____

Morning Snack and Drink
_____
_____
_____

Lunch
_____
_____
_____
_____
_____
                                    TOTAL_____

Afternoon Snack and Drink
_____
_____
_____

Dinner
_____
_____
_____
_____
_____
_____
                                    TOTAL_____

Evening Snacks and Drinks
_____
_____
_____
                        TOTAL FOR THE DAY_____

CALORIC OUTGO (Average Day)

Activity	Length of Time	Calories	Activity	Length of Time	Calories
Morning			Morning		
_____	_____	_____	_____	_____	_____
_____	_____	_____	_____	_____	_____
_____	_____	_____	_____	_____	_____
_____	_____	_____	_____	_____	_____
_____	_____	_____	_____	_____	_____
_____	_____	_____	_____	_____	_____
Afternoon			Afternoon		
_____	_____	_____	_____	_____	_____
_____	_____	_____	_____	_____	_____
_____	_____	_____	_____	_____	_____
_____	_____	_____	_____	_____	_____
_____	_____	_____	_____	_____	_____
_____	_____	_____	_____	_____	_____
Evening			Evening		
_____	_____	_____	_____	_____	_____
_____	_____	_____	_____	_____	_____
_____	_____	_____	_____	_____	_____
_____	_____	_____	_____	_____	_____
_____	_____	_____	_____	_____	_____
_____	_____	_____	_____	_____	_____
Night			Night		
_____	_____	_____	_____	_____	_____
_____	_____	_____	_____	_____	_____
_____	_____	_____	_____	_____	_____

TOTAL FOR THE DAY   TOTAL FOR THE DAY

PART #3

STICK WITH IT*

*Some things they never told you at the health spa.

10
How To Avoid Being A Weight Control Dropout

I don't know how many times I've seen people with good intentions start doing calisthenics, or play handball, or begin jogging. They really go gung ho. Never miss a day. For about two or three weeks. Then they lay off a day here and a couple of days there. Before you know it, they've dropped out entirely.

My friend Wade Oplinger, whom I introduced to you earlier, was a lot like that. He usually began exercising each New Year. You know. Start the year out on the right foot. Burn some calories. Get in shape. He had very good intentions and was doing it for the right reasons. But he never stayed with it for more than a few weeks. Poor Wade. He had a closet filled with double-knit running suits and fancy shoes for every sport imaginable, but he still carries 240+ pounds on a body designed to hold 170.

Obviously, the program I've outlined in this book will not work if you fail to follow it regularly. It is imperative that you get a minimum of 30 minutes of target heart rate activity four days a week. Three days a week is better than nothing, but one or two days a week will not contribute to a significant fat loss. Of course, dropping out altogether denies you of any chance of fat loss and may even cause a more rapid weight gain. That's because the usual reaction to quitting is guilt. You get down on yourself for not having the discipline to do something you know is good for you. And psychologists tell us a possible side effect of guilt is overindulgence. So you stuff yourself to overcome the guilt, only to cause more depression when you step back on the scales.

It doesn't have to be that way. With exercise, like anything else, good intentions aren't enough to keep you going. You need specific guidelines and helps. It's a lot like choosing your career. Your chances of sticking with your job—showing up every day and even liking it—are better if you pick a field that is suited to your interests and personality. You wouldn't choose accounting if you didn't like working at a desk with numbers and adding machines. Yet many people decide to start running even though they can't stand the thought of running.

The key to sticking to your program depends a great deal on your interests, health status, body type, age, and time availability. By choosing an activity that corresponds with these factors, you will enhance your chances of sticking with your weight control program indefinitely. Let's look at specific ways you can avoid being an exercise dropout.

How To Avoid The Word Quit

Quit to me is a four-letter word. I think it should be dropped from the English language. This chapter is so important that I feel you should dog-ear it. The information here will not lose its validity regardless of your physical condition. It will serve as a constant reinforcement for exercise. This part of the book should be well used and heeded.

Set a Goal

First things first. You're not going to get anywhere without a specific objective. You must set a goal. Goals are important in life, and they're important in an exercise program, too. They give you something specific to work toward and a standard on which to measure your progress. When you're setting a goal, avoid vague generalizations: "I want to lose the spare tire on my waist." Or "I want to lose weight." Instead, set specific long, intermediate, and short-term goals.

For example, after you determine the best weight for yourself you might determine that this is your long-range goal. Perhaps by six months or a year from now you want to lose 20 pounds. The short-term goal may be three pounds by the end of the first month. Ten pounds after three months (intermediate goal) and 20 pounds by the end of the year.

Once you have established these goals you need to establish a goal of how many minutes of exercise you need to achieve your long-range goal. At first, your short-term goal may be 20 minutes of walking a day. Your ultimate goal may be 30 minutes of running. The short-term goal is to get your legs in shape and ready for more vigorous exercise and real fat loss. An intermediate goal might be to move up through Level #3, Step 2 in Chapter #9. Your ultimate goal may be to workout four times a week for 60 minutes.

So it's important to take stock of yourself right now. What would you like to accomplish by exercise? It may include one, two, or more of the following: percent body fat, body weight, time, or mileage. Use Chapter #9 for guidance. Whatever it is, write it down now. Even if it seems unrealistic at this time. Put it on a sheet of paper or a file card. Save it! These are important goals. Once a week, take this sheet of paper out and look at your progress. Write down your progress and what obstacles apparently are in your way. Then try to figure out how to get around these obstacles.

Next, write down how you plan to achieve those goals. Be specific. For example, list the number of minutes walking you're going to increase each week to get to your ultimate goal. What motivators are you going to use to help yourself exercise? Write them down. Some of the suggestions and stories in this book may be helpful. Even this chapter may be helpful. Save this card and look at it daily or weekly to see what kind of progress you're making.

Finally, write down what you're going to do today. Not tomorrow, today. Write down how long you plan to walk, at what time, and where you're going to walk. Each morning do the same thing until you reach your ultimate goal. Place the card with your goals written on it at a spot which will remind you at the time you have scheduled yourself to exercise or walk.

Progress Being Made

For some of us the thing that makes football, basketball, or ice hockey interesting is competition. Well, there's no reason why you can't make your exercise program competitive. A progress chart lets you compete with yourself. It shows you and anyone else who looks at it how well you are doing on the program. In addition, it indicates how close you're getting to your goal. Moreover, it gives you a feeling of accomplishment to fill in your chart after an exercise session.

The chart doesn't have to be complicated either. The simplest would be to mark the information on a calendar. Another (and the one I like best) is to record your mileage of walking, running, swimming, etc., on a map. It's great fun to see how long it takes you to get from one city to another and from state to state. We use this principle in our program with the National Y. Individuals record their mileage each week. The group also records its mileage. Those of us in Michigan are always walking to Florida or Southern California during the winter months. We make announcements to newspapers and other groups when we arrive. We do the same thing with individual goals. It may sound corny, but it works.

Time Commitment

You must be willing to set aside a certain period of time each or every other day for exercise. Build it right into your schedule. You don't leave the house without brushing your teeth, and you like to eat lunch between 12 and 1 p.m. every day. These are all part of your schedule. Exercise should be no different. Exercise should fit into your routine. If you can get yourself into the habit of exercising at a certain time every day, you'll accept it as part of your regular daily schedule and not just something to do during odd moments. That way exercise will become habitual.

Whatever you do, don't worry about taking the time. Your co-workers may take a 2 to 3 hour, 3-martini lunch and think nothing of it. But they may cast a scornful eye as you go off to take your walk, run or swim at noon. Don't let them make you feel guilty. You're doing something positive with your body, and it will make you feel better, more productive, more alive, and a better worker. Those put downs by your co-workers are masking jealousy and guilt. With this program, I'm asking for about 1 to 3% of your time. That's a small price to pay for a life of vigor, wellness, a better looking body, and greater productivity.

The Best Time of Day

You will stick with your program more faithfully if you establish a routine geared to your own disposition and living habits. Once exercise becomes as usual (and as necessary) as getting dressed, the evening paper, going to work, or eating lunch; it won't seem like an added burden. Basically, your choices will fall around morning, noon, or evening.

Some people prefer to exercise early in the morning. Some even go out before daybreak. They're the real early birds. And the title fits. If you can get up that early, there are some real benefits. The early birds receive the bonus of empty streets, clean crisp air, and unusual quietness. When I travel to large cities, I try to get up early to do my running in the morning. I don't usually run in the early morning, but in cities that's about the only time you don't have to fight cars, exhaust, people, and noise. This calm, peaceful surroundings of an early morning run can slowly prepare your mind and body for the rigors of a new day.

That's the poetic side of exercise in the morning. But, alas, it has its prosaic side. If you're not particularly interested in being exhilirated at that time in the morning, if you have to be at work by 9 o'clock, and if it takes you an hour and a half to commute; then, of course, you will have to crawl out of bed at an ungodly hour several days a week so you can get in your exercise time. That means you will probably have to forego the late, late show on TV—that is if you don't want to fall asleep at the office. When you are on a solid exercise schedule, sleep is one thing you shouldn't stint on, even though you'll be so charged with energy that you may not need as much as before.

If you exercise before work, it is probably a good idea to nibble on something beforehand so your body has the fuel it needs for the walk, run, swim, or bike ride. There are really no iron-clad rules. I think something very light is best, such as a piece of toast and a small glass of orange juice.

Perhaps you want to exercise in the morning, but don't want to get up extra early. You may want to try getting your exercise while "commuting" to work. For example, if your office or shop is a nice half hour walk from your apartment, you could leave the car in the garage and hoof it. If it's farther, maybe a bicycle is in order. Without working too hard, you could cover six to eight miles in a half hour. Or why not run? Now we get into difficulties, don't we? If you go very fast or work very hard, you may perspire heavily and need a shower or change of clothes. And how do you carry things like books, files, lunch, or extra clothing? If your job requires that you wear a three piece suit, neatly pressed, you may not want to carry it in a backpack while you run to work. If there are no showers at work, your co-workers may not appreciate the way you smell.

Naturally, these potential difficulties must be considered. But with the rising cost of transportation, increasingly busy schedules, and an awareness of the need for exercise, more and more people are turning to this form of activity. I know a man who rides his bicycle to his office eight miles from where he lives. He straps his briefcase on the back of his bike, keeps a rain suit and towel in his backpack, and loves every minute of his ride. With a little planning, you might find that your "ride" to work every day can be a pleasant way to shed fat.

Still, you just may not be a "morning person." You have all you can do to drag your weary body out of bed every morning and get to work on time. But by 10 o'clock or so, you're a dynamo of energy. Perhaps your noon hour would be a good time to exercise. Assuming you have an hour for lunch, try this schedule:

12:00–12:05	Change into comfortable shoes—clothes
12:05–12:40	Walk, jog, or bicycle.
12:40–12:45	Stretching exercises—change clothes.
12:45–1:00	Enjoy a light lunch.

Naturally, this means you carry your lunch instead of waiting in line at the fast food counter. It might also mean you forego the jovial atmosphere of sharing a few drinks with your co-workers at the corner pub. But then, you're interested in losing fat. If you want companionship, encourage your friends to exercise with you. A half hour of pleasant conversation and fat-burning activity is a hard combination to beat.

If morning and noon exercising don't fit your needs, you may find that working out in the evening is best. Many people feel this is an excellent way to work off some of the tension and stress they may have encountered during the day. Exercising at this time provides a nice transition from the market place to the home and can result in an improved family life. Instead of snapping at your kids or arguing with your spouse, try a half hour to 45 minutes of aerobic activity when you get home from work.

Some people prefer to do their exercising late in the evening. There is both good news and bad news about exercising at the end of the day. First, the bad news. When you put exercising as the last item on agenda for the day, that's the way it's usually treated—last. You tend to put everything else in front of it. Consequently, it's easy to forget it or postpone it, rationalizing that you "just don't have the time." I have discovered another drawback to exercising late at night. If you choose running, walking, or cycling on the roads, doing these activities after dark can be dangerous. Personally, I don't enjoy running after dark, because I am constantly wondering if the oncoming cars see me. If you must exercise on the roads or sidewalks after dark, follow these precautions:

1. Wear bright clothing. You can purchase reflective tape and place strips of it on your clothing to enhance your chances of being seen.
2. Move toward oncoming traffic. In this country, that means do your running or walking on the left-hand side of the road.
3. Don't take chances. If two cars are approaching from opposite directions, don't be stubborn and hold your position. Move at least six feet off the pavement. Stop if you must. It is better to interrupt your run or walk than to run the risk of being hit.
4. Avoid going it alone. The lonely pedestrian at night is a target. Reports of joggers being attacked at night and robbed, raped, or otherwise assaulted are increasing. You are much safer if you have someone with you.

Now for the good news. Some people find evening exercise relaxing. Their day unwinds. They feel it's the best sleeping pill ever invented. It's cheap, has no bad side effects, and you don't have to see your doctor about a change in prescription. Some people report, however, that vigorous exercise late in the evening can trigger wakefulness. You'll have to experiment to find out how you react.

When you exercise is an individual thing. Exercise any time it suits you. If you're a morning person and like to get up with the larks, exercise in the morning. But if you're the sort who spends most of the morning groping about, don't force yourself to greet the dawn. Leave it to the larks. Exercise later in the day when it fits in with your metabolism and idiosyncracies. If you are fortunate enough to be on top of things at either end of the day, the possibilities you have for selecting your exercising time are simply multiplied.

Establish A Routine

Once you have decided on the best time for exercise, stick to it! If one day you exercise in the morning, the next at noon, and the third day in the evening; you're not building a strong routine. You should be striving to develop a new habit of exercise and this is much easier to do if you exercise at the same time every day. Any habit is largely a conditioned reflex. And conditioned reflexes come about through repetition. Repetition develops a patterned response in our minds and bodies. And if something interrupts the pattern, most of us feel very uncomfortable.

At one time or another, all of us have felt great distress about a simple thing like not having our newspaper delivered. We feel like skinning the newsboy alive. Our habit of reading the newspaper every day has been interrupted. But it's more complicated than that. We are used to reading it at a particular time, say after a good dinner, and the pattern of contentment associated with it may also be disturbed. When you feel the same way about interruptions in your exercise schedule, you'll be well on your way to a better looking body.

Do It For Enjoyment

Most of us aren't masochists; we're hedonists. We do things for pleasure. When you are totally immersed in an activity of any type, you can actually lose your sense of time and your awareness of the external world. You experience ecstasy. This has been called the flow experience. It's probably the highest form of enjoyment. If you enjoy your exercising, this flow experience can happen to you. Runners talk about their "high" when running more than 30 minutes. Basketball players talk about the "juices" flowing. And other athletes say they're "in the groove" or "in sync." They all mean the same thing. Enjoyment and performance came together and everything was perfect.

Unfortunately, too many people base an exercise program on what they think is "good for them." They've been told it's "good because it hurts." Many follow extremely strict regimens that are doomed to failure. Exercise, for them, is a test of willpower. This approach does not work for most Americans. You should try to pick something you enjoy. In this book, I've tried to give you various options that you can use to build exercise into your lifestyle. You'll probably find that once you have made the time to build it into your lifestyle, you'll never want to let it go. Of course, you'll have to give exercise a chance. One week is not enough. It may take months. Even athletes don't get "in the groove" in one week. They usually peak near the end of the season, after months of training.

Dress The Part

If possible, have a special outfit and wear it only for exercising. Anything comfortable—an old pair of shorts or slacks and a sweatshirt, will do. How you look is not the point; it's how you feel. In changing from regular clothes into an "exercising outfit," you also psych yourself up for the activity. In effect you're telling yourself you mean business and really intend to collect your rewards.

Think The Part

What happens in your head is almost as important to the success of the program as what happens to your body, because if you don't enjoy what you're doing, you'll begin to find reasons.

Before you exercise, think yourself into a positive, active frame of mind. As you exercise, be aware of what's happening to your body. Feel your muscles work. Concentrate on the rhythmic flow of your movements. Exercising can be a pleasurable sensory experience, and it will be if you can learn to think of it that way.

Your Spouse

Your spouse has to be on your side. Research has shown that your chances of sticking to a program are better if your spouse approves and encourages you. A study conducted by Fred Heinzleman, Ph.D., then Chief of Behavioral Science Activities for the Heart Disease and Stroke Control Program, bears this out. In a program where he had men participate in one hour of physical activity three times a week for eight months, he found adherence was good or excellent if the wife encouraged participation. If the wife had neutral or had negative feelings about the exercise, attendance was much poorer. He concluded the spouse's attitude was critical. I agree.

Exercising In A Group

Exercising with a friend or in a group gives you the advantage of companionship and having someone encourage you when you feel like quitting. You probably will exercise more if you have someone to talk to and to keep you company.

An investigation conducted at the University of Toronto bore this out. After acknowledging the merits of both the group and individual programs, the scientists reported a greater dropout rate for individual programs. In their observations of group and individual exercises, they found that only 47% of those on individual programs were still active at 28 weeks, compared with 82% of those in the group programs.

If you feel your motivation is weak, make sure you exercise with a partner or with several friends.

Importance Of Success

Whenever you feel on the verge of quitting, try this. Recall your first exercise session. You may have only walked 10 minutes.

Now repeat this walking program one day. You will be amazed at how easy it is. This can be just the inspiration you need to return to your normal exercising program the next day.

Read about people who exercise in spite of adversity. The man who completed a marathon with one leg, the fellow who wheelchairs his way through a marathon, or the blind marathoner or golfer. Keep stories such as these to read for inspiration.

Concentrate on your own success. Remind yourself that you have been exercising for the last six months, two years, or whatever. The first six months are the roughest. Most people are "hooked" after 3 to 6 months. Think positively: "I've been on this swimming program for 6 months, and I'm not going to quit now!"

Importance Of Variety

Don't be afraid to put variety into your exercising routine. If you are traveling, you may find walking or running the streets of Houston, Miami, or Seattle most stimulating. As you walk or run, look at your surroundings.

If you're not a traveler and find your walking, running, or bicycling route is getting you down, try a new area for a while. You might even schedule a backpacking or hiking trip. But even if you're walking, running, skiing, or bicycling on old terrain, look at your surroundings. You'll notice things you haven't seen before. The old saying is solid: variety is the spice of life.

Be Tough

By being tough, I mean don't worry about what other people think. As you're walking, running, or biking down Main Street, you may think that every eye in town is looking at you. So what! You're doing something good for your body; they're not. You have to learn that some of the stares people are giving you are really nothing more than jealousy and envy. I had a psychiatrist friend tell me one time that the reason he felt people stared at him as he ran was because they wished they had the motivation and will to run.

On the other hand, it may be that someone is looking at you with a good bit of pride. They may be pleased to see you exercising and assuming responsibility for your own health.

You may find yourself somewhat embarrassed by running, walking, or biking alongside the road. When you're doing this, many times people will be asking you questions such as: "Did your car break down?" "Can we give you a lift?" You have several alternatives. You can tell them, "No thanks, I'm walking." Or, you can say, "I only have a few more steps to go." Finally, you can take your dog with you. Everyone knows that a dog needs exercise.

If none of these excuses seem to work, then exercise at a place where you can't be seen. I know of one couple who was so embarrassed by running in daylight that they decided to run in the huge underground parking lot of their apartment complex. They ran the ramps and the empty car stalls. They did their 60 minutes of exercise underground. That's one solution. Personally, I prefer to get out and enjoy God's good, green earth. I don't worry about what others think. It's their problem, not mine. Be tough.

Where To Exercise

Where you choose to exercise is another individual matter, and the range of choices is unlimited. Well, at least unlimited as far as space is concerned. Just look around you—nothing but spaces to roam. Just pick a route. Maybe you're lucky enough to live in a town that offers not just walkng space—but biking routes, parcourse courses, running, and cross country ski trails. You may have your favorite, and you'll probably discover new ones every week, but while making the discoveries, you should always consider safety.

Traffic must always be taken into account. And you don't have to be a genius to realize that some city areas are just not safe enough to run, walk, or bike through at any hour. The best way to protect yourself against these possible dangers is to check over the route you plan to use beforehand.

Health Status

Obviously, your current health status must be taken into account when planning exercise. Certain health problems will affect selection of type, duration, and frequency of exercise. Such problems will also place limits on how much improvement can be expected and at what rate. People with any current or potential health problem should be extremely careful in the beginning not to overstress their bodies. If you have some kind of cardiovascular problem, for example, especially close supervision of the program by a physician is essential. Frequent physical examinations in this situation are necessary to be sure that the exercise program is having a beneficial rather than a harmful effect.

In the next chapter there is a summary of medical considerations to take into account before you start an exercise program. If you have been sedentary, a knowledgeable physician's observations and opinions are absolutely necessary. Even when cleared by the doctor, the activity may be restricted to walking or bicycling. These activities are mild enough to be no danger to the cardiovascular system in most cases and will not predispose the body to major orthopedic problems.

Common sense will tell you, too, that when you have an illness such as a cold, minor infection or injury, it is best to take a few days off. When you resume exercise after a temporary halt (for whatever reason), you should start at a lower workload and work your way up again. Oft-times after a one or two week layoff, you'll feel real good on the first day back exercising, only to feel burned out on the second through fifth day.

Body Type

Your body type also plays a role in helping you select fitness activities for weight control. There can be no joy for the lightly built person who is forced to participate in rugged contact sports. And there's nothing but frustration for the person who aspires to be a long distance runner but is too heavy to win the fight against gravity.

Research has shown that certain types of physique are attracted to certain sports and exercise routines. Thomas K. Cureton, Ph.D., in his book *Physical Fitness Appraisal and Guidance,* points out that the active, wiry, relatively thin types usually do best on endurance-type training such as long-distance running. That's the person who can run five or ten or even twenty miles without feeling ill effects.

For people high in fatness, Dr. Cureton recommends activities such as bowling, sailing, swimming, bicycling, camping, tennis, badminton, shuffleboard, fishing, and skating. He adds that both thin and fat types should be encouraged to keep up their strength and cardiovascular conditioning.

Muscular people, however, as a rule have a relatively high physical fitness status. They seem to enjoy virtually all physical activities, though it may take some time for them to get used to long-distance running because of their body weight.

It all boils down to the fact that you can't do more than your body type will allow. If you choose a sport that does not fit your body type, you can get away with it for a while, but sooner or later you'll simply give up (See Table 16).

Age

Age has already been mentioned as a factor in determining the ideal intensity for your exercise. The target pulse rate was highest for young people and decreased as age increased.

Age enters into exercise planning in other ways too. If you maintain a physically active lifestyle during your developmental and middle years, you'll find that you probably can exercise vigorously even at a relatively old age.

It would be hard to disagree with Paul Dudley White, M.D.: "I'm sure that our health in middle age is very dependent upon what we do in our twenties. And I'm equally sure that the

		BODY TYPE				
Table 16￼**BODY TYPE AND PHYSICAL ACTIVITY**		FAT	MUSCULAR AND FAT	MUSCULAR	MUSCULAR AND THIN	THIN
FAT-BURNING EXERCISES	AEROBIC DANCING		▓	▓	▓	▓
	BICYCLING	▓	▓	▓	▓	▓
	CROSS COUNTRY SKIING	▓	▓	▓	▓	▓
	JOGGING		▓	▓	▓	▓
	ROPE JUMPING			▓	▓	▓
	RUNNING		▓	▓	▓	▓
	RUNNING IN PLACE			▓	▓	▓
	SWIMMING	▓	▓	▓	▓	
	WALKING	▓	▓	▓	▓	▓
OTHER ACTIVITIES	ARCHERY	▓	▓	▓		
	BADMINTON			▓	▓	▓
	BASKETBALL			▓	▓	▓
	BOWLING	▓	▓	▓	▓	
	GOLF		▓	▓	▓	▓
	HANDBALL		▓	▓	▓	
	HIKING		▓	▓	▓	▓
	SKIING		▓	▓	▓	
	TENNIS		▓	▓	▓	
	WEIGHT TRAINING		▓	▓	▓	

health at sixty, seventy, and eighty is very dependent on what we do in middle age."

But what about people who have been inactive? What if you choose to become active after years of sedentary existence? Can you expect to benefit from, or even tolerate, vigorous exercise? In most cases, yes.

The period of maximum physical development is between the ages of twenty-five and thirty. After this, there is a slow decline in maximum strength, decreasing suddenly after fifty (but even at age sixty the loss does not usually exceed 20% of the maximum). Decline in speed of movement and reaction time show a similar pattern. Maximum heart rate, cardiac output (stroke volume times heart rate), and oxygen consumption also show a decline with age, with cardiac output at rest generally showing a decline of 1% after maturity.

These factors combined make for slower improvement and a lower rate of recovery from stress than was experienced at an earlier age. Also, loss of conditioning (when inactive) takes place more rapidly and reconditioning progresses more slowly. Consequently, the overload, intensity, duration, and type of activity must be adapted accordingly. For older persons, strength, speed, and agility take on relatively less importance than flexibility, local muscle endurance, body weight, relaxation, and circulo-respiratory endurance. This should be reflected in the program. There is no current evidence that vigorous exercise will injure a healthy person, regardless of age. Proceed cautiously, realistically—and enthusiastically.

If you find that at the end of exercise you are extremely fatigued, then cut back the next day. If as you are exercising you find it difficult to hold a conversation with someone next to you, cut back. If at any time you are dizzy, suffer chest pains, exceptional fatigue, or pain—stop. If you find you are staggering, have mental confusion, lose facial color, or have deep breathing or nausea; again cut back. Some of these should also be evaluated by a doctor.

Just remember: the older you are the longer it may take you to get into shape. You should spend more time on warm-up and you should definitely listen to your body. But don't let anyone tell you you should get out of recreation and into the rocker. It just isn't so. Exercise is healthful and beneficial to the older citizen.

It's Your Responsibility

Research suggests that most people who try to diet seldom stick with it. Exercise doesn't have to be that way. This chapter has shown you a sensible approach that will make exercise an easy and natural way to lose fat. Once you have taken a few minutes to plan a program that fits your goals and interests, you need not continue the depressing on-and-off syndrome of weight control.

11

How Not To Overdo It

Whenever exercise is mentioned, occasionally someone will express a fear that is valid. They worry about overdoing it and perhaps creating more serious health problems. Though I believe dieting can ultimately be more harmful than exercise, I recommend a good dose of common sense before you go out and run, bike, or walk around the block.

If you're going to plan a program of fat control, you should know or understand several things including:

1. Your health status
2. Your fitness level
3. Your personal feelings
4. Your pulse rate while exercising

All four are important in helping you get the most out of your physical activity and keeping you from overdoing. Let's look at each one.

Your Health Status

To get an idea of just how healthy you are, take the informal inventory* on page 176. Read each question and circle the appropriate answer.

* This inventory was developed by the British Columbia Ministry of Health.

1. Has your doctor ever said you have heart trouble?   YES   NO
2. Have you ever had pains in your heart and chest
   when exercising or at other times?   YES   NO
3. Do you often feel faint or have spells of severe
   dizziness?   YES   NO
4. Has a doctor ever said your blood pressure was
   too high?   YES   NO
5. Has your doctor ever told you that you have a bone
   or joint problem such as arthritis that has been
   aggravated by exercise, or might be made worse with
   exercise?   YES   NO
6. Do you suffer from chronic low back pain?   YES   NO
7. Do you suffer from disease of the lungs, kidneys,
   and/or liver?   YES   NO
8. Are you over the age of 65 and not accustomed to
   vigorous exercise?   YES   NO
9. Do you have a serious question about your ability
   to partake in an exercise program?   YES   NO

If you answered No to all these questions skip down to the entry headed *Your Fitness Level.* If you answered Yes to one or more of the above questions or have any doubts at all about your health, you should check with your doctor before proceeding. If your doctor recommends a checkup because of a question about your health, the checkup should include an examination of your heart, blood vessels, muscles, and joints. Ideally, your blood should be analyzed for cholesterol and triglycerides, and your blood pressure should be measured. A resting electrocardiogram (ECG) should also be performed.

If you are past the age of 40, it's a good idea to take an exercise stress test. A stress test is nothing more than an electrocardiogram taken while you are exercising.

Dr. Kenneth Cooper's recommendations regarding stress testing are good ones. According to Cooper: "If you are under 30, you can start exercising if you've had a checkup in the past year and your doctor has found nothing wrong with you; if you are between 30 and 39, you should have a checkup within three months before you start exercising, and the examination should include an electrocardiogram (ECG) taken at rest; if you are between 40 and 59, your guidelines are the same as those for the 30 to 39 group, plus an ECG taken while you are exercising; if you are over 59, you should follow the same requirements as for the 40 to 59 group, and the examination should be performed immediately before you embark on any exercise program.''

Selecting the right physician to clear you for exercise is important. I think it is crucial. Quite frankly, not all doctors believe in or understand the value of exercise. Some have negative attitudes about it. So follow this advice. When selecting a physician, do this:

1. Look at your physician's waistline. If it seems too big and there is opposition to your exercising, don't trust the exercise advice.
2. Make sure your doctor is a nonsmoker.
3. Find out if the doctor takes part in an aerobic exercise program; that is, exercising three or more times a week. (Golf does not qualify.)

If the physician passes these three hurdles, tell the good doctor you are going to participate in an exercise program. Show him or her this book. Then ask the following:

1. Can you clear me for participation in this program?
2. How long, how hard, and how often am I permitted to exercise?

If your doctor realizes you are serious about exercising, he should be pleased. But if the reaction is a comment like: "Remember, if you walk one mile from home you'll have to walk one mile back," get a second opinion from another doctor.

Unfortunately, most doctors deal with sickness, not wellness.

So physicians tend to think in negative rather than positive terms. Yet if you look around a bit, I'm sure you will find a physician who is in tune with exercise. Ever so slowly, the medical profession is beginning to look at *all* areas of health. Every now and then, I pass a doctor friend of mine running the roads. While that is good, the patients are the real winners.

Your Fitness Level

Once you have passed the checklist and/or have been given the green light from your physician, you may want to take a personal fitness test. While the fitness test is not necessary, many people prefer to have a bench mark from where to measure their fitness program. The test can also give you direction in selecting the best activities for you.

Several fitness tests have been prepared which you can perform yourself. But they are not to replace the medical checkup. Fitness tests provide you only with a rough idea of your physical capabilities—nothing more. Some of the tests are quite vigorous. Others are less so. My favorite test is Cooper's Three Mile Walking Test. It has several advantages including specific fitness categories, age differentiation, and most importantly, an activity many people can do without fear of over-doing— walking. To do this fitness test try to *walk* a three mile course in as short a time as possible. Twelve laps on a ¼ mile high school track would be a good place. You can also measure the distance with your car's odometer. A course that is 1½ miles out and 1½ miles back is best. Make sure the terrain is flat. Caution: When taking the test, if you experience any chest, jaw, or neck pain, if you seem unduly tired, or if you experience any lightheadedness, slow down, stop the test, and report your observations to your doctor.

After taking the test compare your results with those listed on the chart. Remember: Don't view the test as a pass/fail item. Use the test to tell yourself how fit you are. Then retake the test three months later to determine your progress.

Table 17
THREE MILE WALKING TEST (NOT RUNNING)

FITNESS CATEGORY		AGE (Years) 13–19	20–29	30–39	TIME (Minutes) 40–49	50–59	60+
I. Very poor	(men)	>45:00*	>46:00	>49:00	>52:00	>55:00	>60:00
	(women)	>47:00	>48:00	>51:00	>54:00	>57:00	>63:00
II. Poor	(men)	41:01–45:00	41:01–46:00	44:31–49:00	47:01–52:00	50:01–55:00	54:01–60:00
	(women)	43:01–47:00	44:01–48:00	46:31–51:00	49:01–54:00	52:01–57:00	57:01–63:00
III. Fair	(men)	37:31–41:00	38:31–42:00	40:01–44:30	42:01–47:00	45:01–5):00	48:01–54:00
	(women)	39:31–43:00	40:31–44:00	42:01–46:30	44:01–49:00	47:01–52:00	51:01–57:00
IV. Good	(men)	33:00–37:30	34:00–38:30	35:00–40:00	36:30–42:00	39:00–45:00	41:00–48:00
	(women)	35:00–39:30	36:00–40:30	37:30–42:00	39:00–44:00	42:00–47:00	45:00–51:00
V. Excellent	(men)	<33:00	<34:00	<35:00	<36:30	<39:00	<41:00
	(women)	<35:00	<36:00	<37:30	<39:00	<42:00	<45:00

*< Means "less than"; > means "more than."

The Walking Test, covering 3 miles in the fastest time possible *without running*, can be done on a track over any accurately measured distance. As with running, take the test after you have been training for at least six weeks, when you feel rested, and dress to be comfortable. From K.H. Cooper, *The Aerobics Way* (New York: M. Evans, 1977).

Besides taking the test, I think it's a good idea to check your pulse rate immediately after the test. Pulse rate should be taken within 10 seconds of stopping. Take your pulse for 6 seconds, multiply it by 10, and record it on a sheet of paper. For an accurate record you may want to record it here. My post walk pulse rate was _____.

I suspect many of you will not like what you discover from the test: that you're not in as good shape as you thought you were. If that happens:

1. DON'T get discouraged. Your body is amazing. Just as it can become sluggish from underuse, it can be revitalized with increased activity. It just takes time. As a rule, I figure it takes one month of activity for every year of sedentary living. That means if you've been out of shape for 10 years, plan on at least 10 months of regular aerobic activity to get back into shape.

2. DON'T ignore the results. If the test placed you in the FAIR category, you can assume you're not in good or excellent shape as far as fitness is concerned. To ignore the results would cause problems for you in your exercise program. Instead, face the facts and press on toward your goal to do something about it. If you still need a boost, turn ahead to the last page where you made a promise to yourself.

One Final Note: If the prospect of walking three miles seems rather difficult even before you take the test, place yourself in the very poor category. It is also my position that you shouldn't take this test until you have walked for six weeks. That way the chances of hurting yourself are greatly reduced.

Personal Feelings

Your personal feelings when exercising are extremely important. They probably will tell you more about how you are responding to exercise than anything else. Here are three things you should consider:

1. First, you should be able to hold a conversation with some-one beside you as you exercise. Even when you are exercis-ing alone, you can use your imagination: do you feel like talking? If not, you can probably conclude that you're exer-cising too fast for your present age or fitness level. I call this the Talk Test. The Talk Test is especially important during the first 6 to 12 weeks of exercising.
2. Second, your exercising should be painless. If you experi-ence any jaw, chest, or neck pain, slow down. If that doesn't stop the pain, see your doctor and describe what happened. Try to recall the circumstances: "I was walking up the hill," "It occurred during the first few minutes of exercise," or "The weather was cold."
3. Third, if after exercising you seem excessively tired for an hour or longer, the exercise was too strenuous. Next time, go slower and not as hard. Or as long. Your exercising should be exhilirating, not fatiguing. If you experience dizzy or light-headed feelings, if your heart is beating too fast while you are exercising, it's time to back off. If you have a strange hollow feeling in your chest, feel like vomiting, or are tired for at least a day after exercising, take it easy. If you can't sleep at night or if your nerves seem shot, it means that you've been pushing too hard. The same thing is true if you've lost your zing or can't get your breath after a few minutes of exercise. These are your body's warning signs.

All three points emphasize "listening to your body." This listening is something you'll have to learn but you'll probably find it fun. You will enjoy your body more. It will let you know when to slow down and when to speed up. You are the best judge of your exercise.

See the following chart for a listing of possible warning signs to slow down and reassess your progress.

Figure 2. Possible warning signs

COMPLAINT	CAUSE	TREATMENT
1. "My heart feels funny." (This may be a hollow feeling, fluttering, or sudden racing, or slowing of the heart rate.)	Your exercise is too vigorous.	Slow down level of exercise and see your doctor.
2. "I have this sharp pain or pressure in my chest."	Your exercise is too vigorous	Slow down level of exercise and see your doctor.
3. "I am dizzy or lightheaded"; "My head feels funny"; "I break out into a cold sweat"; or "I almost fainted."	Your exercise is too vigorous. Not enough blood gets to your brain.	Slow down level of exercise and see your doctor
4. "My heart seems to be beating too fast 5 to 10 minutes after exercising" or "I seem breathless 5 to 10 minutes after exercising."	Your exercise is too vigorous.	Work at a lower level of target heart rate range, about 70%. In some instances you may need to work below that. If this doesn't correct the problem, see your doctor.

5. "I feel like vomiting" or "I vomit right after exercising." | Your exercise is too vigorous or you need a better cool-down. | Work at a lower level of target heart rate range, about 70%. Take longer for a cool-down.

6. "I'm tired for at least a day after exercising" or "I'm tired most of the time." | Your exercise is too vigorous. | Work at a lower level of target heart rate range, about 70%. Work to a higher level more gradually or you may need more sleep/rest.

7. "I can't sleep at night after exercising." | Your exercise is too vigorous or done too late in the evening. | Work at least 2 to 3 hours before retiring or work at a lower level of target heart rate, about 70%.

8. "Even though I'm exercising my nerves seem shot"; "I'm jittery"; or "I'm hyper all the time." | Too much exercise or too much competition. | Lay off the competition, cut back on your intensity, and/or switch to another activity for a short time.

9. "I've lost my zing" or "I'm no longer interested in my favorite activity." | Too much exercise or too much competition. | Lay off the competition, cut back on your intensity, and/or switch to another activity for a short time.

10. "During the first few minutes of exercise I can't get my breath." | Improper warm-up. | Spend more time in your warm-up, at least 10 minutes, until you get to your target heart range.

Your Pulse Rate

Your final check on trying not to overdo when exercising is your pulse rate. Earlier I showed you how your pulse rate increases as your oxygen demands increase. I also told you that most people can safely exercise between 70 and 85% of their maximum heart rate.

The 70 to 85% range, however, is only a guideline. A good starting point. In all probability it's your ultimate goal. While it seems to work for most people, you must remember everyone is different. Therefore, don't be a slave to the 70 to 85% figure. If you find the target heart rate exercise too demanding (can't get your breath, experience pain, etc.) back off. Work at a lower level. I strongly believe your personal feelings are much more important than your pulse rate.

There you have it. The guidelines you need to keep from overdoing exercise. Use common sense. If switching TV channels has been your most strenuous activity for the last couple of years, it's just not a good idea to start off with a half hour of vigorous exercise. It's probably too sudden a shock for your body to absorb all at once. Even those of you who are rather young. Problems are bound to crop up in the area of muscle, joint, tendon, and ligaments. I don't care how big of a hurry you're in to lose weight; if you've been fairly inactive for a long time, I urge you to be cautious during the first few weeks and months of exercise. Work up gradually to more vigorous exercise. Although the guidelines that I've given may slow you down a bit at first, do follow them, and you'll be giving your body a chance to make the necessary physiological adjustments to benefit from more vigorous exercise.

You now know how not to overdo it. Now it's up to you. Dance, walk, run, swim, bicycle, cross country ski, move your way to a slimmer, trimmer body.

12

The Gimmicks And Gadgets That Don't Work

"Finally, a new once a day pill has been discovered that will burn your fat away, even while you sleep! Just $13.95 for a two month supply!"

"The incredible new Slim-Nickers are guaranteed to remove 9 to 18 inches of fat from your waist. Just pull them on, hook them up to your vacuum cleaner and feel the fat disappear. Just $9.94 a pair!"

"Dream Cream is a scientifically formulated ointment that draws the fat out of your body. Just rub it on those problem areas and watch the new you appear. Only $10.95! Hurry! Supply is limited!"

Because everyone wants a painless, easy way to lose weight, ads such as these help rake in millions of dollars each year. For their "small" investment, the unsuspecting obese receive nothing but an empty promise. Though I wish it weren't so, modern science has not designed an effortless way to burn calories and fat. The great majority of those "amazing weight loss devices" achieve their greatest effectiveness in the area of separating you from your money. They also improve the fitness of the postal and shipping clerks who have to carry the bloody things around.

The Fallacy Of Sweating It Off

For years, sweating has been equated with weight loss. Because of this unfounded belief, products that make people sweat are pushed as weight loss devices. Nothing could be further from the truth. Your body sweats for one reason, and one reason only. That's to keep your body cool. The human body can be compared to an engine with a thermostat. Except for one very important difference: the human thermostat cannot be turned off. To understand the effects—and perhaps dangers of trying to lose weight by sweating, a look at your cooling system is in order.

Your body produces heat in many ways. By cell activity, muscular activity, digestion of food, and production of hormones. It will also pick up heat from rays of the sun bouncing off sand or snow. Wherever or however the body gets this heat, it must protect itself from accumulating too much. Under normal conditions, heat is lost in a number of ways—through the skin, through sweat, through the lungs, and through waste materials.

When you exercise the situation changes. Sweat becomes the most important way to keep the body cool. For sweat to produce a loss of heat, it must evaporate (sweat that is wiped away or permitted to run off the body has no cooling function). As sweat evaporates, it cools the blood close to the surface of the skin. That blood returns to the body's inner core tissues. At the same time, the interior blood is carrying heat from the deeper tissues toward the skin where the heat can be lost to the environment. Circulation is speeded up during exercise, which makes the heat exchange more efficient.

When the atmosphere has a low humidity, sweat will evaporate very quickly in the air. Likewise, when a breeze is blowing, the air currents will aid evaporation. But if the humidity is high (which means the air is saturated with water), sweat cannot be taken up by the air and the water simply drips off the body. The blood near the skin surface is not cooled. The temperature of the core tissue is not lowered. And the body temperature continues to rise.

If the body temperature is not checked, heat exhaustion, dehydration exhaustion, or heat stroke can occur. Each is more serious than the other. The basic signs are profuse sweating, very moist skin, and rapid pulse, followed by difficulty in breathing, and finally a loss of consciousness. These are considered serious and are a medical emergency. Naturally, heat stroke is far more serious than heat exhaustion, but there is a continuum in which people are in a dangerous state if they are not given a chance to recover and placed into an environment that will help their body temperature cool.

Coupled with this fact that water is lost, the body may also lose some electrolytes (sodium and potassium). A prolonged loss of electrolytes and water may cause nausea, diarrhea, and fatigue. It may impair kidney function to the point where kidney tissue damage occurs. In fact, muscle cramping and irregular heart beats are also common factors of an electrolyte imbalance.

Rubberized Sweatsuits

It is a medically accepted fact that allowing your body to overheat will produce dangerous conditions that could even lead to death. Therefore, any device that is based on increased and unchecked sweating is potentially hazardous to your health. Though the claim of weight loss may sound attractive, remember that what is being lost is water. And water is one of the substances your body needs in order to exist. When you perspire, you are not losing fat. Eventually, the water that you lose must be replaced. Hence, whatever weight you lose will be regained. It's just not worth the risk.

A rubberized sweatsuit prevents air from reaching the surface of the skin and at the same time traps heat radiating from the body. Therefore, sweat is prevented from evaporating. If sweating continues, with little or no evaporation, heat exhaustion, deep dehydration exhaustion, and even heat stroke may occur. During very strenuous exercise, the body might lose—sweat away—as much as 8 quarts of water in an hour and a half. If profuse sweating continues and the fluid loss is not replaced, then heat stroke will occur—a medical emergency. A doctor must be called immediately. Unless body temperature is promptly lowered, brain cells may be permanently damaged and the victim might die.

So I don't think anyone should ever wear a rubberized sweatsuit for exercise. Even heavy cotton knit suits ought to be avoided. Like the rubberized kind, they also cause profuse sweating. Either could lead to the sort of complications we've just described.

The question arises, why does anyone wear these things anyway? Well, a lot of people really believe that sweatsuits will make them lose weight. When I expressed my concern to the elderly man who was wearing a sweatsuit and running in place in the steamroom, he informed me rather peevishly—as though I had better get back to minding my own business—that he'd be "five pounds lighter after his workout."

He was right in a sense. After a strenuous workout, the kind that makes sweat drip from every pore, you may step on the scales and find you are three, four, and maybe five pounds lighter. That is similar to the phenomenon of the water lost when people drastically change their diet. I could make the same claim as the fad diet people: "You'll start to lose weight immediately." But all you've lost is water. With your first glass of something wet, you'll start to regain all the "weight" you have "lost." By the following day you'll weigh just about what you did before donning the sweatsuit. In other words, any weight loss you experience immediately after a strenuous workout is a false one.

Steamrooms

Steamrooms are popular in many health clubs. I think that's

because they provide a great place to hide from the people who want to exercise. The temperature in a streamroom is maintained at 110 to 130° F. Since the humidity is also very high, a person who sits in the steamroom will, of course, sweat profusely. But due to the high humidity, sweat cannot evaporate and have a cooling effect on the body. As a result, body temperatures can rise to dangerous levels. Clayton R. Myers, Ph.D., Lawrence Golding, Ph.D., and Wayne Sinning, Ph.D., say that "there is growing concern among physicians that . . . steam booths may be detrimental to health. Heat stress is not tolerated well by most middle-aged people. Heat exposure can lead to heat exhaustion. The dangers of heat exposure are increased if an individual enters the bath after exercise, when the body is trying to reduce temperature."

Sauna

Ah . . . a lovely Nordic looking couple relaxing nude in a redwood paneled sauna. The picture of health. Of course, the implication is that sitting around in a sauna will give you a sexy body. Perhaps even your hair will turn blonde and you will ski better, too. Many claims have been made for the sauna. The great majority have appeared in newspapers, popular magazines, and articles thin in research but fat with personal testimonials. Claims have also been made, of course, by sauna manufacturers. Two are that sauna bathing will cause a loss of weight and possibly a loss of body fat. We have already said that the only way to lose weight is to burn off more calories than you take in. Sitting in a hot sauna just doesn't burn off a significant number of calories. The weight loss in such a hot environment is water—not fat tissue. You may be three pounds lighter after the sauna bath, but you'll gain it back almost as soon as you eat or drink.

Nowadays, most any health club or gym worth its name is equipped with a sauna. They're even beginning to turn up in beauty parlors, country clubs, and private homes.

While temperatures inside a sauna are high (the AMA recommends an upper limit of no more than 185°F), the humidity is low. So, while you do sweat in a sauna, the perspiration quickly evaporates and the body is better able to regulate its own internal temperature.

Recent research shows that spending time in a sauna untenses the muscles somewhat, and this contributes to a nice relaxed feeling. But like sweatsuits and steamrooms, saunas have no real value when it comes to helping people lose weight. And again, like sweatsuits and steamrooms, the sauna should be approached with caution. Sauna users must keep the following guidelines in mind:

1. The temperature should be no higher than 185° F and the humidity should be kept low—about 10%.
2. Wear as little clothing as possible. Stark naked is best—no towel, no jewelry, watch, or eye glasses.
3. Beginners should spend no more than eight to ten minutes in the sauna and should be sure there is another person in attendance. Maximum time for the veteran sauna user is 15 minutes.
4. Never go into a sauna with a full stomach. Wait at least an hour after a heavy meal—two hours are better.
5. Never use a sauna when you are under the influence of alcohol or narcotics, or when you've taken antihistamines, tranquilizers, vasoconstrictors, vasodilators, stimulants, or hypnotics.
6. Elderly people and those who suffer from diabetes, heart disease, or high blood pressure should probably avoid saunas altogether.

Sauna Shorts

A few years ago inflatable outfits were the rage. Sweat belts, girdles, or rubberized Bermuda shorts promised to take off ten inches around the waist in two weeks without dieting. I recall quite vividly one young woman, Shirley, who was very impressed by the advertisements featuring testimonials from people who had used the shorts. She brought one of those ads to show me. Under the photograph of a beautiful brunette there was a caption running something like "In one day I lost two inches from my hips. Sauna shorts, I love you."

I looked at the ad, shrugged, and handed it back to Shirley. "Don't waste your money," I said.

But that ad really got to Shirley, and the next day she ordered a pair of shorts for $12.98. Now they're $30 or more. Before getting into the shorts, she measured her hips—38 inches. After wearing the shorts around the house for several hours, she took them off, and—Lo and behild!—her hips measured 36 inches. She phoned me to tell me I was all wet. "See, Kuntzleman, you don't know everything!"

But I still had a trump card. I asked her to measure her hips again the next morning. She did and sure enough, she was back to 38 inches.

Here's what happened: the sauna shorts generated intense heat. Consequently, the cells directly under the shorts lost a great deal of water. By the end of the day when Shirley took off the shorts, the depleted cells had "shrunk" in size and she seemed to have lost inches. But, as Shirley ate and drank normally that evening and during the night, these cells took up as much water as they had lost and she "regained" inches.

"But what if I don't drink anything? What happens then?" Shirley countered. The answer is that she will die of thirst. By limiting food and drink she might be able to prolong the effect of the shorts. But the body demands fluids. (You can do without food for 72 days, but you can't do without water for more than 72 hours.) And as soon as she returned to normal eating and drinking habits, she'd be back where she started.

Sauna shorts and belts are not dangerous, but they're a useless waste of money. Soon after taking the shorts off, the dehydrated cells begin to draw water from the normal cells and return to their normal size.

In short, the theory of losing inches using inflatable outfits is bunk. Research supports this stand. Researchers conducted a study in which they compared the weights and measurements of several groups of people. Some wore inflatable garments, some did not, and some were on a low calorie diet. All subjects performed comparable exercise routines. The only significant difference among the groups after the exercise and diet regimens was a greater loss of weight among those who had dieted. The conclusion was that "inches can be lost using an inflatable apparatus only if the user is on a 900 to 1,000 calorie per day diet."

Clayton Myers, Ph.D., reached a similar conclusion. He said, "there is no evidence that 'sauna belts' will contribute to any fat reduction." Furthermore, "A recent Federal Trade Commission decision has restricted advertising these devices since the evidence in support of these claims was insufficient."

Massage

There is nothing better at the end of the day than a massage. It feels great—puts me right to sleep. We all love to have our neck, shoulders, arms, and legs gently kneaded and rubbed. A massage is a perfect relaxer—it beats a cocktail any day. Unfortunately, massage has also been touted as a great way to remove body fat. Nonsense! The only person who loses weight with massage is the masseuse or masseur. Certainly not the person on the table.

To understand massage it's important to know a little bit more about your fat tissue. The number of fat cells that you have in your body is determined early in life. In adulthood, it is the size—not the number—of fat cells that increases. When you are young and physically active, the fat cells are relatively low in fat content. But as you become more sedentary and burn off fewer calories, your fat cells fill up with fat. Exactly where these fat cells occur in your body is determined in a large measure by heredity.

Fat gets in and out of the fat cells by a combination of factors including circulatory, nervous, endocrine, and muscular systems. And a key element appears to be the hormonal action.

Massage has been defined as a systematic manipulation of soft tissue of the body for therapeutic purposes. And the benefits of massage, according to experts in the field, is that it helps to relax muscles and reduce muscle tension. Occasionally, the mechanical effects may improve circulation and blood and lymph, stretching adhesions between muscle fibers, and mobilizing the accumulation of fat. But the effects of massage do not include reducing body fat. How could it? All indications are that almost every system in the body, including the nervous, circulatory, endocrine, digestive, and muscular systems are involved in getting fat in and out of the cells.

Unfortunately, there are many misconceptions about exercise. Far too often, the teaching of massage has been done by people who knew very little about physiology. For example, one writer said, "Massage breaks down fat so it can be carried away by the bloodstream." No documentation is given for this kind of interpretation because there is none.

We would have funny shapes if we could massage fat out of a cell. All we would have to do is massage the fat from one area of the body and it would appear at another. Our bodies don't work that way.

Of course, there are many machines which proport to massage the fat out of areas of your body. Massaging machines include vibrators, rollers, and hydromassage (whirlpool) units of various types. Some devices are comfortable vibrating chairs, others are machines that perform kneading and stroking movements. There are also appliances that rely on revolving wooden rollers or vibrating belts to produce light stimulation to various body parts.

These various "reducing" machines touted as a means to painless, effortless fat control are certainly impressive with their chrome plating and their push-button controls. No wonder so many people are taken in by them. It hardly seems possible that mechanical devices so handsomely designed—and so expensive— should turn out to be utterly worthless at doing the job they're supposed to do. But they are.

These elaborate contraptions have no significant effect on your weight, fat, or calories, because it is physiologically impossible to shake, jiggle, roll, vibrate, bump, slap, or massage fat from the body. Anyone who tells you that it is, is either misinformed or lying.

Belt Vibrators

To pin down the true value—or lack of it—of these machines, the late Dr. Arthur Steinhaus of George Williams College and later Michigan State University, subjected 13 men (some markedly overfat) to a 15-minute period of vigorous vibration by a belt massager, with a belt placed aroung their abdomen. He found that they used about 11.4 extra calories for a 15-minute bout (about $\frac{1}{23}$rd of an ounce of body fat). Steinhaus also measured blood fat levels and learned that there was no increase in the amount of fat circulating in the bloodstream. According to his calculations, one would have to use the vibrator 15 minutes a day for a full year to lose one pound of fat. (A 15-minute walk daily would take off 10 pounds a year!) His conclusion was that "The vibrator is not to be taken seriously as a device to assist in fat reduction or in shifting of fat deposits within the body."

Hydromassage Units

A hydromassage unit is a portable or self-contained unit whose purpose is to direct streams of water forcefully at your body. The water provides a massage, sometimes gentle and sometimes not so gentle. Some people claim this device will help to redistribute fat. The fact, however, is that they have no real fitness value. They may be helpful in bringing temporary relief to minor aches, but they do not change your body composition.

Cellulite

Within the past eight years American women have been told that their "orange peel fat"—ugly bumpy fat—is caused by an entrapment of toxic wastes left over in various parts of the body—particularly the abdomen, hips, thighs, arms, knees, back, and ankles. This fat has been recently called cellulite. Cellulite is supposed to be connective tissues saturated with water and wastes. It is also supposed to be a very unusual kind of "fat" that requires very special corrective measures.

These measures include: dieting, exercise, massage, high pressure water, relaxation, deep breathing, and working the kidneys, intestines, and skin overtime. Which means sauna bathing and consuming lots of natural laxatives and diuretics.

To be very honest with you, I never heard of cellulite until Nicole Ronsard's book, *Cellulite: Those Lumps, Bumps, and Bulges You Couldn't Lose Before* appeared in this country in 1973. To determine the existence and/or value of cellulite, I searched more textbooks than I care to mention, talked to several reputable nutritionists and physiologists, read several articles, carefully scanned *Index Medicus,* and used my own gray matter. My conclusion: cellulite is simply perpetrated on the American public.

First, I could not find a single reference to cellulite in numerous medical physiology texts, or books on adipose tissue. In *Index Medicus,* an index of medical literature, there were only five papers in ten years referring to cellulite and then they referred to the fat as "so-called cellulite."

Second, Dr. Philip L. White, director of the AMA's Food and Nutrition Department, calls cellulite a figment of Mme. Ronsard's imagination. Dr. Morton Glen, past president of the American Nutrition Association, said there was no such thing in medical science.

Third, the *Medical World News,* in an excellent review of the problem, noted that if Mme. Ronsard had presented any facts to substantiate her thesis, she would have dramatically altered our notions about the causes and treatment of obesity.

Fourth, I have seen several people with what appears to be "orange peel fat" or the "cottage cheese" look. As far as I'm concerned, that is fat of the good old fashioned variety. It is caused by a lack of activity, and is cured by initiating activity. You cannot remove the fat out of those fat cells either by massage or high pressure. Relaxation and deep breathing have nothing to do with fat removal. Working the kidneys overtime only reduces water stores in the body which are refilled after taking in more liquids. The only good recommendation Mme. Ronsard gives is exercise—that's what will do it.

Cellulite is nothing more than just plain fat that has accumulated near the surface of the skin. Since it is near the surface of the skin it's more obvious. And apparently women have a greater problem with fat being deposited near the surface of the skin than men.

Figure Wrapping

Figure wrapping comes in many packages. Some of the most popular include the "Shape Wrap," "Body Wrap," "Continental Miracle Wrap," "Swiss Trim," "Insta-trim," "Suddenly Slim," "Suddenly Slenda," and the "Benne Method" treatments. Of the many ridiculous claims made by figure wrapping experts, the most abominable is that "You must lose four to twelve inches with your first treatment."

For those of you who don't know what figure wrapping is, let me explain. In a figure-wrapping treatment, you remove your clothing and are measured at predetermined locations on your body. Naturally, an expensive "expert" must perform this task. That is because you do not know the technique for arriving at certain measurements (whether four inches from the shoulder, three above the knee, etc.). Another trick the expert may use is to hold the tape measure in such a manner the customer is not able to read it to verify the measurement recorded by the attendant.

After measuring, you are wrapped mummy fashion from neck to ankle with special tapes that have supposedly been soaked in a "magical solution." Parts of the body that do not need reducing may be omitted from the wrapping. Then you don a rubberized sweatsuit with elastic cuffs and neck to prevent air circulation. Finally, covered with a blanket, you relax in a lounge chair and listen to music or watch television. At the end of one hour the tapes and suit are removed and presto! You're skinny. And a whole lot more.

Work by Dr. Ruth Lindsey, then professor of health and physical education and recreation at Oklahoma State University, working in cooperation with the American Medical Association and the U.S. Food and Drug Administration, surveyed figure-wrapping salons. She concluded that the treatment may be risky. She said there are dangers of dehydration and heat exhaustion from the figure wrapping techniques. Furthermore, the "magical solution" in which the wrapping tapes are soaked often contain aluminum sulphate, which produces skin irritation as well as a softening of the tissue itself.

Of course, the figure wrapping technique does give the illusion of real weight loss. Cold air may be used to constrict the saturated victim's superficial blood vessels, thereby creating a temporary reduction in his or her body measurements. The dehydration effect of the "magical solution" and the pressure from the wrappings may add to the apparent reduction in body size. But the changes caused by these factors are temporary at best. In a few hours, the person is back to normal size.

Dr. Lindsey's conclusions are clear: "There is no chemical substance known to science which can be applied to the body to produce a permanent effect and/or 'react with the fat' to make it disappear. Aside from the possible health hazards . . . it appears that the efficacy of such a reducing treatment is highly questionable . . . There is no way to reduce weight or bulk except through exercise and diet control."

Exercise Machines—The Good, The Bad, & The Ugly

Of course, claims of weight and fat reduction extend beyond saunas, steamrooms, massage devices, and figure wrapping. The all time winners for claims with respect to weight loss are exercise machines.

Surprisingly, some of these can be effective in controlling your body weight and fat. But the effectiveness is contingent upon you doing the work. Not the machine. William · Zuti, Ph.D., Director of Health Enhancement for the National Board of YMCAs, has said it most succinctly: "Exercise equipment is not a necessity for fitness, but people like to use equipment for motivational purposes, which is okay, provided they use them. Some equipment is good . . . while others are out and out quackery."

The following chart may help you sort out the good from the bad.

Exercise Equipment: Separating The Good From The Bad

Motorized treadmill	Good—may be boring.
Non-motorized treadmill	Fair—for walking only.
Motorized stationary bicycle	Poor—does the work for you. Very few calories expended.
Non-motorized bicycle	Good—can be boring.
Rowing machine	Good—except for people with heart problems or high blood pressure.
Weights for lifting	Poor—only good for muscle strength.
Exercise wheels	Poor—can injure your back.
Rubber or spring chest stretchers	Poor—difficult to adjust for improved fitness.
Body trimmers	Poor—difficult to adjust for improved fitness.

Health Clubs For Weight Reduction

Health spas and figure salons often hold the promise that they will be able to help you lose fat. Some of them make really incredible advertising claims: "If you wear size 14 now, you'll be wearing a size 10 in just 30 days, or your money back." Of course, with all this it is implied that the wonderful chrome-plated mechanical devices are going to miraculously melt away pounds and inches, with no effort whatsoever exerted by the customer. The ads do not, however, state that the cost for using the machines is high—from $100 to $400 a year. But what is most deceitful is that if the customer wants a money-back guarantee, he or she must agree to follow a very strict exercise and diet regimen. That way, if the customer does not lose the specified number of pounds or inches, the manager can disclaim responsibility; obviously the customer "cheated" and didn't adhere to the prescribed program. Goodbye money-back guarantee!

After reviewing hundreds of exercise clubs, spas, and organizations around the country, I've come to the conclusion that there are several things you can do to protect yourself. Here are some guidelines you can use to establish the right fitness facility for you.

1. If you get a high-pressure pitch, leave.
2. Go over the contract with a fine-toothed comb.
3. Tour the facilities and as you do be observant for:
   a. A discussion of your individual problems.
   b. Is the person conducting the tour an instructor, a manager, or what?
   c. Does the spa manager or instructor emphasize cardiovascular fitness and weight control or is the emphasis on muscular strength and endurance?
   d. Visit the club at the time of day you plan to use it.
4. Before signing anything, talk to several people who are members of the club.

5. Find out how long the club has been in your area.
6. Make sure the club belongs to the Association of Physical Fitness Centers.
7. Find out if their staff is adequately prepared and trained in physiology of exercise and fitness. That means they have a bona fide degree and certification by the American College of Sports Medicine or some other certifying board.
8. Finally, remember this all-important thing: the spa needs you more than you need the spa.

In many ways technology has been a boon to humankind, but as we all know, its blessings are mixed. Along with newer, better ways of doing things it's given us pollution, overprocessed food and—just as harmful in the long run—it's robbed us of many opportunities to be physically active, making us a nation too sluggish, too fat, and prone to diseases that our hardier, better-exercised ancestors never had to worry about. Trained in technology's school to be always on the lookout for the newest, the trickiest, the easiest solutions to our weight and health problems, we're inclined to reject the oldest but simplest trick of all: using our bodies the way they were meant to be used.

13

But Why Do I Always Lose Weight At The Wrong Places?

I wish I had a dollar for everyone who told me, "I want to lose inches, Charlie, but I don't want to lose any inches off my bust." Then there are those who ask, "How come whenever I lose weight I lose it in my face?" I've concluded that people who lose fat want to reserve the right to decide just which fat to give up. Everyone wants a perfect figure.

Unfortunately, there is little evidence to indicate that we have control over where our fat gets deposited or from where it is removed. In fact, the research only confuses the issue.

First, some researchers feel that fat comes off the area of greatest concentration. You lose weight mostly from those areas that have the most fat. Yet I've known some people who have a tremendous amount of fat on their hips and thighs, and when they've lost weight, they don't seem to lose much from that particular area. Second, there are other researchers who feel that fat comes off the area where it was last deposited. If your recent TV watching, sit-down strike, or cramming for finals added an inch to your waist, that's where it's going to come off first.

I'm not sure which is true. It's probably a combination of the two. There are also probably some genetic reasons why you lose fat or gain fat in particular areas. So, you have no guarantee that you'll look like a movie star. You'll probably end up looking like your mother, dad, uncle, aunt, or brothers and sisters. If they have skinny shoulders and large hips, you'll probably end up looking the same way. So you might say that if you start off with a big pear shape, after you've lost all your weight you're still going to be a pear . . . only a smaller one.

I know this is frustrating but it is the truth. Of course, all this implies that there is no such thing as spot reducing. Sit-ups flatten the muscles of your stomach. But you need target heart rate exercise to burn off fat which is located there or any other place on your body. If spot reducing worked, people who chew gum would have thin faces. Research supports this statement.

Frank Katch, Ed.D., and his associates at the University of Massachusetts had people do 5,000 sit-ups over a period of 27 days. At the end of the study the researchers found out that there was a decrease in the fat cells of the abdomen, back, and buttocks despite the fact that all of the exercise was of an abdominal nature. The researchers concluded that there was no difference between the fat lost in all these areas, which ruled out the possibility of spot reducing. They did note, however, that their abdominal muscles were quite strong and well defined.

Vigorous movement of a single localized group of muscles—the stomach muscles, for instance—will not cause fat to be released only from around those muscles. There is no physiological pathway for such a direct outlet. Instead, your nervous system triggers the release of small quantities of fat from the cells all over your body. The circulatory system then picks up the fat and takes it to the liver where it is converted into energy which is used by the muscles.

Perhaps a concrete illustration will help you here. Let's say that you've got quite a few fat cells around your waist. So your fat tends to be deposited there. Let's also assume that you're out of caloric balance and your waistline is expanding. You might decide that the best way to trim your waist is to do sit-ups. Let's say you decide to do 30. Before you begin you measure your waist and it is 38 inches. You do your sit-ups faithfully for a month. At the end of the month you measure your waist again. Now it's no longer 38 but 38½ inches. At this point you conclude you are probably not doing your sit-ups correctly. So you bend your knees. And you increase the number of sit-ups to 50. You do the exercises without fail for a month. At the end of the month you measure your waist. It's now 39 inches. Disgusted, you give up. You conclude that exercise doesn't work.

The real problem is that you are out of caloric balance. The sit-ups had nothing to do with your failure. The sit-ups that you did—maybe even the 50—burned only an extra 10 calories. In the beginning you may have been out of caloric balance by maybe 100 or 200 calories. As a result your weight and waist continued to increase despite the fact that you were doing sit-ups. If you had been involved in an exercise program that burned a lot of calories, your waistline would have been reduced, simply because you would have burned off more calories than you had eaten.

To sum up, your rule of thumb is this: if you have too much fat, then you must go into caloric deficit with a big muscle activity that permits you to exercise at your target heart rate level. If, however, your muscles seem weak, then various calisthenics can be used to help firm particular areas of your body. In all probability, you'll need a combination of both calisthenics and target heart rate exercise.

Many times, people who have excessive fat on one area of their body will find weak muscles in the same area. So I've included some specific exercises that will *firm up* the various problem areas of the body. Done in a traditional way, they will not necessarily fight fat. Use these as a warm-up or cool-down to your regular 30 to 40 minutes of fat-burning exercise. Or use the exercises as I describe them on pages 217 to 218. You'll like the results.

Bust—You can restore that youthful look to your bustline by developing the pectoral muscles that lie beneath your breasts. These exercises allow the muscles to hold your breast high, thus giving them a youthful appearance. Remember that behind every curve there is a muscle. Well-conditioned muscles give your body shape.

1. Arms Over—Hold a book in each hand (hands at sides) while lying on your back. Raise the books over your head, reaching as far back as possible, and return hands to sides. Perform three sets of eight.

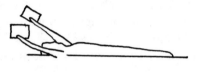

2. Right Angles—Lie on your back with your arms at right angles to your body and a book in each hand. Raise your arms so that they come together (arms straight) above your chest. Pull in your abdomen at the same time. Again, perform three sets of eight repetitions.

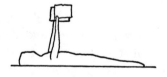

3. Barrel Roll—Lie on your back with a pillow under your shoulders. Raise your arms above your chest as though you were holding a barrel. Holding books in both hands, open your curved arms as far as possible and return slowly.

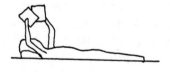

4. Arm Arc—Lie on your back with your arms extended toward your knees. Holding a book in each hand, sweep your arms out to the sides as though you were making an arc to at least shoulder height. Return.

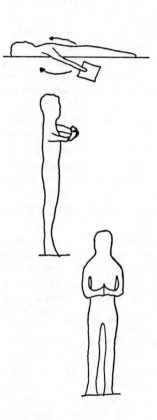

5. Pectoral Push—While standing or sitting, grasp the left elbow with the right hand and your right elbow with your left hand. Push your arms together as hard as possible and then relax. Perform three sets of eight repetitions.

6. Hand Push—Clasp your hands at various heights in front of your body: waist, chest, and forehead. Push your hands together for 6 seconds then relax. Repeat three times in each position in the morning, at noon, and evening.

Arms & Shoulders—Arm and shoulder muscles can be toned and firmed by doing the following:

7. Arm Circles—Stand erect, arms extended sidewards at shoulder height, with palms up. Make small circles backward with your hands. Keep head erect. This helps keep the shoulder joints flexible and strengthens the muscles of the shoulders.

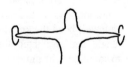

8. Wall Push-Ups—Stand about three or four feet away from the corner of wall or a room. Place your hands on each wall at shoulder height. Keeping your body rigid, slowly bend the arms and touch the chin to the wall or corner. Return. Wall push-ups strengthen the arm and shoulder muscles.

9. Punching Bag—Stimulate punching a punching bag by beginning with the arms extended, then alternately drawing them back from in front of the body. Do for the specified period of time. This tones both the triceps and biceps muscles.

10. Modified Push-Ups—Start in a lying position, hands outside the shoulders, fingers pointed forward, knees bent. Lift yourself off the floor by straightening your arms and keeping your back straight. Return to the starting position. Repeat. This firms the muscles in the back of the arms.

11. Alternate Arm Swing & Bounce—Stand with the feet parallel, shoulder-width apart and the knees bent at a 45° angle. The body should lean forward and the arms and hands relaxed. Swing one arm forward as the opposite arm swings back. Continue by reversing the position of the arms in an easy swinging motion. As the motion is continued, bend the knees to a 45° angle and straighten them. Try to coordinate the movements. This exercise firms the leg muscles and improves shoulder flexibility.

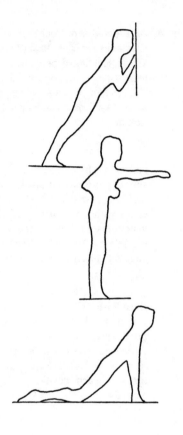

12. Push-Ups—Assume a prone position on the floor with the feet
together and the hands beneath
the shoulders. Keeping the body
straight, extend the arms fully,
then return to the starting position.

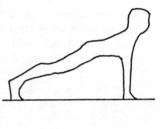

Thighs—Thigh muscles that are soft
and flabby can be firmed up by trying
these exercises:

13. Sitting Single Leg Raise—Starting
position: Sit erect, hands on side
of chair seat for balance, feet on
floor. Raise left leg waist high.
Return to starting position. Repeat with opposite leg.
14. Standing Leg Swing—Stand erect,
feet together, hand on chair. Swing
the right leg forward and then
back and up. Return to starting
position. Repeat with left leg. This
exercise is good for firming up
the thigh, hips, and buttocks area.
15. One-Half Knee Bend—Stand
erect, with the feet close together
and hands on hips. Bend the knees
to a 90° angle (the heels are allowed to come off the floor). Return to the starting position.
16. Skiers' Exercise—The Skier's
Exercise is identical to the previous exercise except when the
knees are bent to a 90° angle,
they are turned alternately to the
left and right. When the knees
are bent to the left, move both
arms to the left. When the knees
are bent to the right, both arms
go to the right. This exercise
strengthens the thigh muscles and
stretches the calves.

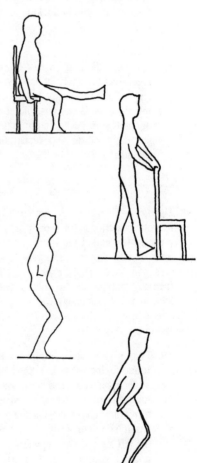

17. Side Stretch—Stand erect with your hands on your hips and your feet spread wider than shoulder width. Lunge to the right, bending the right leg, keeping the left leg extended. Return to the starting position, and repeat to the opposite side. This is also good for the hips and buttocks.

18. Standing Side Leg Swing—Stand erect, feet together, let hand on a chair. Swing the right leg out to the right as far· as possible. Do not arch your back. Return to the starting position and repeat on the other side.

Derriere—Though it may not feel like it, your posterior is (or should be) all muscle. It's called the gluteus maximus and is one of the largest muscles you have. These exercises will firm up that muscle so that it will look and feel less pudgy.

19. Two Way Stretch—Kneel on all fours. Bring your left knee up under your chest and bend your head toward your chest. Then return your head to the starting position simultaneously extending the left leg back and upward. Do not arch your back. Return to the starting position and repeat with the right leg.

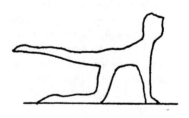

20. Leg Raise—Standing, place your hands on top of your desk. Try to keep your upper body as straight as possible. Your feet should be approximately 12 to 18 inches from the desk. Now slowly raise one leg backward and upward as high as possible. Do not arch your back. Return to the starting position. Alternate.

21. Bench Step—Locate a step or a stack of securely tied newspapers 12 to 18 inches high. Standing tall with your feet together step up with your left leg, follow with your right, stand erect. Now step down with your right leg followed with your left. Do this with a steady rhythm. Alternate legs periodically. You should step at a rate of about 20 to 30 steps a minute (counting the left leg only). This exercise firms up the leg muscles, derriere, and improves circulo-respiratory fitness.

22. Mountain Climber—Assume a push-up position. Bring the right leg up under the chest with the right knee bent. The left leg is extended backward. The exercise action is to switch the legs and continue alternating fairly rapidly. Each time a leg is brought up under the chin count one repetition.

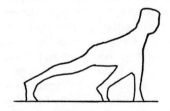

Hips—The exercises for the thighs may also help the hips, because the most common hip complaint is actually the condition of "saddlebags" at the top and sides of the thigh area. Hip size is determined mostly by bone structure, but a sedentary lifestyle can soften the muscles surrounding the hips, giving them a baggy appearance. When that occurs, these four exercises will help.

23. Standing Side Leg Raise—Stand erect, hands on hips, feet together. Raise your left leg sideways and up as high as possible. Return to the starting position. Repeat with the right leg.

24. Side Leg Double Leg Raise—Lie on your right side, legs extended, head supported with the right arm. Raise both legs together as high as possible, then lower to the starting position. Do a few times then repeat on the opposite side.

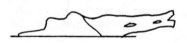

25. Leg Cross Over—Lie on your back, legs together, arms extended sidewards for balance. Raise your left leg to a vertical position. Keeping the legs straight, lower the leg to the floor on your right side. Return to the starting position. Repeat with the right leg. This exercise firms the hip muscles.

26. Fire Hydrant—Assume a kneeling position with your hands on the floor. Keeping your knee bent, raise your right leg parallel to the floor. Then straighten and extend the leg to the side perpendicular to your body. Return to a bent leg position. Then place your knee back down on the floor. Repeat with the left leg. Do this several times.

These exercises are particularly good for the thighs, derriere, and hips.

27. Walk in Place—Stand erect, eyes forward, chest elevated, and shoulders and arms in a relaxed position. Toes and heels should point straight ahead. Raise your left knee to waist height, then return it to the floor. Repeat with the right foot.

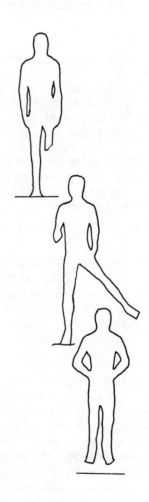

28. Fitness Lope—Stand erect and relaxed. Kick your legs alternately to the sides. Stay on your toes, hopping as your weight shifts from one leg to the other. Continue for the specified time.

29. Toe Hops—Stand erect, your feet close together and your hands on your hips. Spring lightly from your toes into the air. Land on your toes and spring immediately back up. Don't touch your heels to the floor. Continue hopping for the specified period of time.

30. Stride Hops—Stand erect, hands on your hips, left foot forward in a striding position. Lean forward slightly. Hop up and reverse the position of your feet. For rhythm and balance, be sure you hop from both feet at the same time and land on both feet at the same time. Immediately repeat the movement from the reversed position.

31. Rope Jumping—Good form while jumping is important. You should remain relaxed. Keep your body erect and look straight ahead while you are jumping. Land on the balls of your feet. Hold the rope at above hip level and use as little arm movement as possible to keep it moving. Jump on a soft surface to avoid injuring the balls of your feet.

32. Run in Place—Lift the feet at least four inches off the floor while running in place. For greater stress, lift the knees up to waist height.

Waist—When the tape measure tells you your waist needs some work, remember it may also be the fault of sagging abdominal muscles. These next eight exercises are especially good for the waist. But I also recommend the set of exercises for the abdomen.

33. Side-Bend-Up—Lie on your side with your legs held down by a partner or a piece of furniture. Raise your body sideward from the waist as high as you can. Repeat several times on both sides.

34. Body Twist—Step forward with the left foot. Twist the upper torso to the left as far as possible and swing both arms to the left. Then step forward with the right foot and twist the upper torso to the right as far as possible and swing both arms to the right.

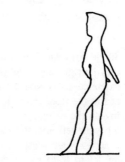

35. Side Trunk Bend—Stand erect with your feet shoulder-width apart, left hand on hip and right arm extended at shoulder height. Bend your trunk to the left, reaching over beyond the head with the right arm. Return to the starting position and repeat with the opposite side.

36. Side Single Leg Raise—Lie on your right side, legs extended, right hand supporting the head. Raise the left leg as high as possible. Lower to the starting position. Do on the right side and then on the left side.

37. Trunk Twister—Stand with your hands clasped behind your neck and elbows drawn back. As you walk in place, raise your knee as high as possible and turn the body to the left, having your right elbow touch your left knee. The touching of the right elbow to your left knee is one repetition. Repeat to the other side.

38. Single Arm And Leg Raise—Lie on your right side, your right arm extended above your head (palm agains the floor), your head resting on the extended arm. Keeping your left arm straight, place it across your waist. Raise your left leg to at least a 45° angle. As you lower your leg, simultaneously raise your left arm. By the time your leg is back to the starting position, your arm should be at about a 45° angle. Return your arm to the starting position. As you do so, raise your leg again. Repeat for the specified period of time. Then turn and do the exercise on the other side.

39. Side Curl-Ups—Lie on your right side, arms extended downward in front, hands about six inches in front of your hips. Have a partner hold your feet down or brace them under a piece of furniture. Curl your body upward several inches. Return to the starting position. Repeat for the specified period of time.

40. Double Knee Lifts—Lie on your back, arms extended at right angles to your body, knees drawn up to your chest. Keeping your knees together, touch the floor to the right of your body with your right knee. Return to the starting position. Touch the floor to the left of the body with the left knee and return. Repeat for the specified number of seconds.

Abdomen—Perhaps the most unsightly and yet common problem of men and women is the sagging or protruding abdomen. Given such colorful names as bay window, pot belly, and spare tire; this problem plagues many people. The following exercises will help strengthen the muscles that should be holding that area firm and flat. But remember, only daily aerobic exercise will remove the fat.

41. Look-Up—Lie on your back, knees slightly bent and arms at your sides. Raise your head and shoulders slightly from the floor until you can see your feet. Lower your head to the floor. Repeat several times.

42. Curl-Down—Start from a sitting position with the knees bent and hands across the chest. Lower the upper body until you feel a pull on your tummy. Hold that position several seconds and then return. Repeat.

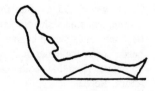

43. Abdominal Curls—Lie flat on your back with the lower back touching the floor; knees bent. Curl the head and upper part of the body upward and forward to about a 45° angle. At the same time, contract your abdominal muscles. Return slowly to the starting position.

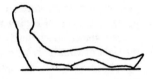

44. Bicycle Pump—Sit with your legs extended and hands resting on the floor on or beside your hips. In this inverted position, simulate a bicycle riding or pedaling action. Ride your bike in this manner for several seconds.

45. Sit-Ups—Lie on the back with knees bent and arms locked behind the head or at the sides. Curl the body up into a sitting position by first placing the chin on the chest and then lifting the upper body off the floor. Keep the back rounded. Touch the elbows to the knees, then return to the starting position. Repeat.

46. Curl Down-45° Angle—Start from a sitting position with your knees bent and hands placed behind the head. Lower the upper body to a 45° angle. Hold that position and return. Repeat.

I know there are many people who would like to do calisthenics to burn fat. So I've taken some selected exercises from the previous pages and put them into a six level program which will help remove fat from your body. The program is designed to give you a good warm-up, target heart rate or fat-burning exercise, and cool-down exercises along with muscle toning. The program not only burns calories, but attacks your fitness problem areas as well.

You will notice there are six levels of exercise, and within each level there are four steps. This allows you to begin at a level of intensity that will not be too difficult, yet allow you to gradually increase the intensity and duration of your exercise as your fitness level improves. For most people who have been relatively inactive in the past, it is best to start at Level I, Step 1. As your fitness level improves over the weeks, your body will seem to call for more exercise. That is, at the end of a session of exercise, you will feel as if you could do a little bit more. As this happens, move your way up through the various steps until you reach the final level. Move from step to step at a pace that seems best for you. Also notice that the emphasis is placed on time, not repetitions. Simply do as many exercises as seems reasonale for you in the time allotted. Remember, the key is to reach your target heart rate and to feel good about your exercise level.

Do these exercises a minimum of four times a week. An alternate day basis is best. Don't get overanxious, and see how fast you can get through the various levels. For your exercise program to be successful, you should progress at a rate that corresponds with your fitness level and ability. Progress gradually and carefully. Listen to your body. If it seems as though your body can tolerate more exercise, move to the next step. If the exercise level seems appropriate, stay there until you think and feel you need more exercise. How long you remain at each step depends upon you. But a minimum of one day at each step in the early stages is recommended. You may need to spend several weeks or more before moving to the next step. You will probably find Level V of the program to be challenging enough. Level VI is for the guy or gal who has become a real fitness enthusiast.

Warm-Up and Cool-Down Exercises

In Chapter #9 it was mentioned that a proper warm-up and cool-down are important to you in your exercise program and fat-burning exercise. Make sure you include the five to ten minutes of the warm-up exercises suggested there and five minutes of stretching and slower activity at the end of your exercise session. That will enable you to approach your next exercise session with a minimum of soreness and stiffness.

Now get into something comfortable and make sure you are wearing a good pair of shoes. It's time to get started on a body shaping program that will help you look and feel good.

Added note: The running in place, walk in place, toe hops, etc., are not to be neglected. They are to be done between each exercise as illustrated on the various levels. These exercises will help keep your heart in a target heart rate zone and burn a significant number of calories.

The
Six Level
Activetics
Exercise Program

Exercise Number	Exercise	Level I				Level II			
		1	2	3	4	5	6	7	8
	Walk & Warm-up	5–10 minutes				5–10 minutes			
27.	Walk in place	10 seconds				15 seconds			
7.	Arm Circles	5–10	11–15	16–20	21–25	26–30	31–35	36–40	41–45
27.	Walk in place	10 seconds				15 seconds			
8.	Wall push-ups	5–10	11–15	16–20	21–25	26–30	31–35	36–40	41–45
27.	Walk in place	10 seconds				15 seconds			
41.	Look up	5–10	11–15	16–20	21–25	26–30	31–35	36–40	41–45
27.	Walk in place	10 seconds				15 seconds			
42.	Curl down	5–10	11–15	16–20	21–25	26–30	31–35	36–40	41–45
27.	Walk in place	10 seconds				15 seconds			

	1 minute				2 minutes			
21. Walk stairs or bench step	1 minute				2 minutes			
27. Walk in place	10 seconds				15 seconds			
36. Side single leg raises	5–10	11–15	16–20	21–25	26–30	31–35	36–40	41–45
27. Walk in place	10 seconds				15 seconds			
15. ½ knee bends	5–10	11–15	16–20	21–25	26–30	31–35	36–40	41–45
27. Walk in place	10 seconds				15 seconds			
40. Double knee lifts	5–10	11–15	16–20	21–25	26–30	31–35	36–40	41–45
27. Walk in place	10 seconds				15 seconds			
Walk	2 minutes				2 minutes			
Cool-Down	5 minutes stretching				5 minutes of stretching			
Record 10 seconds pulse rate; multiply by 6.								

Exercise Number	Exercise	Level III				Level IV			
		9	10	11	12	13	14	15	16
	Walk & Warm-Up	5–10 minutes				5–10 minutes			
32. 28.	Run in place or fitness lope	15 seconds				20 seconds			
9.	Punching Bag	15–20	21–25	26–30	31–35	36–40	41–45	46–50	51–60
32. 28.	Run in place or fitness lope	15 seconds				20 seconds			
10.	Modified push-ups	15–20	21–25	26–30	31–35	36–40	41–45	46–50	51–60
32. 28.	Run in place or fitness lope	15 seconds				20 seconds			
43.	Abdominal curls	15–20	21–25	26–30	31–35	36–40	41–45	46–50	51–60
32. 28.	Run in place or fitness lope	15 seconds				20 seconds			
46.	Curl downs—45° angle	15–20	21–25	26–30	31–35	36–40	41–45	46–50	51–60
32.	Run in place or lope	15 seconds				20 seconds			

	3 minutes	4 minutes
21. Bench stepping	3 minutes	4 minutes
32. / 28. Run in place or fitness lope	15 seconds	20 seconds
38. Single arm & leg raises	15–20 21–25 26–30 31–35	36–40 41–45 46–50 51–60
32. / 28. Run in place or fitness lope	15 seconds	20 seconds
17. Side stretch	15 seconds	20 seconds
32. / 28. Run in place or fitness lope	15 seconds	20 seconds
25. Leg crossovers	15–20 21–25 26–30 31–35	36–40 41–45 46–50 51–60
32. / 28. Run in place or fitness lope	15 seconds	20 seconds
Walk	2 minutes	2 minutes
Cool-Down	5 minutes of stretching	5 minutes of stretching
Record pulse rate 10 seconds; multiply by 6.		

Exercise Number Exercise	Level V				Level VI			
	17	18	19	20	21	22	23	24
Walk & Warm Up	5–10 minutes				5–10 minutes			
32. Run in place, 28. fitness lope, 30. toe hips, stride 29. hops, or rope jumping	25 seconds				30 seconds			
11. Alternate arm swing & bounce	15–20	21–25	26–30	31–35	36–40	41–45	46–50	51–60
32. Run in place, etc.	25 seconds				30 seconds			
12. Push-ups	15–20	21–25	26–30	31–35	36–40	41–45	46–50	51–60
32. Run in place, etc.	25 seconds				30 seconds			
45. Sit-ups	15–20	21–25	26–30	31–35	36–40	41–45	46–50	51–60
32. Run in place, etc.	25 seconds				30 seconds			

	15–20	21–25	26–30	31–35	36–40	41–45	46–50	51–60
44. Bicycle pumps			25 seconds				30 seconds	
32. Run in place, etc.			25 seconds				30 seconds	
21. Bench stepping			5 minutes				30 seconds	
32. Run in place, etc.			25 seconds				30 seconds	
24. Side double leg raises	15–20	21–25	26–30	31–35	36–40	41–45	46–50	51–60
32. Run in place, etc.			25 seconds				30 seconds	
22. Mountain climbers	15–20	21–25	26–30	31–35	36–40	41–45	46–50	51–60
32. Run in place, etc.			25 seconds				30 seconds	
39. Side curl-ups	15–20	21–25	26–30	31–35	36–40	41–45	46–50	51–60
32. Run in place, etc.			25 seconds				30 seconds	
Walk			2 minutes				2 minutes	
Cool-Down			5 minutes of stretching				5 minutes of stretching	

(Continued)

| Record pulse rate 10 seconds; multiply by 6. | | | | | | | |

14

Doing Exercise For Better Health

Many of the men and women who come to my fitness classes are so pleased with the prospect of diet-free weight loss that even if the program has nothing else going for it, that's fine with them. I think the benefits of fat-burning exercise are some of the best reasons for sticking to the program.

Perhaps you may feel the same way. On the other hand, you may be wondering about some of the other statements I made at the beginning of the book—statements unrelated to weight control. I've mentioned that this program can improve heart and lung function, relieve tension and stress, make you feel peppier, more energetic, and even sharpen your thinking process. In short, that it can boost you toward a new zest for living.

Sound too good to be true? Some people would say so. But the fact is, all these highly desirable developments are the natural, predictable outcome of increased physical activity. There are so many benefits that I even hate to mention it. It sounds almost hucksterish, but the fact of the matter is, exercise has a pervasive effect on life itself.

Reduces The Chance Of Heart Attacks

There are a series of risk factors which predispose a person to heart disease. These include:

1. Someone in your immediate family has or had heart disease (heredity).
2. You have difficulty handling stressful situations (stress and personality type).
3. A diet that is too rich—too much sugar, fat, and salt (diet and nutrition).
4. Too much cholesterol and triglycerides in your blood (lipid or fat abnormalities).
5. High blood pressure (hypertension).
6. Occasional irregular heart rhythms (ECG abnormalities).
7. Diabetes mellitus.
8. Too much body fat (obesity).
9. Smoking.
10. The older you are the greater the risk (age).
11. Physical inactivity.
12. If you are a male (sex).

Let's face it. You can't do much about heredity, age, or sex. Those are the absolutes over which we have little control. The other nine risk factors can be controlled or minimized. It really *is* in your hands. Exercise plays an important role in reducing the effects of these factors. Specifically, exercise may improve your heart, blood, and blood vessels in the following manner:

1. Increase the number and size of your blood vessels (better and more efficient circulation).
2. Increase the elasticity of blood vessels (less likelihood of breaking under pressure).
3. Increase the efficiency of exercising muscles and blood circulation (muscles and blood better able to pick up, carry, and use oxygen).
4. Increase the efficiency of the heart (able to pump more blood with fewer beats—better able to meet emergencies).

5. Increase tolerance to stress and give you more joy of living (this means you will be less likely to be caught in the stress/pressure syndrome).
6. Decrease clot formation (less chance of blood clot forming and blocking blood flow to the heart muscle).
7. Decrease triglyceride and cholesterol levels (less likelihood of fats being deposited on the lining of the arteries).
8. Decrease blood sugar (reduce chances of blood sugar being changed to triglycerides).
9. Decrease obesity and high blood pressure (most people who are obese and have high blood pressure are more prone to heart disease).
10. Decrease hormone production (too much adrenalin can cause problems for the arteries).

How much exercise is necessary to achieve these changes is not known. But work done by Ralph Paffenbarger, M.D., professor of Epidemiology at the Stanford University of Medicine, gives us a clue. Paffenbarger reported on a 10 year study that focused on almost 17,000 Harvard alumni men aged 35 to 74. He found that those men who used less than 2,000 calories a week in exercise were 64% more likely to suffer a heart attack than those who burned more than that. Of the 572 heart attacks suffered by the group, he estimated that 166 would never have happened if the men had exercised vigorously. Paffenbarger was recommending that the best types of exercises for burning the 2,000 calories weekly were walking, jogging, swimming, and other similarly demanding activities.

The final answer, of course, is not in. But Paffenbarger's research suggests that you may decrease your chances of suffering a heart attack if you burn an additional 2,000 calories a week.

Other studies have shown that people who are more active have about ⅓ to ½ less the incidence of heart disease. And more importantly, if you have a heart attack your chances of surviving are about 4 to 5 times greater than that of the average sedentary person.

There is one more important study. Ken Cooper, M.D., conducted research which demonstrates that as a person's fitness level improves, selected coronary heart disease risk factors drop. The heart disease risk factors most affected by the fitness level were cholesterol, triglycerides (lipid abnormalities), glucose, uric acid, systolic blood pressure, and body fat. His study shows that men with very poor or poor fitness levels show poor results. Men with fair fitness levels appear to be better than those in the very poor and poor categories. But, those with the best scores were those who had good or excellent fitness. They had the lowest scores on selected coronary heart disease risk factors. Cooper was not talking about young men or a few subjects. His study involved almost 3,000 men who were an average age of 44+ years. Cooper concluded that exercise plays a role in many risk factors. I agree. In fact, exercise may improve all of the risk factors except age and heredity. Of course, smoking and diet are not altered by exercise itself. But usually people who exercise on a regular basis adopt a more healthful lifestyle. They often stop smoking (or cut back substantially) and start eating less. They also tend to eat more wholesome foods.

Low Back Pain

A lack of physical activity is probably a major cause of low back pain. Hans Kraus, M.D., President Kennedy's physician and perhaps one of the most famous physicians in the area of treating low back via exercise, knows that most of the pain in the lower back is muscular in origin. At first, you may think that's not new. Except we're not talking about the back muscles. We're talking about the stomach muscles. Studies show that in the majority of cases, the abdominal muscles of a person with chronic back conditions are less than ⅓ as strong as their back muscles. Prevention and treatment of potentially disabling back disorders is so simple it's almost overlooked, according to Dr. Kraus. And the major culprits, as you may have guessed, are inactivity and tension.

Seventy million Americans will have back pain sometime during their lifetime. And probably 80% of these are caused by sedentary living. A lack of physical activity causes our abdominal muscles to weaken and sag. Because these muscles sag, we develop a "pot belly." To compensate for this sagging waistline we have to shift our weight to the back. Consequently our pelvis tips forward, the derriere sticks out, and the last joints of the spine require a lot of muscle to hold them up. Eventually, the muscles of the lower back tire of carrying the load and begin to hurt. Dr. Kraus feels that physical activity helps to correct that situation by reducing and toughening up that bulging belly.

Productivity And Job Performance

Working capacity is, of course, linked to endurance and stamina. With conditioning comes a greater capacity to get things done. You are able to do more before feeling fatigued. The body that is physically conditioned has more pep.

Exercise physiologists say that to have more energy you must spend energy—not get more rest. That seemingly paradoxical statement summarizes the theory of "aerobic power." Aerobic power refers to the body's ability to process oxygen.

The beneficial effect of sound exercise on job performance has been widely acknowledged. In one study, Roy Shephard, M.D., Ph.D., of the University of Toronto's Department of Physiological Hygiene, noted the benefits of exercise in increasing endurance on the job. In studying elderly men and women, he saw that many were unable to work an eight hour day without suffering fatigue. The introduction of a regular exercise plan to this group led to Dr. Shephard's observation that "through the use of an appropriate training program, it is possible to improve the working capacity by at least 15 to 29%."

Dr. Victor Linden, of Bergen Trygdleasse, Bergen, Norway,

points out that employees with high rates of absenteeism are less physically fit and less active during their leisure time than their co-workers with good performance records.

Aging

Ernst Jokl, M.D., from the University of Kentucky, has said, "There is little doubt that proper physical activity as part of a way of life can significantly delay the aging process."

We all know that changes occur as we get older. Among the most common are fatigue, decreased vigor and strength, increased weight, reduced joint flexibility, a change in bowel and bladder habits, a decline in sex drive, failing sight and hearing, a decrease in mental agility, and general lack of stamina.

The process of aging varies a great deal from one person to another. It's impossible to determine the exact time of life when it will begin. We usually associate aging with the age of 65 or so, but the signs begin to appear in most of us as early as 30 or 35 years of age. Some people seem washed out before the age of 40. On the other hand, we all know people who seem young and vigorous at 70 or more years of age.

Unfortunately, the average American assumes that the changes that occur after the age of 30 are a natural part of the aging process. This is probably incorrect. Current research suggests that such changes may be the result not of passing years, but of passive lifestyle.

A three day conference on exercise and aging held at the National Institute of Health in Bethesda, Maryland, spelled out the relationship between exercise and aging:

1. Walking is the most efficient form of exercise—and the only one you can safely follow all the years of your life.
2. As people get older, their bones start to demineralize and lose their resistance to breaking. Exercise, such as walking, slows the bone demineralization process, particularly in the legs. Through exercise your bone-growing cells are stimulat-

ed. Bones remain tougher and less likely to break. This also promotes a greater range of motion.

(A Reno, Nevada, orthopedic clinic did extensive tests on a man, at least 60 years old, who had exercised vigorously for 12 years. The tests included x-rays of his legs. At the conclusion of their study, one of the doctors sent a letter to him which said, "Your bone age is approximately 12 years less than your chronological age. This indicates to me that your exercising has been effective in slowing the aging process.")

3. As people get older, particularly those who have smoked or who have worked in high pollution areas, they develop emphysema-like changes in their lungs. Those individuals who exercise may still exhibit such changes, but they still have far greater lung capacity than sedentary people.

4. As you age, your cardiovascular function declines. It loses its elasticity and vigorousness. Yet the cardiovascular systems of older Americans who exercise show a maximum preservation of function.

5. One obvious phenomenon of aging is an increase in obesity. As people get into their 40s, 50s, and 60s their weight escalates. So does their percentage of body fat. This condition greatly affects health. But exercise is a strong deterrent to obesity.

6. Closely related to obesity is the fact that as people get older they tend to eat less than they used to in an effort to keep their weight under control. When they do this, their nutrition often suffers. Daily exercise permits greater food intake and better blood circulation, which improves each cell's nourishment while preventing obesity.

7. Besides heart disease and cancer, many older Americans fear late-onset diabetes. Even though this disease can be controlled, it kills, maims, and reduces a person's well-being. Interestingly, late-onset diabetes is almost entirely reversible by exercise if you are overweight.

8. Rheumatoid arthritis and osteoarthritis are common in older people. It has been estimated that more than 90% of all Americans over the age of 60 have some form of osteoarthritis. The conference studies show that arthritics can perhaps benefit from exercise more than other older people, provided the exercise is increased slowly but steadily.

9. Many Americans fear getting older. They fear that they will be "turned out to pasture," and become unwanted. This increases stress, depression, and fear. Walking seems to stem the tide. Exercise improves their quality of life. Research comparing exercise to a widely prescribed tranquilizer found exercise to be superior in relaxing and elevating one's mood—with none of the drug's negative side-effects.

Longevity

Closely allied to aging is the phenomenon of longevity. And exercise may not only be adding life to your years but also years to your life. A large-scale health survey based on the study of 7,000 adults in California over a long period of time demonstrated a 11.5-year greater life expectancy for people whose lifestyle incorporated six or seven basic health habits versus those who followed three or fewer of them. These habits were: (1) moderate, regular exercise; (2) normal weight; (3) breakfast every day; (4) normal meals with no snacks in between; (5) seven or eight hours of sleep per night; (6) moderate drinking (one small drink or less daily); and (7) no smoking. These findings were duplicated in a Wisconsin study of almost 2,000 people.

Furthermore, Charles L. Rose, M.D., and his associates at the Veterans Administration Outpatient Clinic of Boston explored the relationship between exercise and longevity. The researchers interviewed close relatives of 500 men who died in Boston in 1965. They asked many questions about smoking, eating, exercise, sleeping, recreation, and occupational habits—more than 200 factors. The researchers then arranged the data, looking for interactions of these factors relative to longevity. The results were fascinating: (1) physical exertion during leisure hours benefited people more than exercise on the job; and (2) physical exertion off the job, particularly during the years 40 to 49, were among the best of all longevity predictors.

A Better Sex Life

It has been reported that exercise can improve your sex life. The former Surgeon of the United States, Jesse Steinfeld, M.D., said, "Those people who are in good physical condition even enjoy sex more. If that isn't a motivating factor, I don't know what is."

Exactly why this occurs is not well known, but it seems to be related to the fact that improved fitness makes a person look better. That not only improves their self-concept but also improves their physical attractiveness. Also, there is some speculation that exercise even increases the sex drive. Thomas K. Cureton, Ph.D., used to say that many men, as they became sedentary, were afraid to be physical beings. They were afraid they might get hurt, or have a heart attack. When they became more fit, their courage returned. So did their interest in physical things. And sex is a physical act. Cureton felt that increased sex drive was due to this change in attitude.

There is further research to support the concept that a male's sex drive is affected by his fitness level. A male's sex drive is influenced by the level of the hormone testosterone. In the past, it was assumed that men inherited a tendency to produce more hormones. Although scientists still disagree, there is evidence now suggesting that different factors in life may influence the production of testosterone. One of these factors seems to be physical exercise.

J. R. Sutton, M.D., and his colleagues at the Gavin Institute of Medical Research at St. Vincent's Hospital in Sydney, Australia, studied two groups of athletes—14 oarsmen of a rowing team and seven swimmers. These were not typical college athletes, but highly trained men who had achieved Olympic standards. Their training was rigid, involving two sessions daily—one extremely intense and another somewhat less demanding. Sutton tested blood testosterone levels for all men before and after each of the two sessions. He found that when the exercise was less than maximum, there was no change in testosterone levels, but when the physical effort was all out the testosterone levels increased dramatically.

You don't have to train as hard as an Olympic athlete to increase your testosterone level. Dr. Sutton conducted further research with more reasonable levels of exercise. Here he selected four more subjects. These were medical students in good health, but not athletes. He had them exercise for 20 minutes on a stationary exercise bicycle and he collected blood samples before, during, and after their performance. After 10 minutes of activity, testosterone levels began to rise, reaching their peak at 20 minutes, when the exercise was discontinued.

Work on women has also revealed some interesting findings. Dr. J. Sonka and associates did experiments involving hormone levels in obese women. His researchers discovered that obese women who dieted had a drop in certain hormones. When those who dieted exercised, they did not have this reduced production. Which, of course, suggests that exercise may slow the destruction of certain sex drive hormones.

Perhaps a more common sense explanation for a better sex life for exercisers is their increased energy levels. How many times have you heard or used the excuse, "Not tonight honey, I'm just too tired."? That's too bad. One of the most beautiful gifts given to mankind is being missed by a lot of people who simply don't have the energy to enjoy it. I'm not saying that exercise is an aphrodisiac. There is no such thing. I do say, however, that the couple that plays together . . . well, you finish the sentence.

Summary

"Exercise will *not* cure all that ails you." Good health involves a combination of factors. However, your chances of a healthy, happy life are practically nil if you don't engage in a regular program of sustained physical activity. If we expect to get more out of whatever time we have here in the good life, it is mandatory that we exercise. Exercise is not going to help you grow a leg, cure some catastrophic disease, or make you a superman. But it will help you get the most out of life.

15

Questions And Answers

After all this discussion on fat, perhaps you have a few more questions on fatness, exercise, and fitness. Here are a few of the more popular questions that are asked of me after I give a talk on diet-free fat loss.

Q: I'm not very active and I really picture myself as a klutz.
A: I remember one woman who seemed to get a certain amount of pride in her lack of ability. I got the feeling she thought it was cute. "My coordination is just unbelievably bad," she said. And then proceeded to tick off all the things she couldn't do. "I don't know how to ride a bike. I never learned to swim. I can't ice skate. I've never even held a tennis racquet." And so on.

She was 5'4" and she weighed 185 pounds—precisely because she'd never learned how to use her body. She told me later that her mother had considered sports and physical activity "unlady-like." So here she was, locked into patterns of sedentary living and inventing excuses for not breaking out.

I asked her if she liked to dance. "Yes," she answered. "But you didn't say anything about dancing."

Well maybe I hadn't mentioned dancing to her, but I certainly should have. Athletic ability has nothing to do with this exercise program. Sports are fun. Tennis, swimming, and bicycling are fun. Which is why I tend to refer to them so much in my examples. But walking, running, jogging, and skipping rope are among the highest energy using activities, and you need no special ability or equipment to do any of these.

Q: I'm really concerned that if I exercise my appetite will increase.
A: Not so. There is conclusive (and voluminous) scientific evidence that for a sedentary person an increase in activity absolutely does not lead to an increase in appetite, except possibly during the first few days. After that, the appetite will return to normal and remain so. The myth that increased activity leads to increased eating dies hard.

In fact, it's been demonstrated by Jean Mayer and others that the opposite is closer to the truth; the more sedentary a person is, whether male, female, adult, or teenager, the greater the appetite. At the same time, there's a tendency to reduce caloric consumption upon engaging in increased physical activity.

I realize this goes counter to popular assumption, but think about it for a moment. If you're like most people, you're far more likely to reach for a beer or a piece of cake when you're bored or just lazying around watching TV than when you're busy or actively involved in something interesting.

One more important point. If you increase the activity level of a highly active person, you will find their appetite increases. This is for self-preservation. But then they don't have a weight problem and they don't have to worry about it. The real problem seems to stem with the sedentary person.

Q: But I hate to exercise.
A: By saying that it implies that you like to diet. So, I'm giving you a choice. You can diet to lose weight, but you'll have to put up with it for 24 hours, and I'm sure you'll hate it. In fact, you'll hate what you see in the mirror because your figure won't look good. Or you can exercise, and you only have to put up with that for a half hour or so. The choice is yours.

Q: Won't exercise make me tired?
A: Possibly. Some people certainly do tire more quickly than others and need more rest. But I'll bet you 5 to 1 that when you become more active, you won't need as much rest as you did before. In fact, you'll probably feel a lot peppier and more alive.

There's a good bit of research that documents how a sedentary life promotes sluggishness and the feeling of being chroni-. cally tired. In other words, the less you do, the less you feel like doing. Activity, on the other hand, generates energy and increased vitality. The more you do, the more you'll want to do.

I know what it is with me. When I don't exercise regularly, either because I'm traveling or because my schedule is interrupted by unusual domestic, professional, or social obligations, I really feel I need 8 to 8½ hours of sleep a night. When I'm active—and for me that means running or bicycling on a regular basis—I find I get along very well with only 7 hours of sleep. In effect, a half hour of activity a day results in an extra hour or more of energy-charged wakefulness.

But you needn't take my word for it. "All my life I had to rest in the afternoon. Now I can stay up through a day's work without any fatigue, and I seem to need less sleep." Evangelist Billy Graham said it, a few months after beginning a low-gear fitness program—consisting of stationary exercise and walking two miles a day—suggested by Dr. Thomas Cureton, director of the University of Illinois physical fitness laboratory.

The fact is, more and more experts are convinced physical activity, not more rest, is the key to increased endurance and energy—and less fatigue.

Q: Why should I feel renewed energy after exercise?
A: One explanation for this feeling of energy is that during inactivity the body accumulates adrenalin. The adrenalin products are stored in the brain and in the heart. Exercise literally speeds up the metabolism and burns up the accumulated adren-

alin stores. This improves the function of the body cells and also affects brain cell function.

Along these lines, it is possible some people are fatigued simply because of psychological drain on the job. The pressures of the day and added responsibilities take their psychic toll. Exercise can play a role here too. You may have mental fatigue from job pressure or even boredom. But the exercise gives you a sense of accomplishment—you've covered so many miles on your bicycle, exercised for so many minutes or whatever. All that is good for your psyche. It gives you a sense of personal fulfillment and also helps to achieve a meaningful goal.

By conditioning your body through exercise, your 8 hours on the job do not tax you as heavily as they did before you exercised. The explanation is that exercise makes you stronger physically. Because you are stronger, you work more efficiently—getting the same amount done with less fatigue.

Q: Up to this point, you've said very little about the difference between weight lifting and weight training.

A: Weight lifting is a competitive sport, the object of which is to lift a greater total poundage than your competitors in three basic lifts. Weight training, on the other hand, refers to the process of developing muscular strength and/or endurance by exercising with weights or resistive devices. The whole concept of weight training is based on the principle that the body is capable of adapting to the stresses placed on it. That is called overload. Under no circumstances is weight training to be thought of as a complete fitness program. Weight training may help you improve in sports, but it does absolutely nothing for the most important muscle of the body—your heart. It also increases muscle mass but tends to do very little in removing body fat. Because of this, more and more weight trainers are now involved in running programs or some other type of aerobic type exercise that will help their heart muscle and reduce their body fat.

Q: What about isometrics?
A: Isometrics are special exercises that exert a muscle or a group of muscles against an immovable object. The object you're working against could be a wall, a steel bar, a taut rope, a towel, or even another set of muscles.

Q: Do isometrics really help you?
A: They increase body strength but they do absolutely nothing for your heart or reducing your body fat. Therefore, I don't advocate them at all for a weight control program.

Q: What about yoga?
A: Yoga may be great for relaxation, meditation, and improvement of flexibility. But it does very little in the area of fat control. It burns too few calories. I would advocate your getting involved in things such as those items listed as moderate to very high physical activities. Forget about yoga except as an adjunct to your program.

Q: Throughout the entire book you've talked about the obese, but should the *really* obese people exercise?
A: There is no doubt about it. Obesity is dangerous. But obesity can be helped through exercise. Over the years many doctors and experts on obesity have felt that obese people either will not or should not exercise. But the rate of success of many people in walking programs has prompted some new thinking. Obese people will probably not lose weight through extremely strenuous activities. It's just too demanding for them. Yet they can achieve excellent results through walking, because it is not too difficult. If you're obese, you can exercise provided you do it in the manner I have outlined. And then consider the "go slow" approach. This is a hard lesson to learn, especially if you are a competitive individual. Don't walk at an unrealistic pace. You'll become exhausted and discouraged. Use distance (or time) and go at a pace you can cope with. Follow the tables set

forth in this book and focus on going a minimum of four times a week. If you are extremely obese and find this difficult, you can follow the program below. Your goal should be to work at your target heart rate for a minimum of 30 minutes. When this amount of walking no longer allows you to reach your target heart rate, gradually increase to 60 minutes or more of walking a day.

Table 18
EXTREME OBESITY PROGRAM

Level 1	3 to 5 minutes	3 times a week
Level 2	6 to 8 minutes	3 times a week
Level 3	9 to 11 minutes	3 times a week
Level 4	12 to 14 minutes	4 times a week
Level 5	15 to 17 minutes	4 times a week
Level 6	18 to 20 minutes	4 times a week
Level 7	21 to 23 minutes	4 times a week
Level 8	24 to 26 minutes	4 times a week
Level 9	27 to 29 minutes	4 times a week
Level 10	30 to 32 minutes	4 times a week
Level 11	33 to 35 minutes	4 times a week
Level 12	36 to 38 minutes	4 times a week
Level 13	39 to 41 minutes	4 times a week
Level 14	42 to 44 minutes	4 times a week
Level 15	45 to 47 minutes	4 times a week
Level 16	48 to 50 minutes	4 times a week
Level 17	51 to 53 minutes	4 times a week
Level 18	54 to 56 minutes	4 times a week
Level 19	57 to 59 minutes	4 times a week
Level 20	60 minutes	4 times a week

Q: What if I get discouraged from going so slowly?
A: Unfortunately, the obese can get discouraged quite easily. You have been frustrated for a long time and you want to make

changes now. Even though you are very obese, it seems likely that a three-minute walk will be easy, and you also probably figure it won't do you any good. Of course, you have an alternative. Don't do anything. Sit and add on a few more pounds. The result will be depression, anxiety, resentment, low morale, decreased stamina and vigor. No joy of life. You might as well be dead. Here's where positive thinking comes in. Constantly remind yourself of the following facts:

1. Complete inactivity will not help you live longer. You cannot entirely escape activity. Sooner or later your body will be called upon to do a difficult task. Whether it's a seemingly routine romp with your children or an unexpected emergency, you'll be forced to perform some duty that will present physical stress.
2. Mild, regular exercise is the only way to eventual good cardiovascular shape. No gadget or device will get your heart back into shape and remove your body flab. Your heart muscle will have to be retrained, and the muscles of your body have to be reacquainted to the idea of movement. Proceeding gradually, your body will become stronger and you will be able to work more efficiently.
3. Remember that though progress is slow, at least you're going in the right direction. Somewhere between 25 and 50% of the adult population probably carries too much fat. In fact, in Canada it has been estimated that 75% of the population carries too much body fat. So you're not alone.

Q: I'm not as concerned about my weight as I am about my looks. Aren't there ways I can lose fat to improve my figure?
A: There's no such thing as spot reducing. When you burn calories to lose weight, you will lose weight all over. Your figure is not so much a fat problem as a muscle problem. That's why diets don't always return your body to that youthful look. A diet may help you look skinnier, but you will still be soft and

flabby and may have those same unsightly bulges.

That's why exercise comes out on top when you are interested in a better looking body. The way to improve your figure is to firm up the muscles that accentuate your curves. Problem areas such as the thighs, hips, derriere, and breasts get their shape from muscles. Consequently, exercises like running and swimming are good all-around body shapers because they use so many muscle groups.

Q: If you had to come up with a single best reason why exercise is superior to dieting, what would you say?

A: Exercise has a profound effect on your basal metabolic rate. For example, you not only burn more calories when engaging in the exercise, you burn calories after the exercise. If at rest you burn one calorie a minute, after you jog (in which you burn 300 extra calories in a half hour) your basal metabolic rate may stay at.1.1 calories per minute. That slight increase is truly significant. It can amount to a tremendous amount of calories over a year's time.

But there is a more profound reason. Everyone knows that as you grow older, your metabolism slows down. In fact, your basal metabolic rate slows about ½ percent each year past the age of 26. One-half percent doesn't sound like much. But let's assume that you're 26 years old and you eat. 3,000 calories a day. You also burn off 3,000 calories a day as you work and play your way through the day. You maintain your body weight and there is no weight problem. At the age of 27, you're probably still eating 3,000 calories as you did the year before and doing the same kinds of things physically. But because your metabolism rate dropped a half percent you're now burning off 15 fewer calories a day. You're burning only, 2,985 calories a day instead of 3,000. That doesn't sound significant: only 1½ pounds per year. But if you follow this pattern over 30 years, the weight problem is astronomical—15% fewer calories each year. At the end of 30 years you'll be out of balance by 450 calories a day! All because of a slower basal metabolic rate.

And consistent exercise habits can slow down the change in your overall basal metabolic rate. A study by physiologist Ancel Keyes, Ph.D., found that people who keep their percent body fat low and lean body tissue high as they grow older have a basal metabolic rate decline of only 1% in 30 years.

I can't think of a better reason. We all slow down as we age. Regular vigorous exercise keeps you from slowing down before your time.

Q: Although you've talked about diets and their futility, you've said little about good nutrition. How come?

A: Read the next chapter.

16

Food: A Friend For Life

Earlier I talked about counterproductive eating—dieting. I mentioned diets to avoid. Now's the time to talk about what constitutes good eating and the importance of good food in better living and well-being.

Food is not the culprit in weight and fat gain—a lack of physical activity is the problem. Food is not an enemy. Don't believe people who say that if they breathe food they gain weight. Food is for your enjoyment and refreshment.

One of the main reasons why dieting will never effectively work is the fact that you *need* food. You cannot live without it. If you deny yourself the proper balance of nutrients, you will become ill—physically and mentally. All of your body systems depend upon food for survival.

Many nutritionists talk about the four basic food groups (milk, meat, bread-cereal, and vegetable-fruit). This classification system may be simple and adequate to educate young school children. But it is misleading and, according to Jean Mayer, a world-renowned scientist, not satisfactory. Dr. Mayer states: "There is no reason, for example, to classify potatoes and spinach together. It would make more sense to group together the main sources of animal protein and good quality vegetable proteins (milk, meat, fish, eggs, peas, and beans), and separate starch fruits (bananas) and roots (potatoes) from green, leafy vegetables and other fruits.

A still better approach is to use the seven basic food groups listed below. That is:

1. Leafy, green and yellow vegetables.
2. Citrus fruits, tomatoes, raw cabbage, and salad greens.
3. Potatoes and other vegetables and fruits.
4. Milk and milk products.
5. Meat, poultry, fish, eggs, dried beans and peas, and nuts.
6. Bread and cereals.
7. Butter and fortified margarine.

You should eat one serving of food from each of the basic seven groups every day. More servings may be added if desired, depending upon your eating habits, physical activity, and body size. A teen-age boy or adult man doing hard work may need several helpings because of greater physical activity, while a young child may need only about half the adult serving.

By using the seven basic groups you stand a better chance of getting all of your six essential nutrients: carbohydrates, fats, proteins, vitamins, minerals, and water. Nutrients provide energy (carbohydrates, fats, and occasionally proteins), build tissue (protein), and assist in the building of both energy and tissue (vitamins, minerals, and water). Without these six nutrients, good health, in fact life itself, would be impossible. That's why I tell people, "Don't quit eating!"

Let's look at some of these nutrients. Vitamins and minerals will not be discussed. Although they are essential to your health, they are found in the other foods we will discuss, and they will never, never make you fat.

Carbohydrates

Carbohydrate foods are your body's most preferred nutrients. They are also the most maligned. They are usually those good tasting treats from your grandmother's kitchen that are too tempting to pass up. In addition, they are the easiest foods for your body to digest. Aside from providing quick energy, high quality carbohydrate foods usually contain important proteins, minerals, and vitamins.

When the carbohydrate stores in your body become inadequate, as in prolonged, strenuous muscular activity or starvation, the body can adjust and allow you to use fats and, infrequently, proteins and fulfill your energy needs. Unfortunately, the use of fats and proteins in place of carbohydrates is less efficient and chemically more complex. The use of fats and proteins can continue for only a limited amount of time before other body functions begin to suffer. (See Figure #3 for a summary of how your body uses carbohydrates.)

Carbohydrates are derived from beets, onions, carrots, turnips, and sweet potatoes. Complex carbohydrates are found in grain and grain products such as breakfast cereals, noodles, pastries, and other vegetables.

Most carbohydrates come in the form of double sugars or poly-sugars. When these carbohydrate foods are eaten, they are digested by your body and broken down into the simple sugars of glucose, fructose, and galactose. The carbohydrates may also be stored as glycogen.

Glycogen is stored in animal tissues instead of plants. Glycogen is called animal starch. But only small amounts are stored in the muscles and the liver. The glycogen is also used up quickly during exercise or in starvation. When it is needed, it must be changed into glucose. Since most animals cannot store much glycogen, little of it is found in meat.

Cellulose is a carbohydrate but is harder to digest than starches. It must be cooked to be digested. Even then, most of the cellulose remains undigested. Cellulose helps elimination by giving bulk to the digestive tract. It comes from the seeds of fruits, leaves, stems, and roots.

While sugar comes in many forms (sucrose, lactose, glucose, and fructose), it is sucrose that is getting all the attention. In the

Figure 3. Molecular composition of carbohydrates

Simple Sugars (Monosaccharides):

Glucose: plants

Double Sugars (Disaccharides):

Maltose: malted milk, malted breakfast foods, corn syrups, grains

Fructose: fruits

Sucrose: sugar cane, beets, sap sugars

Galactose: milk, milk products

Lactose: milk, milk products

Starches (Polysaccharides): whole grains and whole grain products, beans, peas, and root vegetables, i.e., potatoes

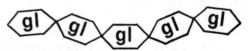

The above would be a small section of the molecule, since a polysaccharide is made up of hundreds of units of sugar.

The simple and double carbohydrates are referred to as sugars, while the multiple ones are called starches. All carbohydrates consist of oxygen, hydrogen and carbon atoms.

last few years many nutritionists have come to feel that Americans eat too much sucrose (table sugar) for their own good. Numerous books and articles have been published in support of this viewpoint.

Figure 4. **Summary of how carbohydrates are used**

Step #1—Carbohydrates are eaten in the form of simple sugars (single or double) and starches. The single and double sugars are mostly in the form of sucrose (cane or beet sugar), lactose (milk sugar), or fructose (fruit sugar).

Step #2—In the small intestine almost all sugars and starches are broken down into the simple sugars of glucose, fructose , and galactose. Eighty percent end up being glucose, 1% fructose, and 10% galactose.

Step #3—As these three sugars move out of the small intestine, glucose and galactose move rapidly into the liver's blood system. Fructose, however, moves through slowly. And as it does, *most* of the fructose is changed to glucose.

Step #4—Insulin along with a small protein molecule helps transport the glucose and galactose across the liver cell membrane. Surprisingly, fructose does not need insulin to get into the liver cell. Insulin is to move the galactose and glucose across the cell membrane rapidly.

Once in the liver almost all remaining galactose and fructose are converted into glucose.

The liver has another role in that if the blood glucose level is too high the liver acts as a buffer and converts the excess glucose into glycogen for future use.

Step #5—From the liver the glucose and remaining fructose and galactose are released into the bloodstream and delivered to the cells of the body.

Step #6—To get into the various cells of the body a pattern similar to Step #4 is followed. Galactose and glucose get into the cells with the assistance of insulin.

The brain cells are an exception since insulin is not needed. As with the liver, insulin is not needed for the passage of fructose into the cell. Once in the cell the glucose and the fructose are used readily. Any glucose or fructose left over is converted into glycogen. The galactose, however, is released from the cell and sent back to the liver for conversion into glucose.

Naturally, some people are confused over the controversy surrounding their product. The president of one said: "Most authorities agree that sugar, in moderation, is one of the most useful foods as well as an economical source of energy. Yet, sugar is frequently accused of being detrimental to health. Some of these accusations come from food faddists and non-scientists with an ax to grind. And some come from physicians and researchers whose views are not generally accepted."

I agree that using sugar in moderation is not harmful. But what is moderation? Certainly, sugar (sucrose) is being used in excess when it constitutes 15 to 20% of one's total caloric intake, which is "average" in the United States!

It's often forgotten that sugar is not only a basic ingredient in the obvious foods such as candy, soft drinks, pastries, and desserts. It is also added to commercially prepared soups, rice, peanut butter, baked beans, crackers, ketchup, mustard, chow mein, blue cheese, cereals, fruit drinks, juices, frankfurters, bread, vitamins, medicines, and almost anything else you can think of.

That wasn't always the case. At one time sugar was purchased by the ounce. In England during the 1750's the average person ate about four pounds of sugar per year. Today, in the United States, the average person eats between two and three pounds a week!

Although I could go on about the suspected relationship between high sugar consumption and increased risk of heart disease, diabetes, hypoglycemia (low blood sugar), and dental decay, I'll confine this discussion to fat control.

The trouble with table sugar (sucrose) is that it tricks the appestat and floods the body with calories—quick energy—so fast that the body cannot handle them properly.

Earlier I told you that the appetite is regulated by the center in the brain called the appestat. When your blood sugar (glucose) is low, the appestat calls for a greater production of glucose by the liver, and you'll feel hungry. When blood sugar is high, the appestat tells the liver to shut down its glucose production, and you'll feel satisfied and probably pass up that extra helping of food.

When you're hungry and attempt to satisfy your appetite with something heavily saturated with sugar, your blood sugar level skyrockets. The appestat is temporarily satisfied and signals a shutdown of glucose production by the liver. However, the appestat reading is a false one; the blood sugar level soon plummets, causing the appestat to quickly signal for *more* food. The result: fresh hunger pangs. If the appestat is placated with more sugar, the process is repeated.

In short, then, a high intake of sugar interferes with the natural operation of the appestat by producing erratic and sometimes constant feelings of hunger, which encourage overeating. Better to have some other kind of food and provide longer term gratification of the appestat than to continue in the attempt to satisfy it with "quick energy" sugar.

Eating excessive amounts of sugar can also lead to an imbalance that causes the pancreas to produce either too much or too little insulin. When there is too much insulin, hypoglycemia (too little sugar in the blood) develops. With too little insulin, the result is hyperglycemia (too much sugar in the blood), which may in time lead to diabetes mellitis.

Blood sugar—glucose—is essential to the body. But all foods, whether carbohydrates, fats, or proteins are sources of glucose. Your body doesn't need refined sugar to produce glucose, or for "quick energy." In fact, since refined sugar is devoid of vitamins and minerals and contains only naked calories, there's no reason for eating it at all, except that it tastes good. But then, so do a lot of other foods, right?

Cutting down on sugar may help you stabilize your appestat— which means you'll feel hungry less often. Certainly, you'll be consuming fewer calories if you reduce your sugar intake, and these will be the kind of calories you'll never miss, since they're not "tied" to vital nutrients.

By following the guidelines below, you should be able to cut your sugar consumption in half—so that only about 10% (as opposed to the norm of 18%) of your total daily calories come from refined sugar.

1. Don't put sugar on cereal or in coffee or tea. (If you can't do completely without, compromise by using only half of what you normally use.)
2. Never eat presweetened cereals.
3. Cut your consumption of soft drinks and candy by 50%.
4. Drink fruit *juices* rather than fruit *drinks*. Also, check fruit juice labels. They should say "no sugar added" rather than "unsweetened." "Unsweetened" can mean that some sugar, usually in the form of fruit sugar, has been added.
5. Keep sugar off fruit.
6. Use fresh rather than canned fruit.
7. Carefully check all labels and select foods that are low in sugar or simple carbohydrates. If you have a choice, choose the can or box with no sugar listed among the ingredients—or with sugar listed *after* several other ingredients, rather than a product where sugar is listed among the first few. (The same rule applies for "sucrose," "glucose," "dextrose," "inverted sugar," and "corn syrup." All get into the bloodstream very quickly and can affect the appestat and trigger the yo-yo reaction of hunger-satiety, hunger-satiety, etc.) Remember, those ingredients are listed according to weight. For example, if sugar is listed first, that means there is more

sugar in that package than any other of the ingredients listed. Increase your complex carbohydrate eating. To do that eat more fresh fruits, vegetables, and whole grain products.

Still, probably the best food that you can eat is carbohydrates. Provided it's the right kind of carbohydrates: complex carbohydrates. They take much longer to metabolize and as a result release a slow, constant stream of glucose into the bloodstream (about two calories per minute).

Complex carbohydrate foods contain many vitamins, minerals, protein, and fiber. They are real winners. Some of the best kinds of carbohydrate food that I advocate are wheat, oats, barley, brown rice, and buckwheat. I also recommend raw vegetables, citrus fruits, beans and peas, sweet potatoes, and squash.

Fats

Fats are a class of nutrients made up of fatty acids and glycerin (an organic alcohol). Most fat nutrients are supplied by animals, in products such as butter and other dairy products, fatty meats, fish, egg yolks, and poultry. But fat is also found in salad and cooking oils, margarine, chocolate, nuts, and peanut butter. Pound for pound, fats provide more usable energy fuel than either carbohydrates or proteins. They also take longer to digest and, therefore, have a longer lasting satisfying effect on appetite and hunger.

There are three general kinds of fatty acids. They are called saturated, unsaturated, and polyunsaturated. These terms refer to the manner in which the hydrogen and carbon atoms of the fat are fastened together. If you could look at a saturated fat under a microscope, you would see the hydrogen and carbon atoms linked together (See Figure #5). The less hydrogen present, the more unsaturated the fat is.

There are some very good reasons for knowing the difference between saturated, unsaturated, and polyunsaturated fats. A diet high in saturated fat tends to produce some undesirable changes in blood chemistry. Not only do cholesterol levels tend to increase, but the low density lipoproteins also increase. These changes apparently encourage the development of heart disease.

Here are some more helpful hints about saturated, unsaturated, and polyunsaturated fats.

- Every fat has its melting point. Fats known as oils are fluid at room temperature. Butter and lard melt with only a little heat. Sheep fat has a high melting point. The difference in the melting points of the different fats is due to the type and amount of fatty acids they contain. Usually, the liquid fats are unsaturated. The solid fats like butter, margarine, and vegetable shortening are saturated.

- Many unsaturated fats are made into saturated fats by food manufacturers through a process called hydrogenation. Since hydrogenated fats don't spoil, they last longer on the shelf. So manufacturers extend the shelf-life of the product by hydrogenating their oils.

  Doctors feel that hydrogenated fats are a real problem for the body and are possibly related to heart disease. So read the labels when you buy peanut butter or any other product containing fats. If the label says "partially hardened" or "hydrogenated," it's a saturated fat. Your circulatory system will be much healthier when you learn to use liquid oils and less butter and margarine.

- There is a distinction between cholesterol and saturated fat. Saturated fat is a true fat and is found in both plants and animals. Cholesterol, on the other hand, is an alcohol with fat-like properties. It belongs to a group of compounds called sterols. Although it seems to have considerable physiological importance in some relationship to the development of atherosclerosis, it has an obscure biochemistry. It is found abundantly in the digestive bile and in all animal fats such as butter, cream, egg yolk, and the fat in meat.

All of this is not to say that fat is bad. Fats should not be totally removed from your diet. Presently, about 40% of the average American's calories come from fats. As you know, it has been recommended by the United States Senate Select Committee on Nutrition and Human Needs that Americans should reduce their calorie quota of fat to about 30% of their diet. If you have a family history of heart disease, however, high blood pressure and the like, a reduction to 20% or less may be best for you.

Figure 5. Three types of fat

Saturated	Unsaturated	Polyunsaturated
beef	almonds	corn oil
butter	cashews	fish
cheese (whole milk)	chicken	herring oil
chocolate	duck	margarine
coconut	olive oil	(special)
cream	peanuts	safflower oil
eggs	peanut oil	soybean oil
ice cream	pecans	walnuts
lamb	turkey	wheat germ oil
margarines		
(ordinary)		
milk (whole)		
pork		
shortenings		
(hydrogenated)		
veal		

Here are some guidelines on eating fats:

● Cut back on your red meat consumption. Supplement with

chicken, turkey, and fish. Try not to eat red meat more than three times a week. And then three to four ounces is plenty. Make sure you cut off any extraneous fat.

- Eat nuts, dried beans, and peas instead of meat.
- Eat egg yolks no more than two or three times a week. This will help to reduce cholesterol content. Eat as many egg whites as you want, but not yolks.
- Eat and drink milk products that are low in dairy fats.
- Use polyunsaturated liquid oils instead of butter and lard when cooking.
- Avoid non-dairy cream substitutes. (They are actually higher in fat than real cream.)

With the above guidelines in mind, do what you can to keep your fat intake as low as possible. This includes unsaturated, polyunsaturated, and saturated fats. The reasons? All fats, animal and vegetable, have a common effect on your bodies. They form a fatty film around the red blood cells and platelets— causing them to stick together so that they cannot function properly. Consequently, small blood vessels and capillaries become plugged and shut down. This can mean that a certain percentage of your blood circulation is severely affected.

There's one more thing that I don't like about fat. Pesticides and other chemical pollutants seem to be attracted to fat cells. Experimenters have shown that the highest amount of pesticides are found in meat, fish, poultry, dairy products and oils. And the least amount is found in leafy vegetables, fruits, grains, and root vegetables.

And there's enough evidence to convince me that too many pesticides in your body is carcinogenic.

Proteins

Imagine a machine that can take a loaf of bread and automatically separate all the ingredients. In goes a loaf, out come piles of flour, sugar, shortening, eggs, baking powder, etc. Then, the ingredients move along a conveyor belt to be picked up by anyone who wants a specific ingredient. If you need a couple of eggs, you grab them as they come by. If someone else needs sugar, he takes what he needs.

This homely example illustrates how the body uses proteins. First, they must be broken down into their appropriate amino acids by the digestive system. Then they can be absorbed by the blood and carried to the tissues where they are selectively removed by cells in need of specific amino acids. The amino acids are then moved to form new protein to carry out specific life functions of the cell.

This occurs over and over again throughout every corner of the body every minute of every day. Since the known 22 amino acids can be used by the body in literally trillions of different combinations, they are called protein building blocks. They make up your eyes, skin, bones, teeth, muscles, hair, organs—you name it. The body literally rebuilds itself daily. And amino acids provide the raw materials for this process. Without amino acids, life would be impossible, indeed non-existent.

The unique thing about amino acids is that while the cells manufacture needed proteins from simple amino acid building blocks, the amino acids themselves cannot be manufactured. They must be eaten as part of your diet. Your body can take protein from plants and animals and break the protein into the various amino acids. When broken down, these amino acids are passed along to the various cells of your body. Here the amino acids are reassembled into whatever type of protein the cells need. Of all the 22 amino acids, 14 can be manufactured from any other amino acid. But eight cannot be. These eight are called essential amino acids. Your body can only be healthy if you have access to all eight of them. When you discuss nutrition, these eight amino acids are the only ones you have to be concerned about.

For good health you need all eight amino acids at one time. If some of these amino acids are not in the food that you've eaten, then the protein cannot be built and your tissues start to die. The job is further complicated because your body cannot wait until the next day hoping that a new meal will bring the missing amino acids. By the next day the previous day's amino acids have either been used for protein or energy or have been excreted. They are not saved. It is thus vital that a meal have all eight essential amino acids and not just some of them. Of course, an occasional incomplete meal is not going to harm you, but if this becomes a habit, you're going to be headed for some protein deficiency problems.

On the basis of current evidence, it seems best to have about 12% of your diet as protein. The protein, however, need not come from what most people consider the primary source, red meat. Chicken, turkey, other fowl, fish, egg whites, soybeans, corn, peas and beans, whole wheat and oats, potatoes, rice and millet, and dairy products all supply you with a good amount of complete protein or essential amino acids.

Dr. Jean Mayer has prepared a list of some of the best sources of good quality or essential protein in your diet.

Table 19
SOME GOOD SOURCES OF PROTEIN*

Food	Amount	Protein (Grams)
Milk	1 cup	9
Cheese, Swiss	1 oz.	8
Beef, ground	1 oz.	7
Chicken	1 oz.	7
Fish, white	1 oz.	7
Dried beans, cooked	½ cup	7
Yogurt	1 cup	7
Egg	1	6
Cheese, cottage	1 oz.	4
Peanut butter	1 Tbsp.	4

Two cups of skim or low fat milk provide the average person with 18 grams of protein which is almost 40% of the protein requirement of a woman. On top of that, if she has a cup of low fat yogurt and three ounces of chicken, she would have all the protein needs for the day.

There are some other sources of protein which Dr. Mayer thinks are worthy of your consideration. I have listed them here.

Table 20
OTHER SOURCES OF PROTEIN*

Food	Amount	Protein (Grams)
Green peas	1 cup	9
Noodles	1 cup	7
Broccoli	1 med. stalk	6
Macaroni	1 cup	5
Pecans	½ cup	5
Dandelion greens, cooked	1 cup	5
Spinach, cooked	1 cup	5
Bran flakes	1 cup	4
Rice	1 cup	4
Potato, baked	1 med.	3
Asparagus pieces	1 cup	3
Beet greens	1 cup	3
Oatmeal	½ cup	3
Corn	1 ear	3
Bread, whole wheat	1 slice	3
Green beans	1 cup	2
Cornflakes	1 cup	2
Bread, white	1 slice	2

* Jean Mayer, *Protein How Much Is Enough?* New York, NY: Newspaperbooks, 1975, p. 9.

**Ibid, p. 10.

Although proteins are necessary if life is to continue, they are not required in large amounts. Foods which are rich in protein include meats, fish, eggs, and nuts. Other foods which contribute lesser amounts of proteins are dry cereals, breads, and most fruits and vegetables. Many of the foods that are rich in proteins also provide some minerals and vitamins. Eating a wide range of proteins is conducive to health and is necessary during periods of rapid growth of cell formation, as in adolescence, pregnancy, and convalescence. It is a common practice among doctors to prescribe high-protein diets for pregnant women and individuals with disease in which there is a high degree of cell destruction.

Water

Water accounts for about 70% of body weight. All of the body fluids are basically watery solutions. The three main fluid compartments of the body are:

1. Intracellular fluid which exists win the cells.
2. Extracellular fluid which exists between the cells and provides the environment in which they exist and perform their respective functions.
3. Plasma, a fluid which consists of 92% water.

These fluids are made up of water and dissolved inorganic mineral substances. The chemistry of animal life involves exchanges between these fluids and combinations of the various solutions.

Water is acquired in three ways: water taken in as drink, water contained in ingested foods, and water formed within the body as a result of the oxidation process. Water is lost from the body through urination, defecation, perspiration, and evaporation. In the average adult, the daily water loss amounts to about three quarts, the amount which must be replaced daily. Two quarts of that requirement are provided by the food ingested.

The other quart, approximately four glasses, must be taken daily as drink. Naturally, the thirst mechanism is sufficient to induce us to take enough water. The fluid requirement varies from day to day depending on certain factors, the most important of which is perspiration, temperature, and exercise or strenuous work. Under conditions of extreme exertion, heat, and excessive perspiration, a special effort is necessary to meet the water loss.

Food is not the sinister villian you thought it was. In fact, food can be your companion to good health and weight loss. Any plan that calls for drastic cuts of certain types of food will only be counter productive. I do suggest, however, that you examine your intake to make sure you are getting the recommended amount of nutrients each day. If you eat one serving of each of the seven basic food groups, you will find that food will work for you instead of against you. So eat and enjoy!

Many people ask me; "How can I be sure I'm getting the best nutrition for me?" I've put together a nutrition guide which allows you to evaluate your current eating patterns. The guide is simple to use. In each of the groups, you should get the maximum number of points allocated. For example; if you eat one serving of leafy, green, or yellow vegetables, you receive 15 points. If you eat one serving of citrus fruits, you get 15 points. Follow that pattern for all of the groups. When finished for the day, total your score. One hundred points is your goal. If you get that many points, you will be getting all the essential nutrients—fats, proteins, carbohydrates, vitamins, minerals, water, and fiber.

Bear in mind that this chart does not account for excesses. That is, too much fat, protein, and simple carbohydrates.

Table 21
NUTRITION GUIDE FOR ADULTS

Group	Score	Food Groups & Number of Servings	Day 1	Day 2	Day
1	15	One serving (about ½ cup) of leafy, green or yellow vegetables.			
2	15	One serving (about ½ cup) of citrus fruits, tomatoes, raw cabbage or salad greens.			
3a.	7½	One serving (about ½ cup) of potatoes or other vegetables not listed in groups 1 & 2.			
3b.	7½	One serving (about ½ cup) of non-citrus fruits.			
4	15	Two cups of milk or milk products. 1 inch cube of cheese equivalent to ½ cup of milk.			
5	15	Two servings (Total: approx. 4 oz.) of meat, poultry, fish, dried beans, peas, nuts or eggs.			
6	15	Two or more servings of whole grain bread or cereals.			
7	10	Two to four servings of polyunsaturated margarine or vegetable oils.			

GROUP 1 — Leafy, green or yellow vegetables.

Asparagus, broccoli, carrots, chicory, collards, endive, escarole, green peas, kale, mustard greens, parsley, pumpkins, rutabagas, spinach, squash, string beans, sweet potatoes, wax beans.

EAT IN MODERATION: Canned vegetables

GROUP 2 — Citrus fruits, tomatoes, raw cabbage or salad greens—juice is permitted.

Berries, cantalope, cabbage, grapefruit, lemons, limes, mangoes, oranges, papayas, lettuce, green peppers, celery, tomatoes.

EAT IN MODERATION: Canned fruits and fruit drinks

GROUP 3a.— Potatoes or other vegetables not listed in Groups 1 & 2.

Beets, corn, cucumbers, egg plant, onions, parsnips, potatoes, white turnips.

EAT IN MODERATION: Instant potatoes, french fries, or any of above fried and canned vegetables.

GROUP 3b.— Non-citrus fruits—juice is permitted.

Apples, bananas, figs, grapes, peaches, pears, pineapples, plums, prunes, raisins.

EAT IN MODERATION: Canned fruits and fruit drinks.

GROUP 4 — Milk and milk products.

Buttermilk, cottage cheese, farmer cheese, non-fat milk, skim milk, yogurt.

EAT IN MODERATION: Sweet cream, sour cream, cream cheese, whole milk, ice cream, ice milk, puddings.

GROUP 5 — Meat, poultry, fish, dried beans, peas, nuts or eggs.

A. Four oz. of any of the following:
1. Fish or poultry (organs excluded) at least 5 times a week.
2. Beef, lamb, or pork no more than 4 times a week.
3. Dried beans, peas, and nuts one time a week—maximum.
B. A maximum of two eggs per week.

EAT IN MODERATION: Bacon, corned beef, pastrami, salami, sausage, other luncheon meats, sardines, smoked fish or meat.

GROUP 6 — Whole grain breads and cereals.

Whole wheat, cracked, wheat, rye, pumpernickle breads. granola (unsweetened) grape nuts, wheat germ (unsweetened), 100 or 40% bran, shredded wheat.

EAT IN MODERATION: Cakes, cookies, pastries, pies, muffins, biscuits, pre-sweetened cereals, pancakes, spaghetti, waffles and pretzels.

GROUP 7 — Polyunsaturated margarines, or vegetable oils.

> Corn oil, special margarines, safflower oil, sunflower oil, wheat germ oil. To be used as table spread or in salad dressing and in cooking.

> EAT IN MODERATION: Hydrogenated or hardened oils, margarine, salad dressing, butter, and mayonnaise.

This guide considers several factors:

1) It is extremely low in sucrose (table sugar).
2) It is low in saturated fat.
3) It is low in sodium (salt).
4) It is high in Food Group #1 (leafy, green, and yellow vegetables) and therefore is high in vitamin A. This group also supplies iron, calcium, thiamine, riboflavin, niacin, vitamin C, and fiber.
5) It is high in Food Group #2 (citrus fruits, tomatoes, raw cabbage, and salad greens) and therefore is high in vitamin C. This group also supplies vitamin A, iron, and calcium.
6) It is high in Food Group #3 (potatoes and other vegetables and fruits) and therefore is high in vitamin C, carbohydrates (starches and sugars), and is a good source of other minerals and vitamins.
7) It is high in Food Group #4 (milk and milk products) and therefore is high in calcium, vitamin A, riboflavin, and high quality proteins. Skim milk is low in vitamin A unless so fortified.

8) It is high in Food Group #5 (meat, poultry, fish, dried beans, nuts, and eggs) and therefore is high in protein, fat, iron, phosphorus, thiamine, and niacin. The vegetable proteins also provide starch (carbohydrate).

9) It is high in Food Group #6 (bread, flour, cereals) and therefore is high in minerals, vitamins, and fiber. This group also provides protein and starch.

10) It is high in Food Group #7 (butter and fortified margarine) and therefore is high in vitamin A and fat.

Below are seven daily sample menus. These can be used to show you how the Nutrition Guide on page 264 can be put into practice. These menus provide a variety of foods that are pleasing to the great majority of people. They give you selectivity yet moderation in designing menus. Selectivity, moderation, and variety are essential elements in putting into practice the Nutrition Guide.

The menus provide the appropriate amount of calories for the average male and female in the United States. That means, according to the latest evidence the average woman needs 1,600 calories a day and the average man 2,200 calories a day to maintain their body weights.

Of course, by incorporating the fat burning activities and the exercise supplements recommended in this book, you will be able to "have your cake and eat it too!" You can lose pounds and inches the diet-free way.

Please remember that these menus are not the final word. They are guidelines. They simply give you direction to show you that the charts do work and that a person can get adequate nutrition based on the United States Government Recommended Daily Allowances. These menus are particularly good because they are low in saturated fat, salt, and sugar; yet they are high in complex carbohydrates, and other essential nutrients.

Sample Menu #1

#1 BREAKFAST	Female	Male
Bowl of oatmeal—½ cup cooked w/ 3 tsp. of honey & ½ cup of skim milk	245	245
Diced banana or peach	75	75
One slice of whole wheat toast w/ (optional pat of butter or margarine)*	65	105
4 oz. glass of orange juice (optional 8 oz.)	55	110
8 oz. glass of skim milk	80	80
	520	615

LUNCH

	Female	Male
8 oz. cup of vegetable soup	100	100
Water packed tuna, small amount of mayonnaise w/ lettuce on 1 slice (optional 2 slices) of whole wheat bread	190	225
Cup of herb tea	0	0
Sliced pear	75	75
	365	430

DINNER

	Female	Male
4 oz. serving of broiled skinless chicken	250	250
Baked potato w/ a pat of margarine or butter	165	165
Tossed salad with French dressing-small serving (optional-average serving)	200	400
(optional ½ cup of corn)		140
8 oz. glass of skim milk	80	80
(optional muffin)		125
	1160	695

TOTAL FOR DAY = 1,580—2,205

*Foods in parentheses are additional items which the male may eat to get his 2,200 calories a day.
One pat of butter or margarine = 1 to 1½ teaspoons.

Sample Menu #2

#2 BREAKFAST

	Female	Male
1 poached egg on slice of cracked wheat toast	205	205
Cup of strawberries or cherries	100	100
4 oz. glass of grape juice (optional 8 oz.)	38	75
8 oz. glass of skim milk	80	80
	423	460

LUNCH

	Female	Male
Cup of yogurt w/ fruit	225	225
1 medium carrot & celery sticks	25	25
½ small grapefruit	50	50
Whole grain muffin or slice of whole wheat bread w/ (optional pat of butter or margarine)	65	105
Herb tea (optional 8 oz. glass of skim milk)	0	80
	365	485

DINNER

	Female	Male
4 oz. spaghetti w/ meat sauce (optional 6 oz.)	275	413
1 slice of French bread	50	50
Tossed salad w/ lettuce, tomato, & Italian dressing—small (optional—medium)	200	400
8 oz. glass of skim milk	80	80
	605	943

| Snack morning, afternoon, or evening— 20 peanuts | 200 | 200 |

TOTAL FOR DAY = 1,593—2,088

Sample Menu #3

#3 BREAKFAST | Female | Male

	Female	Male
1 cup of granola w/ ½ cup of skim milk	265	265
½ cup of dried fruit w/ raisins, prunes, and/or figs	225	225
4 oz. glass of tomato juice (optional 8 oz.)	25	50
8 oz. glass of skim milk	80	80
	595	620

LUNCH

	Female	Male
8 oz. cup of potato soup (optional—cream of)	175	275
Grilled open face—low fat cheese with shaved turkey breast on slice of whole grain toast	250	250
Cup of herb tea (optional 8 oz. glass of fruit juice)	0	50
	425	575

DINNER

	Female	Male
4 oz. trout w/ slivered almonds (optional 8 oz.)	90	180
Asparagus 4 to 6 stalks w/ cheese sauce	200	200
½ cup of buttered beets (optional 1 cup)	70	140
1 peach	50	50
Whole wheat muffin w/ (optional pat of butter or margarine)	125	165
Cup of herb tea	0	0
	535	735

	Female	Male
Snack morning, afternoon, or night—3 saltine crackers w/ peanut butter (optional 6)	100	200

TOTAL FOR DAY = 1,655—2,130

Sample Menu #4

#4 BREAKFAST
                                                            Female   *Male*

	Female	Male
2 whole wheat pancakes w/ 1 pat of butter or margarine (optional 3 pats of butter or margarine)	240	360
Fresh fruit—⅙th melon	65	65
4 oz. glass of apple juice (optional 8 oz.)	60	120
8 oz. glass of skim milk	80	80
	445	625

LUNCH

	Female	Male
⅙th slice mushroom pizza	200	200
Small tossed salad with oil and vinegar	200	200
Cup of herb tea	0	0
	400	400

DINNER

	Female	Male
Beef stew w/ meat, carrots, potatoes, & onions—1 cup (optional 1½ cups)	250	375
1 to 2 small sourdough biscuits w/ (optional pat of butter or margarine)	115	230
Fresh or frozen mixed fruit 1 cup	200	200
8 oz. glass of skim milk	80	80
	645	885

	Female	Male
Snack morning, afternoon, or evening—1 bran muffin (optional pat of butter or margarine)	100	145

TOTAL FOR DAY = 1,590—2,055

Sample Menu #5

#5 BREAKFAST

	Female	*Male*
Bowl of shredded wheat w/ ½ cup of skim milk	125	125
(optional fresh fruit—blueberries—1 cup)		100
Wheat germ toast w/ (optional pat of butter or margarine)	65	105
4 oz. glass of pineapple juice (optional 8 oz.)	63	125
8 oz. glass of skim milk	80	80
	333	535

LUNCH

	Female	*Male*
Cheese wedges 1 oz. (2 oz. optional) w/ fresh fruit—½ of an apple sliced, ½ cup grapes, 1 cup strawberries	280	430
Cucumber salad w/ sour cream and onions	190	190
Corn muffin w/ (optional pat of butter or margarine)	100	150
Cup of herb tea	0	0
	570	770

DINNER

	Female	*Male*
4 oz. of roast beef (4 oz. meatloaf)	200	225
1 cup of cream of spinach soup	175	175
1 boiled potato w/ (optional pat of butter or margarine)	125	165
1 cup of broccoli	45	45
1 sliced orange	75	75
8 oz. glass of skim milk	80	80
	700	765

TOTAL FOR DAY = 1,603—2,070

Sample Menu #6

#6 BREAKFAST

	Female	Male
1 cheese omelette w/ 2 eggs—one yolk	200	200
½ small grapefruit	50	50
1 slice of granola bread w/ (optional pat of butter or margarine)	75	115
4 oz. glass of vegetable juice (optional 8 oz.)	50	100
8 oz. glass of skim milk	80	80
	455	545

LUNCH

	Female	Male
1 serving of stir fried vegetables	200	200
¾ cup of brown or white rice w/ (optional pat of butter or margarine)	100	150
1 medium banana	100	100
(Optional 1 blueberry muffin w/ pat of butter or margarine)		140
8 oz. glass of orange juice	100	100
	500	690

DINNER

	Female	Male
Broiled fish—cod or whitefish w/ lemon juice (optional pat of butter or margarine)	200	300
¾ cup of white or brown rice w/ stewed tomatoes	145	145
1 cup of peas—fresh or frozen w/ ¼ cup of mushrooms	115	115
(Optional cup of tapioca pudding)		280
Granola-honey muffin	100	100
8 oz. glass of skim milk	80	80
	640	1,020

TOTAL FOR DAY = 1,595—2,255

Sample Menu #7

#7 BREAKFAST

	Female	Male
Bowl of cream of wheat w/ ½ cup of skim milk & 3 tsp. of honey	205	205
Fresh fruit—strawberries—1 cup	50	50
1 slice of whole wheat toast (optional pat of butter or margarine)	75	115
4 oz. glass of prune juice (optional 8 oz.)	85	170
8 oz. glass of skim milk	80	80
	495	620

LUNCH

	Female	Male
8 oz. of tomato soup (optional 16 oz.)	100	200
2 cream cheese filled celery sticks (optional 3)	110	150
1 apple	75	75
1 slice of whole grain bread w/ (optional pat of butter or margarine)	75	115
8 oz. glass of skim milk	80	80
	440	620

DINNER

	Female	Male
1 cup of baked beans	200	200
Spinach salad w/ bean sprouts (optional dried egg)	50	125
2 pineapple slices	150	150
1 bran muffin w/ pat of butter or margarine (optional 2 bran muffins w/ 2 pats of butter or margarine)	140	280
8 oz. glass of skim milk	80	80
	620	835

| (Optional snack morning, afternoon, or evening—1 oz. of swiss cheese) | | 100 |

TOTAL FOR DAY = 1,555—2,175

AVERAGE TOTAL OF CALORIES CONSUMED PER DAY
= 1,596—2,140

Regular exercise. Good, sound eating. And no diets. It really *does* sound too good to be true. Maybe that's part of the reason why some people never give exercise a chance. They have become so accustomed to the claims of instant success from the diet and pill crowd. Losing pounds the Activetics way will not produce overnight success. You can't start Monday and expect to lose five pounds by Friday. If you plan to put these concepts of diet-free weight loss to work, you must be patient. As you build activity into your life and develop sensible eating habits, the pounds will begin to fall. More important, they will stay off, since you will be developing a new lifestyle. You will no longer worry about extra helpings, but will enjoy eating a variety of foods. You will no longer "starve" yourself after a holiday eating binge, but will enjoy those quiet moments of exercise with your friends or spouse. You will no longer look in the mirror and be disappointed, but enjoy the comments of your friends and family who tell you you never looked better. In short, when you put Activetics— the diet-free plan—to work for you, the biggest reward will be your discovery that losing fat is fun. Have fun!

APPENDIX A

The Physiology of Fatness

Fat has not always been seen as the devil in disguise. Before World War I, it was considered a good guy. A real asset. Fatness was equated with success. Being fat was THE status symbol. Only those people who had servants, slaves, and lots of money were fat. They were the only ones who could afford to be fat. If you wanted to align yourself with the successful segment of society, you put on weight. You flaunted it. Boasted about it. Fat was where it was at.

Yet fatness was more than a social status symbol. People were convinced that fatness was associated with good health. Two generations ago, doctors encouraged parents to fatten their children. Before the discovery of antibiotics, a child's only defense against sickness was his or her body. When fevers attacked and laid the child low, parents and patient were told to "wait it out" and "hope and pray" that the child's immunity system would take over and fight the disease. The doctors reasoned that extra fat helped keep the child from starving to death during this difficult time. Therefore, parents were pleased to see their children put on fat. This attitude, as we shall see, is unfortunate. Underexercising and overfeeding children may be the major reasons for adult obesity and heart attack.

The result of our historical appreciation of fat and our current negative attitudes about it have produced a good deal of confusion. We're just not really sure about fat. We think it's bad so we do all sorts of crazy things to get rid of it. When we can't lose as much as we want, we rationalize our way into accepting the idea that being fat might not be so bad after all.

Ironically, all fat is not bad. Some is necessary. It helps keep us warm, provides us with energy, and is there for some very good biological reasons, i.e., survival during real famine and providing stamina when migrating. So the human body probably has a natural affinity toward getting fat.

Fat is the most misunderstood part of our anatomy. It's essential, but in modern-day American it can also be a liability—socially, health wise, and physically. It adds to your figure or shape in that it gives your body a smooth appearance. But it can also ruin your body with dimples and rolls in the wrong places.

Another plus is that it gives you a reserve of energy when sick, but too much can cause sickness and death. Socially, a certain amount of fat is good (if you're too thin people think you are seriously ill), but if you carry too much fat they brand you as undisciplined and careless. Today, there is a fine line between a necessary amount of fat and too much fat.

The one way out of this dilemma is to change our focus. Instead of worrying so much about fat, perhaps we should understand that some fat is good and too much fat is bad. And we must understand how much and what types are best. To set the record straight, let's take a look at fat as it relates to our appearance and well-being.

Fat is a specialized form of tissue. The main portion of the shape of a class ring (see illustration). The main portion of the cell contains a form of fat called triglyceride. This fat has the function of providing us energy. We need that energy when we think, walk, talk, run, swim, bicycle, or cross country ski. It also provides us with some energy when we fail to get the proper amounts of food—when dieting or starving.

At one end of the cell is the nucleus, which acts as the brain, giving the rest of the cell information on what to do. Collectively, the fat cells supply you with insulation, much like the layers of insulation surrounding a house, to protect you from the cold.

Most of this type of fat lies directly beneath the surface of your skin. Physiologists call it subcutaneous fat. This is the fat that affects your appearance. Triglyceride fat moves in and out of the subcutaneous cells. These cells are constantly replenished as you eat and play your way throughout the day. Should you be so unfortunate as to find yourself shipwrecked on a deserted island, these cells contain a store of energy that will sustain you for a while. The average person has a 40 day reserve of fat. However, if you deposit more fat into these cells than you need, you begin to develop those bulges and sags that create an unattractive shape.

Your body has a second type of fat which provides protection against blows. It is found in and around the vital organs such as the heart, liver, kidneys, spleen, as well as the bones, intestines, brain, and spinal cord. This fat, unlike the subcutaneous fat, is not easily lost. That's good. Even if you were to starve for a year, most of this fat would still be there protecting those vital parts of your body.

Throughout this book the emphasis has been on the fat which lies right beneath the surface of your skin. It is this subcutaneous fat which gives you an appearance problem.

How much subcutaneous fat you have on your body depends upon four factors. They are: 1) your heredity; 2) your sex; 3) your childhood activity and eating patterns; and 4) your activity and eating patterns today.

Heredity

Whether you like it or not, your parents influence you in many ways. One way is in your body type. Everyone comes in different shapes and sizes. Big ones, small ones, fat ones, skinny ones, and many in between. Bone structure, the number of fibers in the muscles, the length of your intestines, the number of fat cells, and many other factors play a major role in your basic body type.

For years, scientists have tried to classify people according to their body type. There have been varying degrees of success. Recently, somatotyping has come into use. Somatotyping is a method of classifying the human body into three basic types by estimating the balance of fat, muscle, and bone.

The three types, according to somatotyping are: endomorphic, mesomorphic, and ectomorphic. Endomorphs possess a roundness or softness to their bodies. They have little muscle development and small bones. Their weight is centered in the front of the body around the abdomen. Endomorphs have a natural tendency for softness and roundness. Consequently, they may always tend to look a little more pudgy than their friends. Fortunately, very few people fall into this extreme category. It may surprise you, but quite a few mesomorphs tend to slide into endomorphy because of poor living habits.

Mesomorphs are muscular and rugged. They are also big boned. Noted for hardness and ruggedness, they normally are of moderate height and are long necked and broad shouldered. Mesomorphs have large chests, relatively slender waists, and broad hips. They also tend to have a weight problem as they get older.

Their body type is the "macho image." Many men in the 1950's and 60's strove for this body type. Today, there's a definite trend toward thinness. But many men still want to develop a mesomorphic build or at least a tendency toward it. And according to a recent *Psychology Today* article, many women want their men to have bodies that look strong and well developed.

Ectomorphs are thin muscled and thin boned. Their bodies look fragile and delicate. The trunk is short. The neck, arms, and legs are long. There is very little fat on their bodies. Generally, however, the posture of the ectomorph is rather poor because it lacks the muscular strength for proper support. This is the body type exemplified by women's fashion magazines. Consequently, it is desired by most women. In reality, few women will ever achieve this body type. So don't frustrate yourself with expecting your body to look like a fashion model's.

Of course, not all of us fall into these three extreme categories. There are very few pure endomorphs, mesomorphs, or ectomorphs. We simply have a tendency towards fatness, muscularity, or thinness; and that tendency is largely determined by heredity.

It's a good idea to decide in which category you belong. It will give you a better idea of goals that you can expect to achieve in a weight and fat loss program. The following points will help you decide.

1. If there's a tendency in your family toward obesity (your mother and father tended to be fat), if you seem to gain weight easily AND have a difficult time losing it, you're probably an endomorph or have endomorphic tendencies. You may have a difficult time losing weight.

2. If you have a good physique [nice arm and leg development, good chest (bust), and flat stomach], it is probably an indication that you are a mesomorph. Maybe you had a good physique at one time, but things have gone to pot. You have mesomorphic tendencies. You gain weight easily and also find it easy to shed pounds. If that's the case, it's an indication that you are more of a mesomorph than anything else.

3. If there's natural tendency toward thinness in your family, you're probably an ectomorph. Especially if you have always found it difficult to put on weight or to develop well-formed muscles. You will always be thin and probably have little or no fat problem. Congratulations, you probably bought this book for someone else.

Look at the members of your family. Chances are they all have similar body shapes. If dad is short and fat, the boys tend to be short and fat. If mother is tall and slender, the girls probably are too. There are exceptions, but the family trend seems to hold true three out of four times. Look at your own family and see what you think.

Research supports this observation. One study showed that when both parents were slender *none* of the children were more than average weight, and most were very slender. On the other hand, when both parents were obese, none of the children were slender. All were of at least average weight and ⅓ were obese. Physiologists and psychologists continue to argue whether the influence of the parents on children has to do with genetics or behavior patterns. They just don't know.

Race, ethnic mix, or nationality also affect your susceptibility to fatness. Some scientists speculate that selected races are fatter because of their vigorous environment. The climate was so demanding that the food supply was not steady or plentiful. Consequently, over the years these races were genetically coded to accumulate fat far more efficiently than people who lived in more temperate and hospitable climates. Additionally, these same people needed more fat near the surface of the skin to keep them warm in harsh winters.

You would expect the people who developed in the colder climates to be heavier and have a greater amount of fat than those who developed in the hot, humid environments. An example would be the Eskimos and Northeast Europeans versus the Africans. Interestingly, height may also be related to this phenomenon of environment. Tall people tend to dissipate heat better while short people tend to conserve it. People who live in tropical climates tend to be taller than those who live in northern climates.

Like most theories, the heredity and environment explanation does not always hold water. The Somoans live in a hot, humid environment, have a lot of fat, and are short. Likewise, the Scandinavians, who live in a cooler climate, are relatively lean yet tall. Frankly, the science of obesity and human development is quite imperfect. The bottom line is that scientists really don't know. I suspect that 50% of your body size is determined by heredity, race, and genetics, and the other 50% has to do with your environment.

Your Sex

Interestingly, sex seems to play a significant role in body fat. Before puberty, girls and boys have about the same amount of body fat. At puberty, girls show a sudden spurt in weight and fat. The cause of the increase is that women need a critical minimum amount of fat deposited before they are able to menstruate, conceive, and bear children. As a result young women have a rapid increase of fat during adolescence. Although there is much variance from woman to woman, most girls tend to gain an average of 35 pounds in stored fat between the ages of 9 and 15. This substantial poundage has been calculated to provide enough energy for a woman to sustain a successful pregnancy and three months of post partum breast feeding without a serious energy drain on the mother and child.

Consequently, by the time a woman has reached full maturity, she has more body fat than her male counterpart. When she becomes pregnant, hormones—insulin, estrogen, and progesterone—act in such a way that fat deposits are encouraged. For example, progesterone may trigger increased appetites in women during the last week before menstruation or during pregnancy. Scientists speculate that when progesterone interacts with estrogen and insulin they trigger an extra deposit of fat in the woman's fat cells—particularly during pregnancy. And if a woman is susceptible to this kind of hormonal response, the problem is compounded. Several pregnancies may make her obese for life unless she's extremely judicious in her diet and very active.

Since women have more body fat than men, and men have more muscle than women, there are additional problems for women. Fat uses less oxygen than muscle; so that, all things being equal, women use fewer calories per minute than men—in *all* activities, including sleeping, studying, walking, working, and playing.

This discussion is confounded by some recent observations on women athletes—runners and gymnasts in particular. These individuals have exceptionally low percentages of body fat—5% or less. The question is, are they thin because of training and diet, or are they special people biologically? My personal feeling on this confusing issue is that you do inherit tendencies toward thinness, heaviness, or muscularity. But what you do in life allows you to move toward that potential. For example, I'm basically a mesomorphic or muscular person. My upper body is fairly well muscled, as are my legs. If I become sedentary (due to travel, study, book writing, etc.), I can put on weight easily. But If I run my allotted distance each day, I remain on the thin side. In fact, since I've been running quite vigorously for several years, I'm now thinner than I've ever been in my adult life.

My daughter Debbie is also a mesomorph. In fact, she has a tendency toward endomorphy. When she is sedentary she gains weight very easily—20 pounds in three months is entirely possible. But when she runs, swims, bicycles, and walks on a regular basis, she loses her fat. Quite frankly, she'll never be a skinny model type. She has too much muscle development. Her calves and legs are bigger than what would be acceptable for a model. Yet she is not fat: her percentage of body fat is normally under 15%. Debbie has a choice. She can become sedentary and have a big derriere and legs that are rather thin. Or she can run, have legs that are well muscled, and a small derriere. The choice is hers.

Once you understand your tendencies, you'll feel a lot better about yourself and place in life. And you'll understand how you can control your shape through exercise.

Your Eating & Activity As A Child

This section and the one that follows (Your Activity & Eating Patterns Today) is where the rubber hits the road. You can't do anything about your sex, race, and parents. But you sure can change your lifestyle. And that's what this book is all about—helping you help yourself to a better looking body.

I'll begin with fat cells, because the number of fat cells you have and the amount of fat in these cells are basic to this discussion.

Almost 20 years ago, Jules Hirsch, Ph.D., from Rockefeller University did some pioneering work on fatness. By studying animals and humans, Dr. Hirsch came up with some very interesting observations and comments about fat and obesity. In his experiments, he found that obesity is caused by either an excessive number of fat cells on the body, a disproportionate amount of fat in these cells, or a combination of the two. His research makes for a fascinating scenario.

First, Dr. Hirsch compared some obese people with non-obese individuals. He discovered that the obese weighed *twice* as much as the lean group and had *three* times more fat on their bodies. The obese had more fat in their fat cells (about 35% more) than the non-obese. In addition, the total number of fat cells in the obese subjects were about three times greater than the number of fat cells in the thin people. In fact, the obese had 75 billion fat cells while the normal weight people had only 27 billion. Obviously, there were some anatomical differences between the two groups. So Dr. Hirsch looked a little further. His analyses showed that obese people with the least amount of fat had the fewest fat cells of the obese. The most obese had the greatest number of fat cells. The amount of fat in the fat cells of the obese people was not much different. This suggested to the good doctor that there is probably an upper biological limit of how much fat a fat cell can hold. After a fat cell becomes a certain size, it can get no larger, so the cell number on your body becomes the key factor in determining your obesity. For even if the fat cells could stretch and increase their size twofold, their size could not account for the tremendous difference in the amount of fat carried by the obese versus the non-obese. Experimenters now conclude that 25 to 30 billion fat cells are the average number of cells in a person of average weight, while 50 billion cells are found on the moderately obese, and over 200 billion cells are found on the extremely obese.

Dr. Hirsch didn't stop with just counting fat cells. He wanted to know what happened when people lose weight. Do they lose cells, fat in the cells or a combination? His further investigations revealed that when obese adults lose weight, they decrease the amount of fat in the cells but not the cell number. In one experiment, 19 of Hirsch's subjects averaged 382 pounds. They also had 75 billion fat cells. When the subjects lost 101 pounds they still had 75 billion fat cells. The amount of fat in the cells had been reduced by about a third, however. When Hirsch had these same 19 people lose another 62 pounds they still had 75 billion fat cells. But the fat in the cells continued to shrink. Dr. Hirsch concluded that the number of fat cells will not change with a weight loss. The only thing that changes is the amount of fat in the cells.

The investigation and reasoning of Dr. Hirsch are basic to understanding the fat on your body: how your fat gets there and how you get rid of it. Frankly, the formerly obese person (from childhood) who reduces his or her body fat and weight to near average levels is not "cured" of obesity—at least in terms of his or her number of fat cells. Further more, a person with a preponderance of fat cells has a much more difficult time shedding pounds. One of the reasons may be that the large number of empty fat cells in the reduced obese person may be related to the appetite center of the brain. It is possible that the empty cells constantly signal the brain to be hungry. This theory has been dubbed "the plight of the starving fat cells."

But Dr. Hirsch wasn't finished. He wanted to explore fat cells in children. He asked these questions:

a) At what age is the fat cell number determined?
b) Can the fat cell number be modified at an early age?
To answer these questions, he conducted several more experiments on animals and humans. His data and the work of others which followed suggested that fat cells start to develop in the last three months of pregnancy. Then, during the first year of life, the cell number increases rapidly. The total number of fat cells is about three times greater at one year than at birth. The fat cell number grows slowly over the next 10 years. Then with the adolescence growth spurt (around 13), the number of fat cells increases until adulthood. At maturity, fat cells no longer increase in number.

As a result of his research, Hirsch and others refer to three critical periods of fat cell number growth. They include: the last three months of pregnancy, the first year of life, and adolescence. While Hirsch was able to identify these critical periods of cell number growth, neither he nor others have been able to determine whether fat cell size and number can be altered before adulthood, or whether the size and number are determined by genetics.

There is tantalizing evidence, however, that the number may be depressed by the prudent living habits of fewer calories and more exercise during childhood and adolescence. Animal experiments suggest that animals which are fed fewer calories in their earlier years have fewer fat cells when they are older. Additionally, animals which are exercised vigorously during their early growth period have fewer fat cells and smaller fat cells when they are adults.

The upshot of this whole discussion is that a prudent life of fewer calories and more exercising during childhood and adolescence make for thin adults. Also, if you gain weight as an adult, you'll probably have an easier time losing it.

So, don't fatten up your children and plunk them down in front of the TV set. Don't shower them with chocolate chip cookies and car rides to and from the store as your method of showering them with love. Show them love by keeping them physically active. Encourage them to run, walk, bike or swim 30 minutes four times a week. And watch their nutrition. They'll love you for it when they're adults.

Your Activity & Eating Patterns Today

Most obese people get that way by being just a few calories a day out of balance. Chapter #1 and the rest of the book highlighted this concept and the theory need not be presented again. By now you know that stepping up your physical activity is the most convenient and healthful way to lose weight. It goes directly to the cause of obesity—a life of sedentary living.

Getting Fat In & Out Of Your Cells

How the fat gets in and out of a fat cell has not been conclusively proven. But scientists are putting the jigsaw puzzle together. It is believed that the number of fat cells, the rate of fat circulation in your blood, enzyme action, and nervous and hormonal factors all play a role.

Each cluster of fat cells is serviced by tiny blood vessels and nerves. When you eat more calories than you burn off, your liver converts these extra calories into a triglyceride. The triglyceride is then carried by the circulatory system to your fat cells. There, complicated biochemical changes and adjustments permit the fat to enter the fat cell. It is stored in the cell temporarily as a triglyceride. It is probable that testosterone and corticoids play crucial roles in depositing the fat.

When your body requires extra energy due to starvation, long distance runs, or temporary body adjustments, fat must be gotten out of the fat cell. It is postulated that adrenalin is released. The adrenalin increases your blood glucose levels and enzymes break down fat and prepare it for release into the bloodstream. A growth hormone may also play a key role in the breaking down of the fat. The circulatory system then transports the fat back to the liver to be broken down into usable energy for the body. Of course, the entire procedure of fat breakdown is probably activated by the nervous system. It is also suggested that testosterone and corticoid may activate fat removal.

Dr. Jerome Knittle, Director of Nutrition and Metabolism at Mt. Sinai School of Medicine in New York City, sums all this up nicely: "Hormonal actions can markedly affect adipose cell size, by virtue of their effect on metabolism and cellular proliferation." In other words, getting fat into and out of the cells is the function of a complicated biochemical mechanism that involves almost every body system. It demonstrates that fat deposit and *removal* is contingent upon a caloric imbalance—not massage, pills, or some exotic spa device.

APPENDIX B

Measuring Your Body Fat And The Fitness Finder

As indicated in Chapter #6, the most accurate method for estimating body fat is through hydrostatic weighing. This technique weighs you both in and out of water. Since fat is lighter than water and lean body tissue is heavier than water the researcher can determine how much of your weight is fat and how much is bone, muscle, and organ tissue. But the test is not practical for most people.

Recently, physiologists and nutritionists have used a device called the skinfold caliper to estimate a person's percentage of total body fat. It is practical for a physician or clinician to use, but rather expensive for the layman—it costs around $150.* Unfortunately, the device is not readily available for most people. To aid you, however, I've devised a less expensive, yet more accurate (and certainly better conceptional) way than height/weight tables to estimate your ideal weight. It's done by taking a few simple measurements with the Fitness Finder. Pages 293 and 294 show how to make your own Fitness Finder.

---

*If at all possible it is best to have this test done by an experienced tester with a caliper which conforms to the specifications established by the Committee on Food and Nutrition of the National Research Council of the United States. You may purchase such a caliper from a local medical supply house or by writing to Fitness Finders, Box 507, Spring Arbor, MI 49283. The cost is $150.00. A plastic model is available for $5.95 from the same address.

The Fitness Finder will help indicate what percentage of your total body weight is fat. Once you have this information, you can establish your ideal weight based on your percentage of body fat.

Before you start measuring, let me explain quickly how and why the Fitness Finder works:

Most people under the age of 50 have at least half of their body fat stored directly beneath the skin (subcutaneous fat). Additionally, when people put on extra fat, most of it is deposited there. By measuring the fold produced when the skin and tissue just under it are firmly grasped, it is possible to get a good idea of how much fat is present on the body.

Since two different studies*—one for men and one for women, were used to determine percentage of body fat, you will be required to follow directions based on your sex and age. The men will take four measurements and the women three.

Note: These are only estimates and not to be taken as a definitive diagnosis of fatness or obesity—for that an experienced tester is recommended.

Procedure

1. Practice taking as many skinfolds as you possibly can. The more you take, the more accurate you will be.
2. All measurements are taken on the right side of the body.
3. When taking measurements, firmly grasp the fold of the skin between the left thumb and forefinger and lift up. Take this measurement by bringing your fingers over the top as illustrated. Once you have the subcutaneous fat between your thumb and forefinger, pinch and lift the fold several times to make sure you do not get into the muscle. It is generally recommended that the fold be the thinnest fold you

---

*Jackson, A. S. and M. L. Pollock. "Generalized Equations for Predicting Body Density of Men." British Journal of Nutrition. 40:497–504, 1978.

Jackson, A. S., M. L. Pollock, and A. Ward. "Generalized Equations for Predicting Body Density of Women." Medicine and Science in Sports and Exercise. 12:175–182, 1980.

Making Your Own Fitness Finder

First, get tracing paper, pencil, thumbtack, cardboard, eraser, and scissors.

Second, make your caliper by tracing the pattern on the next page and transferring it onto some cardboard. Once the parts are cut out, a simple pivot can be made by sticking a straight pin or thumbtack through the hole marks and into an eraser.

Third, get a partner and take the measurements recommended for your sex.

Caution: The measurements are only estimates. It is best to record your total millimeters of fat. Then after you have exercised for 12 weeks, check your total millimeters again. The total should be lower if you have exercised at your target heart rate level for 30 minutes or longer, four or more times a week.

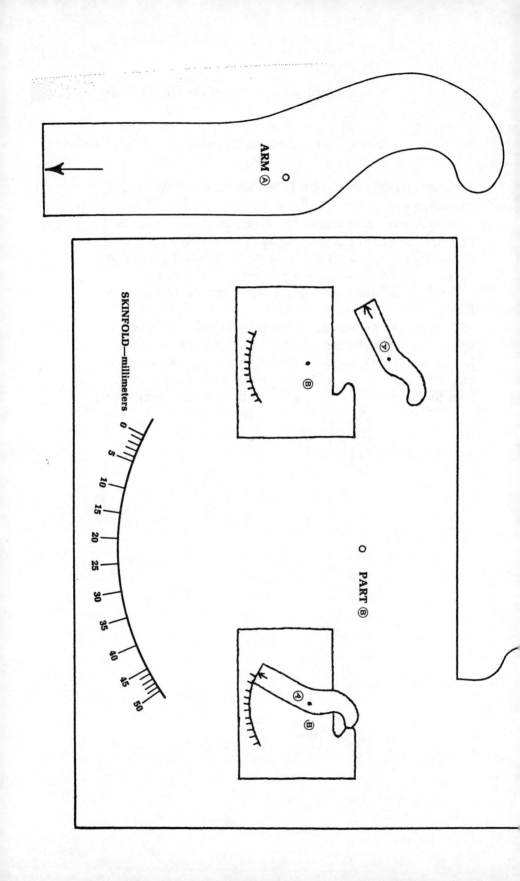

ARM Ⓐ

SKINFOLD—millimeters

PART Ⓑ

can gather without simply pinching the skin.

4. Continue to hold the skinfold *tightly* with the thumb and forefinger and place the contact surface of the Fitness Finder just below the thumb and forefinger. Approximately ¼ of an inch is fine.
5. Do not let go of the skinfold. Move the Fitness Finder in as tightly as possible so you have an indentation. Take the reading to the nearest half millimeter. Release the grip and take at the next site.
6. Measure all of your skinfolds once. Then repeat the sequence two or more times so that you have a total of three measures on each fold. If at all possible, take the additional measurements without looking at your preceding measures.
7. Average the three measures for each site.
8. If you feel that you want a more accurate measure, have someone else take the measurement as well.

Use the procedure just outlined for the various sites listed below.

Men—Four skinfold sites.

Chest—Take a diagonal fold on the pectoral line midway between the nipple and your armpit. My chest measurement is_____.

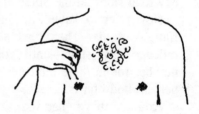

Hip—Take a diagonal fold just above the crest of the illium. My hip measurement is_____.

Abdomen—Take a vertical fold approximately one inch to the right of your belly button. My abdomen measurement is_____.

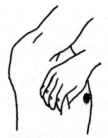

Armpit—Take a vertical fold on the upper part of your armpit at nipple level. My armpit measurement is_____.

My total skinfold measurements are_____.

Now refer to Table 22. On the far left, find the sum of the four skinfolds. Then read across the column horizontally—mileage map style—until you reach your age column. The number found there indicates your percentage of body fat. My percent body fat is_____.

Example: If you had four skinfolds which added up to 75 and you're 35 years of age, you would have 19% body fat.

Table 22
PERCENT FAT ESTIMATES FOR MEN
SUM OF FOUR SKINFOLDS

Age to Last Year

Sum of 4 Skinfolds	18 to 22	23 to 27	28 to 32	33 to 37	38 to 42	43 to 47	48 to 52	53 to 57	58 and older
8 – 12	2	3	3	4	4	5	6	6	7
13 – 17	3	4	5	5	6	6	7	8	8
18 – 22	5	5	6	6	7	8	8	9	10
23 – 27	6	6	7	8	8	9	10	10	11
28 – 32	7	8	8	9	10	10	11	11	12
33 – 37	8	9	10	10	11	11	12	13	13
38 – 42	10	10	11	11	12	13	13	14	14
43 – 47	11	11	12	13	13	14	14	15	16
48 – 52	12	12	13	14	14	15	16	16	17
53 – 57	13	14	14	15	15	16	17	17	18
58 – 62	14	15	15	16	16	17	18	18	19
63 – 67	15	16	16	17	18	18	19	19	20
68 – 72	16	17	17	18	19	19	20	20	21
73 – 77	17	18	18	19	20	20	21	21	22
78 – 82	18	19	19	20	21	21	22	22	23
83 – 87	19	20	20	21	22	22	23	23	24
88 – 92	20	21	21	22	22	23	24	24	25
93 – 97	21	21	22	23	23	24	25	24	26
98 – 102	22	22	23	24	24	25	25	26	27
103 – 107	23	23	24	24	25	26	26	27	28
108 – 112	23	24	25	25	26	27	27	28	28
113 – 117	24	25	25	26	27	27	28	29	29
118 – 122	25	26	26	27	27	28	29	29	30
123 – 127	26	26	27	28	28	29	29	30	31
128 – 132	26	27	28	28	29	30	30	31	31
133 – 137	27	28	28	29	30	30	31	31	32
138 – 142	28	28	29	30	30	31	31	32	33
143 – 147	28	29	30	30	31	32	32	33	33
148 – 152	29	30	30	31	31	32	33	33	34
153 – 157	30	30	31	31	32	33	33	34	35
158 – 162	30	31	31	32	33	33	34	34	35
163 – 167	31	31	32	33	33	34	34	35	36
168 – 172	31	32	32	33	34	34	35	36	36
173 – 177	32	32	33	34	34	35	35	36	37
178 – 182	32	33	33	34	35	35	36	36	37
183 – 187	33	33	34	34	35	36	36	37	37
188 – 192	33	34	34	35	35	36	37	37	38
193 – 197	33	34	35	35	36	36	37	38	38
198 – 202	34	34	35	35	36	37	37	38	39
203 – 207	34	35	35	36	36	37	38	38	39

Women—Three skinfold sites

Back of arm—Take a vertical fold on the back of the arm midway between your shoulder and elbow joint. My back of arm measurement is_____.

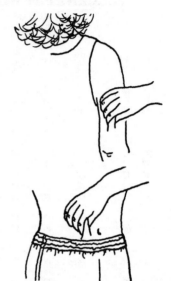

Abdomen—Take a vertical fold approximately one inch to the right of your belly button. My abdomen measurement is_____.

Hip—Take a diagonal fold just above the crest of the illium. My hip measurement is_____.

When you have one reliable measure at each site, add the three measures together. Record your total skinfold measure. My total skinfold measurements are_____.

Now refer to Table 23. On the far left, find the sum of the three skinfolds. Then read across the column horizontally—mileage map style—until you reach your age column. The number found there indicates your percentage of body fat. My percent body fat is_____.

Example: If you had three skinfolds which added up to 56 and you are 31 years of age, you would have 25% body fat.

Table 23
PERCENT FAT ESTIMATES FOR WOMEN
SUM OF THREE SKINFOLDS
Age to Last Year

Sum of 3 Skinfolds	18 to 22	23 to 27	28 to 32	33 to 37	38 to 42	43 to 47	48 to 52	53 to 57	58 and older
8 – 12	9	9	9	9	10	10	10	10	10
13 – 17	11	11	11	11	12	12	12	12	12
18 – 22	13	13	13	13	13	14	14	14	14
23 – 26	15	15	15	15	15	15	16	16	16
28 – 32	16	16	17	17	17	17	17	18	18
33 – 37	18	18	18	19	19	19	19	19	19
38 – 42	20	20	20	20	20	21	21	21	21
43 – 47	21	21	22	22	22	22	22	23	23
48 – 52	23	23	23	23	24	24	24	24	24
53 – 57	24	24	25	25	25	25	25	26	26
58 – 62	26	26	26	26	27	27	27	27	27
63 – 67	27	27	27	28	28	28	28	28	29
68 – 72	28	29	29	29	29	30	30	30	30
73 – 77	30	30	30	30	30	31	31	31	31
78 – 82	31	31	31	31	32	32	32	32	32
83 – 87	32	32	32	33	33	33	33	33	34
88 – 92	33	33	34	34	34	34	34	34	35
93 – 97	34	34	35	35	35	35	35	35	36
98 – 102	35	35	36	36	36	36	36	36	37
103 – 107	36	36	36	37	37	37	37	37	38
108 – 112	37	37	37	38	38	38	38	38	38
113 – 117	38	38	38	38	39	39	39	39	39
118 – 122	39	39	39	39	39	39	40	40	40
123 – 127	39	39	40	40	40	40	40	41	41
128 – 132	40	40	40	40	41	41	41	41	41
133 – 137	41	41	41	41	41	41	42	42	42
138 – 142	41	41	41	42	42	42	42	42	43
143 – 147	42	42	42	42	42	42	43	43	43
148 – 152	42	42	42	43	43	43	43	43	43
153 – 157	42	43	43	43	43	43	43	44	44
158 – 162	43	43	42	43	43	44	44	44	44
163 – 167	43	43	43	43	44	44	44	44	44
168 – 172	43	43	43	44	44	44	44	44	45
173 – 177	43	43	44	44	44	44	44	45	45
178 – 182	43	44	44	44	44	44	44	45	45

How To Find Your Individual Ideal Weight

Let's assume your Fitness Finder results are in, and you now know your body's fat/lean ratio. If you're a woman and the total percentage of fat on your body is 19% or less, congratulations! You may still want to firm up some of those muscles, but you are definitely not obese, and fat poses no real threat to your health. The same goes for any man who comes in at 15% total body fat or less.

But, if your body fat is above 19% (women) and 15% (men), you should attempt to reduce those percentages, for the sake of both your health and looks. If the height/weight tables say your weight is okay, in your case they're wrong.

As we mentioned previously, our society discriminates against those who carry more fat than is good for them, and here's another example of that discrimination: those of you with fat/lean ratios that are too high will have to make another quick calculation—this time to determine your Ideal Weight.

To get this figure, turn to Table 24 or 25· (depends upon your sex) on page 302 or 303 It, too, is meant to be read mileage-chart style. For example: to get the Ideal Weight for a male, presently weighing 175 pounds, whose total body fat is 19%, look down the column of figures under the Percent Fat heading until you find the number 19. Then find the vertical column extending from 175 pounds. Where the two columns intersect, there's the number 167—which indicates that 167 pounds is what this particular man should be aiming for.

For a woman whose total body weight is 25% fat and who presently weights 135 pounds, turn to the woman's table on page 303, then locate the number 25 in the Percent Fat column at the far left. Under the column headed Body Weight, look for the number 135. Where the two columns intersect, you see the number 125 which is the Ideal Weight for this woman.

Now it's time to find your own personal Ideal Weight using your present weight and your percent of total body fat as indicated by the Fitness Finder. If you wish, keep a record of

your Ideal Weight by entering it in the space provided below.
MY IDEAL WEIGHT IS————.

Now that you have your Ideal Weight, you have a goal. Does it jibe with what the height/weight tables say is right for you. If it does, all well and good. If it doesn't, then forget those tables—you're one of the many for whom they are useless.

If your percentage of body fat is below what it's supposed to be, that's great. Don't worry about it. Some people think that gives them an opportunity to gain extra weight. I don't agree. This means that your percentage is lower than what is listed as the "best" for most people. It doesn't mean you're unhealthy.

One more very important point: Some people, when they get to their *ideal* weight and percentage of body fat, may still think they're fat. The figures 15% (men) and 19% (women) refer to percentages which are best for health reasons. Some people are quite demanding on their physique and want extremely low levels of fat. They are usually former athletes, cheerleaders, or models who at one time had very low percentages of fat and keep comparing themselves to how they previously looked. Consequently, for cosmetic reasons, these people may want to have their body fat percentages lower than 15 and 19%.

Table 24
IDEAL WEIGHT TABLE
Ideal Weight for 15% Fat (Men)

Body Weight (lbs.)

	% of Fat	120	125	130	135	140	145	150	155	160	165	170	175	180	185	190	195	200	205	210	215	220	225	230	235	240
Ideal Weight	15	120	125	130	135	140	145	150	155	160	165	170	175	180	185	190	195	200	205	210	215	220	225	230	235	240
	17	117	122	127	132	136	142	146	151	156	161	166	171	176	181	186	190	195	200	205	210	215	220	225	229	234
Borderline	19	114	119	124	129	133	138	143	148	152	157	162	167	171	176	181	186	190	195	200	205	210	214	219	224	229
Phase	21	111	116	121	125	130	135	139	144	149	153	158	162	167	172	176	181	186	190	195	200	204	209	214	218	223
	23	109	113	118	122	127	131	136	140	145	149	154	158	163	167	172	176	181	186	190	195	199	204	208	213	217
	25	106	110	115	119	123	128	132	137	141	145	150	154	159	163	167	172	176	181	185	189	194	198	203	207	211
Range of	27	103	107	111	116	120	124	129	133	137	141	146	150	154	159	163	167	171	176	180	184	189	193	197	201	206
Overfatness	29	100	104	108	113	117	121	125	129	133	137	142	146	150	154	158	162	167	171	175	179	183	188	192	196	200
	31	97	101	105	109	113	117	121	125	130	134	138	142	146	150	154	158	162	166	170	174	178	182	186	190	194
	33	94	98	102	106	110	114	118	122	126	130	134	137	141	145	149	153	157	161	165	169	173	177	181	185	189
	35	91	95	99	103	107	110	114	118	122	126	130	133	137	141	145	149	152	156	160	164	168	171	175	179	183
	37	89	92	96	100	103	107	111	114	118	122	125	129	133	137	140	144	148	151	155	159	162	166	170	174	177
	39	86	89	93	96	100	104	107	111	114	118	121	125	129	132	136	139	143	146	150	154	157	161	164	168	171

For a male presently weighing 175 pounds, whose total body fat is 19%, look down the column of figures under the Percent Fat heading until you find the number 19. Then find the vertical column extending from 175 pounds. Where the two columns intersect, there's the number 167—which indicates that 167 pounds is this man's Ideal Weight.

Table 25
IDEAL WEIGHT TABLE
Ideal Weight for 19% Fat (Women)

Body Weight (lbs.)

	% of Fat	90	95	100	105	110	115	120	125	130	135	140	145	150	155	160	165	170	175	180	185	190	195	200	205	210	215
Ideal Weight	19	90	95	100	105	110	115	120	125	130	135	140	145	150	155	160	165	170	175	180	185	190	195	200	205	210	215
	21	88	93	98	102	107	112	117	122	127	132	137	141	146	151	156	161	166	171	176	180	185	190	195	200	205	210
Borderline	23	86	90	95	100	105	109	114	119	124	128	133	138	143	147	152	157	162	166	171	176	181	185	190	195	200	205
Phase	25	83	88	93	97	102	107	111	116	120	125	130	134	139	144	148	153	157	162	167	171	176	181	185	190	194	198
	27	81	86	90	95	99	104	108	113	117	122	126	131	135	140	144	149	153	158	162	167	171	176	180	185	189	193
	29	79	83	88	92	96	101	105	110	114	118	123	127	132	136	140	145	149	153	158	162	167	171	175	180	184	188
	31	77	81	85	89	94	98	102	107	111	115	119	124	128	132	136	141	145	149	153	158	162	166	170	175	179	183
	33	74	79	83	87	91	95	99	103	108	112	116	120	124	128	132	137	141	145	149	153	157	161	165	170	174	178
Range of	35	72	76	80	84	88	92	96	100	104	108	112	116	120	124	128	132	136	140	145	149	153	157	161	165	169	173
Overfatness	37	70	74	78	82	86	89	93	97	101	105	109	113	117	121	124	128	132	136	140	144	148	152	156	159	163	167
	39	68	72	75	79	83	87	90	94	98	102	105	109	113	117	121	124	128	132	136	139	143	147	151	154	158	162

For a woman presently weighing 135 pounds, whose total body fat is 25%, look down the column of figures under the Percent Fat heading until you find the number 25. Then find the vertical column extending from 135 pounds. Where the two columns intersect, there's the number 125—which indicates that 125 pounds is this woman's Ideal Weight.

APPENDIX C
Pulse Rate And Calories

Whenever I lead a workout class members will ask me, "How many calories did we burn off?" Usually, I could give them an approximate answer. Some time ago, however, someone said to me, "Wouldn't it be nice if you could use your pulse rate to estimate the number of calories you used in a workout, run, or game of tennis." At first, I said no. The only way you can check your calories burned is to use the activity calories charts. But the thought intrigued me. And the more I thought about it I realized that someone just might be able to estimate the calories used via pulse rates. Especially in those situations where researchers had not yet calculated the calories for certain exercises or activity regimens.

Researchers tell us that there's a relationship between calories and heart rate. Because of these correlations I set out to determine if your pulse rate could be used as a guide for guesstimating the number of calories you use when you participate in aerobic type exercise. To make a long story short I did develop a formula and the result is the charts which follow.

To use these charts properly you need to know several things: your sex, weight, physical condition, resting heart rate, and heart rate when exercising. First turn to the male or female charts depending on your sex. Then find the chart which describes your physical condition—that is very poor, poor, fair, good, or excellent. These fitness designations are based on the

Three Mile Walking Test found on page 179 of this book. Of course, some other bona fide cardiovascular test may also be used.

Once you have the proper chart you may then proceed with the following: On the far left of the chart is a space for you to record your resting heart rate. To get your true resting heart rate take it upon awakening in the morning while still lying in bed. It is best if you awaken on your own accord—not by an alarm clock (it will cause your pulse rate to increase).

When you have obtained your resting heart rate record it in the appropriate space (see the example on page 307). After you have recorded your resting heart rate, add each recommended increase (somewhere between 8 to 12 beats depending upon your fitness level). The chart selected will remind you.

For example, if you're classified as being in very poor physical condition you would add a multiple of 12 to your resting heart rate. If your resting heart rate is 60, the next step would be 72, followed by 84, 96, 108, 120, etc. See the following sample chart.

Your Heart Rate		Weight in Pounds		
		90 or less	91–96	97–102
Resting	*60*	.86	.89	.91
12	*72*	1.72	1.78	1.82
24	*84*	2.58	2.67	2.73
36	*96*	3.44	3.56	2.64
48	*108*	4.30	4.45	4.55
60	*120*	5.16	5.34	5.46
72	*132*	6.02	6.23	6.37
84	*144*	6.88	7.12	7.28
96	*156*	7.74	8.01	8.19
108	*168*	8.60	8.90	9.10
120	*180*	9.46	9.79	10.01
132	*192*	10.32	10.68	10.92
144	*204*	11.18	11.57	11.83
156	*216*	12.04	12.46	12.75

Since all of us have different heart rates, the determination of your resting heart rate is crucial. Be certain you get a good reading or the charts will be very inaccurate. I also feel that the charts become more reliable once you are past the double line.

Remember: You are merely guesstimating your calories expended. But I have found many class members to be fascinated by this technique.

The charts work best with aerobic activities. Other exercises make the charts spurious.

Formula Used For Guesstimating Calories Used From Pulse Rate

If you want a formula for how I arrived at the figures on these charts, here it is:

Formula:

$$\frac{\dfrac{\dfrac{B}{M} - R}{\text{(MET) W}}}{\dfrac{C}{1{,}000}} \times 4.825$$

Let B = Total number of beats during exercise.
   M = Minutes of exercise.
   R = Resting heart rate.
   C = Physical condition: 12 = very poor
                                  11 = poor
                                  10 = fair
                                  9 = very good
                                  8 = excellent
MET = Milliliters of oxygen per MET increase
       (See Chart #1).
  W = Weight in kilograms.
1,000 = Used to change from milliliters to liters.

Table 26

VERY POOR—MEN

Calories Used Per Minute Based on Body Weight & Heart Rate

Body Weight (lbs.)

Your Heart Rate	90 or less	91-96	97-102	103-107	108-112	113-118	119-123	124-129	130-135	136-140	141-146	147-152	153-157	158-162	163-168	169-173	174-178	179-183	184-189	190 or more
Resting	.86	.89	.91	.94	.97	.99	1.02	1.04	1.07	1.10	1.12	1.15	1.18	1.20	1.23	1.25	1.28	1.31	1.33	1.36
+12	1.72	1.78	1.82	1.88	1.94	1.98	2.04	2.08	2.14	2.20	2.24	2.3	2.36	2.4	2.46	2.5	2.56	2.62	2.66	2.72
+24	2.58	2.67	2.73	2.82	2.91	2.95	3.06	3.12	3.21	3.3	3.36	3.45	3.54	3.6	3.69	3.75	3.84	3.93	3.99	4.08
+48	3.44	3.56	3.64	3.76	3.88	3.96	4.08	4.16	4.28	4.4	4.48	4.6	4.72	4.8	4.92	5	5.12	5.24	5.32	5.44
+60	4.30	4.45	4.55	4.7	4.85	4.95	5.10	5.2	5.35	5.5	5.6	5.75	5.9	6.	6.15	6.25	6.4	6.55	6.65	6.8
+72	5.16	5.34	5.46	5.64	5.82	5.94	6.12	6.24	6.42	6.6	6.72	6.9	7.08	7.2	7.38	7.5	7.68	7.86	7.98	8.16
+84	6.02	6.23	6.37	6.58	6.79	6.93	7.14	7.28	7.49	7.7	7.84	8.05	8.26	8.4	8.61	8.75	8.96	9.17	9.31	9.52
+96	6.88	7.12	7.28	7.52	7.76	7.92	8.16	8.32	8.56	8.8	8.96	9.2	9.44	9.6	9.84	10.0	10.24	10.48	10.64	10.88
+108	7.74	8.01	8.19	8.46	8.73	8.91	9.18	9.36	9.63	9.9	10.08	10.35	10.62	10.8	11.07	11.25	11.52	11.79	11.97	12.24
+120	8.60	8.90	9.1	9.4	9.7	9.9	10.2	10.4	10.7	11.0	11.2	11.5	11.8	12.	12.3	12.5	12.8	13.1	13.3	13.6
+132	9.46	9.79	10.01	10.34	10.67	10.89	11.22	11.44	11.77	12.1	12.32	12.65	12.98	13.2	13.53	13.75	14.08	14.41	14.63	14.96
+144	10.32	10.68	10.92	11.28	11.64	11.88	12.24	12.48	12.84	13.2	13.44	13.8	14.16	14.4	14.76	15.	15.36	15.72	15.96	16.32
+156	11.18	11.57	11.83	12.22	12.61	12.87	13.26	13.52	13.91	14.3	14.56	14.95	15.34	15.6	15.99	16.25	16.64	17.03	17.29	17.68
+168	12.04	12.46	12.74	13.16	13.58	13.86	14.28	14.56	14.98	15.4	15.68	16.1	16.52	16.8	17.22	17.5	17.92	18.34	18.62	19.04

In order to find the number of calories you have used per minute, enter your resting heart rate in the first space. Then fill in the subsequent spaces of the heart rate column by adding the indicated multiple of 12 to your resting heart rate.

Table 27

POOR—MEN
Calories Used Per Minute Based on Body Weight & Heart Rate

Body Weight (lbs.)

Your Heart Rate	90 or less	91-96	97-102	103-107	108-112	113-118	119-123	124-129	130-135	136-140	141-146	147-152	153-157	158-162	163-168	169-173	174-178	179-183	184-189	190 or more
Resting	.86	.89	.91	.94	.97	.99	1.02	1.04	1.07	1.10	1.12	1.15	1.18	1.20	1.23	1.25	1.28	1.31	1.33	1.36
+11	1.72	1.78	1.82	1.88	1.94	1.98	2.04	2.08	2.14	2.20	2.24	2.3	2.36	2.4	2.46	2.5	2.56	2.62	2.66	2.72
+22	2.58	2.67	2.73	2.82	2.91	2.95	3.06	3.12	3.21	3.3	3.36	3.45	3.54	3.6	3.69	3.75	3.84	3.93	3.99	4.08
+33	3.44	3.56	3.64	3.76	3.88	3.96	4.08	4.16	4.28	4.4	4.48	4.6	4.72	4.8	4.92	5.	5.12	5.24	5.32	5.44
+44	4.30	4.45	4.55	4.7	4.85	4.95	5.10	5.2	5.35	5.5	5.6	5.75	5.9	6.	6.15	6.25	6.4	6.55	6.65	6.8
+55	5.16	5.34	5.46	5.64	5.82	5.94	6.12	6.24	6.42	6.6	6.72	6.9	7.08	7.2	7.38	7.5	7.68	7.86	7.98	8.16
+66	6.02	6.23	6.37	6.58	6.79	6.93	7.14	7.28	7.49	7.7	7.84	8.05	8.26	8.4	8.61	8.75	8.96	9.17	9.31	9.52
+77	6.88	7.12	7.28	7.52	7.76	7.92	8.16	8.32	8.56	8.8	8.96	9.2	9.44	9.6	9.84	10.0	10.24	10.48	10.64	10.88
+88	7.74	8.01	8.19	8.46	8.73	8.91	9.18	9.36	9.63	9.9	10.08	10.35	10.62	10.8	11.07	11.25	11.52	11.79	11.97	12.24
+99	8.60	8.90	9.1	9.4	9.7	9.9	10.2	10.4	10.7	11.0	11.2	11.5	11.8	12.	12.3	12.5	12.8	13.1	13.3	13.6
+110	9.46	9.79	10.01	10.34	10.67	10.89	11.22	11.44	11.77	12.1	12.32	12.65	12.98	13.2	13.53	13.75	14.08	14.41	14.63	14.96
+121	10.32	10.68	10.92	11.28	11.64	11.88	12.24	12.48	12.84	13.2	13.44	13.8	14.16	14.4	14.76	15.	15.36	15.72	15.96	16.32
+132	11.18	11.57	11.83	12.22	12.61	12.87	13.26	13.52	13.91	14.3	14.56	14.95	15.34	15.6	15.99	16.25	16.64	17.03	17.29	17.68
+143	12.04	12.46	12.74	13.16	13.58	13.86	14.28	14.56	14.98	15.4	15.68	16.1	16.52	16.8	17.22	17.5	17.92	18.34	18.62	19.04

In order to find the number of calories you have used per minute, enter your resting heart rate in the first space. Then fill in the subsequent spaces of the heart rate column by adding the indicated multiple of 11 to your resting heart rate.

Table 28

FAIR—MEN

Calories Used Per Minute Based on Body Weight & Heart Rate

Body Weight (lbs.)

Your Heart Rate	90 or less	91-96	97-102	103-107	108-112	113-118	119-123	124-129	130-135	136-140	141-146	147-152	153-157	158-162	163-168	169-173	174-178	179-183	184-189	190 or more
Resting	.86	.89	.91	.94	.97	.99	1.02	1.04	1.07	1.10	1.12	1.15	1.18	1.20	1.23	1.25	1.28	1.31	1.33	1.36
+10	1.72	1.78	1.82	1.88	1.94	1.98	2.04	2.08	2.14	2.20	2.24	2.3	2.36	2.4	2.46	2.5	2.56	2.62	2.66	2.72
+20	2.58	2.67	2.73	2.82	2.91	2.95	3.06	3.12	3.21	3.3	3.36	3.45	3.54	3.6	3.69	3.75	3.84	3.93	3.99	4.08
+30	3.44	3.56	3.64	3.76	3.88	3.96	4.08	4.16	4.28	4.4	4.48	4.6	4.72	4.8	4.92	5.	5.12	5.24	5.32	5.44
+40	4.30	4.45	4.55	4.7	4.85	4.95	5.10	5.2	5.35	5.5	5.6	5.75	5.9	6.	6.15	6.25	6.4	6.55	6.65	6.8
+50	5.16	5.34	5.46	5.64	5.82	5.94	6.12	6.24	6.42	6.6	6.72	6.9	7.08	7.2	7.38	7.5	7.68	7.86	7.98	8.16
+60	6.02	6.23	6.37	6.58	6.79	6.93	7.14	7.28	7.49	7.7	7.84	8.05	8.26	8.4	8.61	8.75	8.96	9.17	9.31	9.52
+70	6.88	7.12	7.28	7.52	7.76	7.92	8.16	8.32	8.56	8.8	8.96	9.2	9.44	9.6	9.84	10.0	10.24	10.48	10.64	10.88
+80	7.74	8.01	8.19	8.46	8.73	8.91	9.18	9.36	9.63	9.9	10.08	10.35	10.62	10.8	11.07	11.25	11.52	11.79	11.97	12.24
+90	8.60	8.90	9.1	9.4	9.7	9.9	10.2	10.4	10.7	11.0	11.2	11.5	11.8	12.	12.3	12.5	12.8	13.1	13.3	13.6
+100	9.46	9.79	10.01	10.34	10.67	10.89	11.22	11.44	11.77	12.1	12.32	12.65	12.98	13.2	13.53	13.75	14.08	14.41	14.63	14.96
+110	10.32	10.68	10.92	11.28	11.64	11.88	12.24	12.48	12.84	13.2	13.44	13.8	14.16	14.4	14.76	15.	15.36	15.72	15.96	16.32
+120	11.18	11.57	11.83	12.22	12.61	12.87	13.26	13.52	13.91	14.3	14.56	14.95	15.34	15.6	15.99	16.25	16.64	17.03	17.29	17.68
+130	12.04	12.46	12.74	13.16	13.58	13.86	14.28	14.56	14.98	15.4	15.68	16.2	16.52	16.8	17.22	17.5	17.92	18.34	18.62	19.04

In order to find the number of calories you have used per minute, enter your resting heart rate in the first space. Then fill in the subsequent spaces of the heart rate column by adding the indicated multiple of 10 to your resting heart rate.

Table 29

GOOD—MEN

Calories Used Per Minute Based on Body Weight & Heart Rate

Body Weight (lbs.)

Your Heart Rate	90 or less	91-96	97-102	103-107	108-112	113-118	119-123	124-129	130-135	136-140	141-146	147-152	153-157	158-162	163-168	169-173	174-178	179-183	184-189	190 or more
Resting	.86	.89	.91	.94	.97	.99	1.02	1.04	1.07	1.10	1.12	1.15	1.18	1.20	1.23	1.25	1.28	1.31	1.33	1.36
+9	1.72	1.78	1.82	1.88	1.94	1.98	2.04	2.08	2.14	2.20	2.24	2.3	2.36	2.4	2.46	2.5	2.56	2.62	2.66	2.72
+18	2.58	2.67	2.73	2.82	2.91	2.95	3.06	3.12	3.21	3.3	3.36	3.45	3.54	3.6	3.69	3.75	3.84	3.93	3.99	4.08
+27	3.44	3.56	3.64	3.76	3.88	3.96	4.08	4.16	4.28	4.4	4.48	4.6	4.72	4.8	4.92	5.	5.12	5.24	5.32	5.44
+34	4.30	4.45	4.55	4.7	4.85	4.95	5.10	5.2	5.35	5.5	5.6	5.75	5.9	6.	6.15	6.25	6.4	6.55	6.65	6.8
+45	5.16	5.34	5.46	5.64	5.82	5.94	6.12	6.24	6.42	6.6	6.72	6.9	7.08	7.2	7.38	7.5	7.68	7.86	7.98	8.16
+54	6.02	6.23	6.37	6.58	6.79	6.93	7.14	7.28	7.49	7.7	7.84	8.05	8.26	8.4	8.61	8.75	8.96	9.17	9.31	9.52
+63	6.88	7.12	7.28	7.52	7.76	7.92	8.16	8.32	8.56	8.8	8.96	9.2	9.44	9.6	9.84	10.0	10.24	10.48	10.64	10.88
+72	7.74	8.01	8.19	8.46	8.73	8.91	9.18	9.36	9.63	9.9	10.08	10.35	10.62	10.8	11.07	11.25	11.52	11.79	11.97	12.24
+81	8.60	8.90	9.1	9.4	9.7	9.9	10.2	10.4	10.7	11.0	11.2	11.5	11.8	12.	12.3	12.5	12.8	13.1	13.3	13.6
+90	9.46	9.79	10.06	10.34	10.67	10.89	11.22	11.44	11.77	12.1	12.32	12.65	12.98	13.2	13.53	13.75	14.08	14.41	14.63	14.96
+99	10.32	10.68	10.92	11.28	11.64	11.88	12.24	12.48	12.84	13.2	13.44	13.8	14.16	14.4	14.76	15.0	15.36	15.72	15.96	16.32
+108	11.18	11.57	11.83	12.22	12.61	12.87	13.26	13.52	13.91	14.3	14.56	14.95	15.34	15.6	15.99	16.25	16.64	17.03	17.29	17.68
+117	12.04	12.46	12.74	13.16	13.58	13.86	14.28	14.56	14.98	15.4	15.68	16.1	16.52	16.8	17.22	17.5	17.92	18.34	18.62	19.04

In order to find the number of calories you have used per minute, enter your resting heart rate in the first space. Then fill in the subsequent spaces of the heart rate column by adding the indicated multiple of 9 to your resting heart rate.

Table 30

EXCELLENT—MEN
Calories Used Per Minute Based on Body Weight & Heart Rate

Body Weight (lbs.)

Your Heart Rate	90 or less	91-96	97-102	103-107	108-112	113-118	119-123	124-129	130-135	136-140	141-146	147-152	153-157	158-162	163-168	169-173	174-178	179-183	184-189	190 or more
Resting	.86	.89	.91	.94	.97	.99	1.02	1.04	1.07	1.10	1.12	1.15	1.18	1.20	1.23	1.25	1.28	1.31	1.33	1.36
+8	1.72	1.78	1.82	1.88	1.94	1.98	2.04	2.08	2.14	2.20	2.24	2.3	2.36	2.4	2.46	2.5	2.56	2.62	2.66	2.72
+16	2.58	2.67	2.73	2.82	2.91	2.95	3.06	3.12	3.21	3.3	3.36	3.45	3.54	3.6	3.69	3.75	3.84	3.93	3.99	4.08
+24	3.44	3.56	3.64	3.76	3.88	3.96	4.08	4.16	4.28	4.4	4.48	4.6	4.72	4.8	4.92	5.	5.12	5.24	5.32	5.44
+32	4.30	4.45	4.55	4.7	4.85	4.95	5.10	5.2	5.35	5.5	5.6	5.75	5.9	6.	6.15	6.25	6.4	6.55	6.65	6.8
+40	5.16	5.34	5.46	5.64	5.82	5.94	6.12	6.24	6.42	6.6	6.72	6.9	7.08	7.2	7.38	7.5	7.68	7.86	7.98	8.16
+48	6.02	6.23	6.37	6.58	6.79	6.93	7.14	7.28	7.49	7.7	7.84	8.05	8.26	8.4	8.61	8.75	8.96	9.17	9.31	9.52
+56	6.88	7.12	7.28	7.52	7.76	7.92	8.16	8.32	8.56	8.8	8.96	9.2	9.44	9.6	9.84	10.0	10.24	10.48	10.64	10.88
+64	7.74	8.01	8.19	8.46	8.73	8.91	9.18	9.36	9.63	9.9	10.08	10.35	10.62	10.8	11.07	11.25	11.52	11.79	11.97	12.24
+72	8.60	8.90	9.1	9.4	9.7	9.9	10.2	10.4	10.7	11.0	11.2	11.5	11.8	12.	12.3	12.5	12.8	13.	13.3	13.6
+80	9.46	9.79	10.01	10.34	10.67	10.89	11.22	11.44	11.77	12.1	12.32	12.65	12.98	13.2	13.53	13.75	14.08	14.41	14.63	14.96
+88	10.32	10.68	10.92	11.28	11.64	11.88	12.24	12.48	12.84	13.2	13.44	13.8	14.16	14.4	14.76	15.	15.36	15.72	15.96	16.32
+96	11.18	11.57	11.83	12.22	12.61	12.87	13.26	13.52	13.99	14.3	14.56	14.95	15.34	15.6	15.99	16.25	16.64	17.03	17.29	17.68
+104	12.04	12.46	12.74	13.16	13.58	13.86	14.28	14.56	14.98	15.4	15.68	16.	16.52	16.8	17.22	17.5	17.92	18.34	18.62	19.04

In order to find the number of calories you have used per minute, enter your resting heart rate in the first space. Then fill in the subsequent spaces of the heart rate column by adding the indicated multiple of 8 to your resting heart rate.

Table 31

VERY POOR—WOMEN
Calories Used Per Minute Based on Body Weight & Heart Rate
Body Weight (lbs.)

Your Heart Rate	90 or less	91-96	97-102	103-107	108-112	113-118	119-123	124-129	130-135	136-140	141-146	147-152	153-157	163-168	169-173	174-178	179-183	184-189	190 or more
Resting	.81	.84	.87	.89	.92	.95	.98	1.00	1.03	1.06	1.09	1.12	1.14	1.15	1.18	1.20	1.23	1.26	1.28	1.30
+12	1.62	1.68	1.74	1.78	1.84	1.9	1.96	2.0	2.06	2.12	2.18	2.24	2.28	2.3	2.36	2.4	2.46	2.52	2.56	2.6
+24	2.43	2.52	2.61	2.67	2.76	2.85	2.94	3.0	3.09	3.18	3.27	3.36	3.42	3.45	3.54	3.6	3.69	3.78	3.84	3.9
+36	3.24	3.36	3.48	3.56	3.68	3.8	3.92	4.0	4.12	4.24	4.36	4.48	4.56	4.6	4.72	4.8	4.92	5.04	5.12	5.2
+48	4.05	4.2	4.35	4.45	4.6	4.75	4.9	5.0	5.15	5.3	5.45	5.6	5.7	5.75	5.9	6.	6.15	6.3	6.4	6.5
+60	4.86	5.04	5.22	5.34	5.52	5.7	5.88	6.0	6.18	6.36	6.54	6.72	6.84	6.9	7.08	7.2	7.38	7.56	7.68	7.8
+72	5.67	5.88	6.09	6.23	6.44	6.65	6.86	7.0	7.21	7.42	7.63	7.84	7.98	8.05	8.26	8.4	8.61	8.82	8.96	9.1
+84	6.48	6.72	6.96	7.12	7.36	7.6	7.84	8.0	8.24	8.48	8.72	8.96	9.12	9.2	9.44	9.6	9.84	10.08	10.24	10.4
+96	7.29	7.56	7.83	8.02	8.28	8.55	8.82	7.0	9.27	9.54	9.81	10.08	10.26	10.35	10.62	10.8	11.07	11.34	11.52	11.7
+108	8.1	8.4	8.7	8.9	9.2	9.5	9.8	10.0	10.3	10.6	10.9	11.2	11.4	11.5	11.8	12.	12.3	12.6	12.8	13.
+120	8.91	9.24	9.57	9.79	10.12	10.45	10.78	11.0	11.33	11.66	11.99	12.32	12.54	12.65	12.98	13.2	13.53	13.86	14.08	14.3
+132	9.72	10.08	10.44	10.68	11.04	11.4	11.76	12.0	12.36	12.72	13.08	13.44	13.68	13.8	14.16	14.4	14.76	15.12	15.36	15.6
+144	10.53	10.92	11.31	11.57	11.96	12.35	12.74	13.0	13.39	13.78	14.17	14.56	14.82	14.95	15.34	15.6	15.99	16.38	16.64	16.9
+156	11.34	11.76	12.18	12.46	12.88	13.3	13.72	14.0	14.42	14.84	15.26	15.68	15.96	16.1	16.52	16.8	17.22	17.64	17.92	18.2

In order to find the number of calories you have used per minute, enter your resting heart rate in the first space. Then fill in the subsequent spaces of the heart rate column by adding the indicated multiple of 12 to your resting heart rate.

Table 32

POOR—WOMEN

Calories Used Per Minute Based on Body Weight & Heart Rate

Body Weight (lbs.)

Your Heart Rate	90 or less	91-96	97-102	103-107	108-112	113-118	119-123	124-129	130-135	136-140	141-146	147-152	153-157	158-162	163-168	169-173	174-178	179-183	184-189	190 or more
Resting	.81	.84	.87	.89	.92	.95	.98	1.00	1.03	1.06	1.09	1.12	1.14	1.15	1.18	1.20	1.23	1.26	1.28	1.30
+11	1.62	1.68	1.74	1.78	1.84	1.9	1.96	2.0	2.06	2.12	2.18	2.24	2.28	2.3	2.36	2.4	2.46	2.52	2.56	2.6
+22	2.43	2.52	2.61	2.67	2.76	2.85	2.94	3.0	3.09	3.18	3.27	3.36	3.42	3.45	3.54	3.6	3.69	3.78	3.84	3.9
+33	3.24	3.36	3.48	3.56	3.68	3.8	3.92	4.0	4.12	4.24	4.36	4.48	4.56	4.6	4.72	4.8	4.92	5.04	5.12	5.2
+44	4.05	4.2	4.35	4.45	4.6	4.75	4.9	5.0	5.15	5.3	5.45	5.6	5.7	5.75	5.9	6.	6.15	6.3	6.4	6.5
+55	4.86	5.04	5.22	5.34	5.52	5.7	5.88	6.0	6.18	6.36	6.54	6.72	6.84	6.9	7.08	7.2	7.38	7.56	7.68	7.8
+66	5.67	5.88	6.09	6.23	6.44	6.65	6.86	7.0	7.21	7.42	7.63	7.84	7.98	8.05	8.26	8.4	8.61	8.82	8.96	9.1
+77	6.48	6.72	6.96	7.12	7.36	7.6	7.84	8.0	8.24	8.48	8.72	8.96	9.12	9.2	9.44	9.6	9.84	10.08	10.24	10.4
+88	7.29	7.56	7.83	8.01	8.28	8.55	8.82	9.0	9.27	9.54	9.81	10.08	10.26	10.35	10.62	10.8	11.07	11.34	11.52	11.7
+99	8.1	8.4	8.7	8.9	9.2	9.5	9.8	10.0	10.3	10.6	10.9	11.2	11.4	11.5	11.8	12.	12.3	12.6	12.8	13.
+110	8.91	9.24	9.57	9.79	10.12	10.45	10.78	11.0	11.33	11.66	11.99	12.32	12.54	12.65	12.98	13.2	13.53	13.86	14.08	14.3
+121	9.72	10.08	10.44	10.68	11.04	11.4	11.76	12.0	12.36	12.72	13.08	13.44	13.68	13.8	14.16	14.4	14.76	15.12	15.36	15.6
+132	10.53	10.92	11.31	11.57	11.96	12.35	12.74	13.0	13.39	13.78	14.17	14.56	14.82	14.95	15.34	15.6	15.99	16.38	16.64	16.9
+143	11.34	11.76	12.18	12.46	12.88	13.3	13.72	14.0	14.42	14.84	15.26	15.68	15.96	16.1	16.52	16.8	17.22	17.64	17.92	18.2

In order to find the number of calories you have used per minute, enter your resting heart rate in the first space. Then fill in the subsequent spaces of the heart rate column by adding the indicated multiple of 11 to your resting heart rate.

Table 33

FAIR—WOMEN
Calories Used Per Minute Based on Body Weight & Heart Rate

Body Weight (lbs.)

Your Heart Rate	90 or less	91-96	97-102	103-107	108-112	113-118	119-123	124-129	130-135	136-140	141-146	147-152	153-157	158-162	163-168	169-173	174-178	179-183	184-189	190 or more
Resting	.81	.84	.87	.89	.92	.95	.98	1.00	1.03	1.06	1.09	1.12	1.14	1.15	1.18	1.20	1.23	1.26	1.28	1.30
+10	1.62	1.68	1.74	1.78	1.84	1.9	1.96	2.0	2.06	2.12	2.18	2.24	2.28	2.3	2.36	2.4	2.46	2.52	2.56	2.6
+20	2.43	2.52	2.61	2.76	2.86	2.94	2.94	3.0	3.09	3.18	3.27	3.36	3.42	3.45	3.54	3.6	3.69	3.78	3.84	3.9
+30	3.24	3.36	3.48	3.56	3.68	3.8	3.92	4.0	4.12	4.24	4.36	4.48	4.56	4.6	4.72	4.8	4.92	5.04	5.12	5.2
+40	4.05	4.2	4.35	4.45	4.6	4.75	4.9	5.02	5.15	5.3	5.45	5.6	5.7	5.57	5.9	6.	6.15	6.3	6.4	6.5
+50	4.86	5.04	5.22	5.34	5.52	5.7	5.88	6.0	6.18	6.36	6.54	6.72	6.84	6.94	7.08	7.2	7.38	7.56	7.68	7.8
+60	5.67	5.88	6.09	6.23	6.44	6.65	6.86	7.0	7.21	7.42	7.63	7.84	7.98	8.05	8.26	8.4	8.61	8.82	8.96	9.1
+70	6.48	6.72	6.96	7.12	7.36	7.6	7.84	8.0	8.24	8.48	8.72	8.96	9.12	9.2	9.44	9.6	9.84	10.08	10.24	10.4
+80	7.29	7.56	7.83	8.01	8.28	8.55	8.82	9.0	9.27	9.54	9.81	10.08	10.26	10.35	10.62	10.8	11.07	11.34	11.52	11.7
+90	8.1	8.4	8.7	8.9	9.2	9.5	9.8	10.0	10.3	10.6	10.9	11.2	11.4	11.5	11.8	12.	12.3	12.6	12.8	13.
+100	8.91	9.24	9.57	9.79	10.12	10.45	10.78	11.0	11.33	11.66	11.99	12.32	12.54	12.65	12.98	13.2	13.53	13.86	14.08	14.2
+110	9.72	10.08	10.44	10.68	11.04	11.4	11.76	12.0	12.36	12.72	13.08	13.44	13.68	13.8	14.16	14.4	14.76	15.12	15.36	15.6
+120	10.53	10.92	11.31	11.57	11.96	12.35	12.74	13.0	13.39	13.78	14.17	14.56	.82	14.95	15.34	15.6	15.99	16.38	16.64	16.9
+130	11.34	11.76	12.18	12.46	12.88	13.3	13.72	14.0	14.42	14.84	15.26	15.68	15.96	16.1	16.52	16.8	17.22	17.64	17.92	18.2

In order to find the number of calories you have used per minute, enter your resting heart rate in the first space. Then fill in the subsequent spaces of the heart rate column by adding the indicated multiple of 10 to your resting heart rate.

Table 34

GOOD—WOMEN

Calories Used Per Minute Based on Body Weight & Heart Rate

Body Weight (lbs.)

Your Heart Rate	90 or less .81	91-96 .84	97-102 .87	103-107 .89	108-112 .92	113-118 .95	119-123 .98	124-129 1.00	130-135 1.03	136-140 1.06	141-146 1.09	147-152 1.12	153-157 1.14	158-162 1.15	163-168 1.18	169-173 1.20	174-178 1.23	179-183 1.26	184-189 1.28	190 or more 1.30
Resting	.81	.84	.87	.89	.92	.95	.98	1.00	1.03	1.06	1.09	1.12	1.14	1.15	1.18	1.20	1.23	1.26	1.28	1.30
+9	1.62	1.68	1.74	1.78	1.84	1.9	1.96	2.0	2.06	2.12	2.18	2.24	2.28	2.3	2.36	2.4	2.46	2.52	2.56	2.6
+18	2.43	2.52	2.61	2.67	2.76	2.85	2.94	3.0	3.09	3.18	3.27	3.36	3.42	3.45	3.54	3.6	3.69	3.78	3.84	3.9
+27	3.24	3.36	3.48	3.56	3.68	3.8	3.92	4.0	4.12	4.24	4.36	4.48	4.56	4.6	4.72	4.8	4.92	5.04	5.12	5.2
+36	4.05	4.2	4.35	4.45	4.6	4.75	4.9	5.0	5.15	5.3	5.45	5.6	5.7	5.75	5.9	6.	6.15	6.3	6.4	6.5
+45	4.86	5.04	5.22	5.34	5.52	5.7	5.88	6.0	6.18	6.36	6.54	6.72	6.84	6.9	7.08	7.2	7.38	7.56	7.68	7.8
+54	5.67	5.88	6.09	6.23	6.44	6.65	6.86	7.0	7.21	7.42	7.63	7.84	7.98	8.05	8.26	8.4	8.61	8.82	8.96	9.1
+63	6.48	6.72	6.96	7.12	7.36	7.6	7.84	8.0	8.24	8.48	8.72	8.96	9.12	9.2	9.44	9.6	9.84	10.08	10.24	10.4
+72	7.29	7.56	7.83	8.01	8.28	8.55	8.82	9.0	9.27	9.54	9.81	10.08	10.26	10.35	10.62	10.8	11.07	11.34	11.52	11.7
+81	8.1	8.4	8.7	8.9	9.2	9.5	9.8	10.0	10.3	10.6	10.9	11.2	11.4	11.5	11.8	12.	12.3	12.6	12.8	13.
+90	8.91	9.24	9.57	9.79	10.12	10.45	10.78	11.0	11.33	11.66	11.99	12.32	12.54	12.65	12.98	13.2	13.53	13.86	14.08	14.3
+99	9.72	10.08	10.44	10.68	11.04	11.4	11.76	12.0	12.36	12.72	13.08	13.44	13.68	13.8	14.16	14.4	14.76	15.12	15.36	15.6
+108	10.53	10.92	11.31	11.57	11.96	12.35	12.74	13.0	13.39	13.78	14.17	14.56	14.82	14.95	15.34	15.6	15.99	16.38	16.64	16.9
+117	11.34	11.76	12.18	12.46	12.88	13.3	13.72	14.0	14.42	14.84	15.26	15.68	15.96	16.1	16.52	16.8	17.22	17.64	17.92	18.2

In order to find the number of calories you have used per minute, enter your resting heart rate in the first space. Then fill in the subsequent spaces of the heart rate column by adding the indicated multiple of 9 to your resting heart rate.

Table 35

EXCELLENT—WOMEN
Calories Used Per Minute Based on Body Weight & Heart Rate

Body Weight (lbs.)

Your Heart Rate		91-96	97-102	103-107	108-112	113-118	119-123	124-129	130-135	136-140	141-146	147-152	153-157	158-162	163-168	169-173	174-178	179-183	184-189	190 or more
Resting	.81	.84	.87	.89	.92	.95	.98	1.00	1.03	1.06	1.09	1.12	1.14	1.15	1.18	1.20	1.23	1.26	1.28	1.30
+8	1.62	1.68	1.74	1.78	1.84	1.9	1.96	2.0	2.06	2.12	2.18	2.24	2.28	2.3	2.36	2.4	2.46	2.52	2.56	2.6
+16	2.43	2.52	2.61	2.67	2.76	2.85	2.94	3.0	3.09	3.18	3.27	3.36	3.42	3.45	3.54	3.6	3.69	3.78	3.84	3.9
+24	3.24	3.36	3.48	3.56	3.68	3.8	3.92	4.0	4.12	4.24	4.36	4.48	4.56	4.6	4.72	4.8	4.92	5.04	5.12	5.2
+32	4.05	4.2	4.35	4.45	4.6	4.75	4.9	5.0	5.15	5.3	5.45	5.6	5.7	5.75	5.9	6.	6.15	6.3	6.4	6.5
+40	4.86	5.04	5.22	5.34	5.52	5.7	5.88	6.0	6.18	6.36	6.54	6.72	6.84	6.9	7.08	7.2	7.38	7.56	7.68	7.8
+48	5.67	5.88	6.09	6.23	6.44	6.65	6.86	7.0	7.21	7.42	7.63	7.84	7.98	8.05	8.26	8.4	8.61	8.82	8.96	9.1
+56	6.48	6.72	6.96	7.12	7.36	7.6	7.84	8.0	8.24	8.48	8.72	8.96	9.12	9.2	9.44	9.6	9.84	10.08	10.24	10.4
+64	7.29	7.56	7.83	8.01	8.28	8.55	8.82	9.0	9.27	9.54	9.81	10.08	10.26	10.35	10.62	10.8	11.07	11.34	11.52	11.7
+72	8.1	8.4	8.7	8.9	9.2	9.5	9.8	10.0	10.3	10.6	10.9	11.2	11.4	11.5	11.8	12.	12.3	12.6	12.8	13.
+80	8.91	9.24	9.57	9.79	10.12	10.45	10.78	11.0	11.33	11.66	11.99	12.32	12.54	12.65	12.98	13.2	13.53	13.86	14.08	14.3
+88	9.72	10.08	10.44	10.68	11.04	11.4	11.76	12.0	12.36	12.72	13.08	13.44	13.68	13.8	14.16	14.4	14.76	15.12	15.36	15.6
+96	10.53	10.92	11.31	11.57	11.96	12.35	12.74	13.0	13.39	13.78	14.17	14.56	14.82	14.95	15.34	15.6	15.99	16.38	16.64	16.9
+104	11.34	11.76	12.18	12.46	12.88	13.3	13.72	14.0	14.42	14.84	15.26	15.68	15.96	16.1	16.52	16.8	17.22	17.64	17.92	18.2

In order to find the number of calories you have used per minute, enter your resting heart rate in the first space. Then fill in the subsequent spaces of the heart rate column by adding the indicated multiple of 8 to your resting heart rate.

APPENDIX D

The Activity Calorie Counter

This Activity Calorie Counter permits you to determine the number of calories your body burns during various kinds of physical activity. It's the key to self-prescribing a diet-free weight-loss program uniquely suited to your individual needs.

As I explained back in Chapter #7, one person may burn a considerably larger—or smaller—number of calories than another person engaged in the same activity for the same length of time. Various factors, the most important being weight, make the difference.

A 100 pound person, for example, burns approximately 285 calories during an hour's worth of gardening, while a 200 pounder burns off about 430 calories. This is primarily because the heavier person's muscles must contend with moving 100 pounds of additional weight, and thus his/her body needs more oxygen (hence more calories) in order to do the same job.

Standard calories expenditure charts which indicate the calorie cost of various activities to an "average" 150 pound, 5 foot, 8 inch man don't allow for individual differences. If you're a woman, or a bigger or smaller than "average" man, the standard charts won't give you the kind of information you need to calculate the number of calories your body burns—either during the course of a normal day or for planning a program of diet-free weight loss through activity.

For this reason, I developed the following more accurate weight-adjusted Activity Calorie Counter. It indicates the number of calories your own body uses during various activities, regardless of your size and shape.

Of course, to use the Calorie Counter it is best to use your ideal body weight (although it is not necessary). The Calorie Counter is meant to be read mileage-chart style. Activities are listed alphabetically in the column at the extreme left. Various weights from 50 to 220 pounds plus are listed across the top. The calories used per minute for the various weights are listed in the space underneath the weight and to the right of the 300 plus activities.

Suppose you want to find out how many calories you'll use during a session of archery, and your present weight is 140 pounds. First, you'd find archery in the activity column at the extreme left of the chart. Then, you'd look in the vertical column headed by your weight of 140 pounds. Where the two columns intersect, you'll see the figure 4.91 which refers to the number of calories you use per minute. If you want to do additional calculations for a half hour's worth of archery, multiply the number by 30. For a quarter of an hour, multiply by 15.

At the extreme right, you'll find my designation of whether these activities are low, mild, moderate high, high, or very high fat burners. Remember: The moderate, moderate high, high, and very high activities are the best ones for losing fat. The low and mild are fat-burning supplements.

Low Intensity Activities

These activities burn few calories. Included here are sleeping, sitting, watching television, standing and driving a car—typical American activities. When you do these activities, the major muscles of your body are not used—except, perhaps, the gluteus maximus. Your body demands little oxygen and expends little energy. At most you double the number of calories you burn while sleeping. Most people (even the infirm) are able to participate in these activities.

The contribution of these activities to your fitness level or to fat control are negligible. These are activities we do day-in and day-out. However, a person who has been bedridden for several weeks (and has had significant disease) may find some of these activities challenging.

Mild Intensity Activities

These activities are relatively easy. They include easy walking, horseshoes, golf and raking the lawn. Practically anyone can engage in these activities without fear of overdoing. Occasionally, however, long hours of participation in Mild Intensity Activities can cause muscles to rebel with pain or aches; but for most people, 30 minutes or so should not cause problems.

Mild Intensity Activities are for almost everyone. Their contribution to fat control, however, is marginal unless done for extended periods of time, five or more days a week. We can call them mini-activetics or fat-control supplements. These are the kinds of activities you should try to do in addition to your regularly scheduled fitness/weight-loss exercises. (Note: persons just recovering from a heart attack, emphysema patients, severely afflicted arthritics and the extremely obese may benefit from these activities.)

Moderate Intensity Activities

These activities get your whole body moving. Thus, your body burns a significant number of calories. Activities such as moderate walking and hiking, fencing, archery, recreational sports and gardening fall into this category.

Moderate Intensity Activites should be approached with some caution. It is best not to do more than 20 minutes of Moderate Intensity Activities four or more days a week. Each week you may then gradually increase the number of minutes per session. Two to three minutes additional per week would be best. Your own body is your best guide. Continue to increase your time until you are able to do a minimum of 60 minutes, four times a week. You can then continue to the higher intensity activities if you wish.

Moderate High Intensity Activities

When you engage in these activities, almost all the major muscle groups are involved. A good number of calories are used in a relatively short period of time. The Moderate-High Intensity Activities are very effective for fat control. Activities such as polka dancing, downhill skiing, water skiing, fast walking, digging, and light snowshoveling fall into this category.

Only those individuals who are in good physical condition or above should participate in these activities. Begin with 20 minutes four times a week. Move up no more than two or three minutes each week. You may find that you need more than one week, so let your body be your guide. Your minimum goal is 45 minutes four times a week. When you reach this goal you're then ready to move to High Intensity Activities if you wish. Remember to use your target heart rate as your guide to prevent you from exercising too hard.

High Intensity Activities

You are now entering the sphere of what we like to call the perfect fat-control activities. These activities get your entire body moving, your major muscles exercising, your heart beating a lot faster, and your breathing deeper. It may take you some time to get to this level, but it will be worth the effort.

Activities such as vigorous handball, running, fast bicycling, race walking and full-court basketball fall into this category. Only those people who are in good physical condition or above should do these. If you are just starting out, I suggest 15 minutes, four times a week. Every succeeding week, you can move up two to three minutes. You may feel that you require more than one week. Take the time. Again, remember your body is your best guide. Your minimum goal is 30 minutes of High Intensity Activity, four times a week.

Very High Intensity Activities

You may never reach this level of intensity. If so, you have a lot of company. In the event that you do reach this plateau, you should be in excellent physical condition before attempting them. The Very High Intensity Activities are great calorie burners. However I do not consider it necessary for you to move to this level. The only advantage is that you burn a lot of calories in a very short period of time.

Some of the activities such as sprinting, heavy snow shoveling, and swimming 55 yards per minute are impossible to do for longer than a few minutes at a time, thereby making the activity somewhat impractical for consistent weight and figure control.

Table 36
CALORIES USED FOR VARIOUS ACTIVITIES
Per Minute

Activity	|	|	|	|	|	| Weight in Pounds	|	|	|	|	|	|	EXERCISE INTENSITY
	71 or less	72-82	83-93	94-104	105-115	116-126	127-137	138-148	149-159	160-170	171-181	182-192	193 or more	
Activetics Calisthenics Program														
a. Low	2.58	2.83	3.08	3.33	3.58	3.83	4.08	4.33	4.58	4.83	5.08	5.33	5.58	Mild
b. Medium	4.16	4.58	5	5.41	5.83	6.16	6.58	7	7.41	7.83	8.16	8.58	9	Moderate
c. High	5.25	5.75	6.25	6.75	7.25	7.75	8.25	8.75	9.25	9.75	10.25	10.75	11.25	Mod./High
Archery	3	3.25	3.5	3.83	4.08	4.33	4.66	4.91	5.25	5.5	5.75	6.08	6.33	Moderate
Assembly & Assembly line work														
a. light/medium machine parts at own pace.	2.08	2.33	2.5	2.66	2.91	3.08	3.33	3.5	3.66	3.91	4.08	4.33	4.5	Mild
b. light/medium machine parts at 500 times per day or more	2.5	2.66	2.91	3.16	3.41	3.66	3.91	4.08	4.33	4.58	4.83	5.08	5.25	Mild
c. working on assembly line where parts require lifting at about every 5 minutes or so lift is for a few seconds and weighs less than 45 lb.	2.5	2.66	2.91	3.16	3.41	3.66	3.91	4.08	4.33	4.58	4.83	5.08	5.25	Mild
d. same as c. but objects weigh more than 45 lbs.	2.75	3	3.33	3.58	3.83	4.08	4.33	4.66	4.91	5.16	5.41	5.66	6	Mild
Badminton														
a. singles recreational	3.33	3.66	3.91	4.25	4.58	4.91	5.16	5.5	5.83	6.16	6.41	6.75	7.08	Moderate
b. doubles recreational	2.83	3.08	3.41	3.66	3.91	4.16	4.5	4.75	5	5.25	5.58	5.83	6.08	Moderate

	4.33	4.83	5.16	5.58	6	6.41	6.83	7.25	7.66	8.08	8.5	8.91	9.33	
c. competitive (doubles)														Moderate
d. competitive (vigorous) singles	5.75	6.33	6.83	7.41	8	8.5	9.08	9.58	10.16	10.75	11.25	11.83	12.33	Moderate
Baking														
a. using mixer	.08	.16	.25	.33	.4	.58	1.66	1.75	1.83	1.91	2.08	2.16	2.25	Low
b. beating cake batter by hand	.58	1.75	1.91	2	2.16	2.33	2.5	2.58	2.75	3	3.08	3.25	3.41	Mild
Bartending														
a. slow	1.25	1.41	1.5	1.58	1.75	1.83	2	2.08	2.25	2.33	2.5	2.58	2.66	Low
b. busy	2.16	2.41	2.58	2.83	3	3.25	3.41	3.66	3.83	4.08	4.25	4.5	4.66	Mild
Baseball														
a. other than pitcher or catcher	2.66	2.91	3.16	3.41	3.66	3.91	4.16	4.41	4.66	4.91	5.16	5.41	5.66	Mild
b. pitcher only	3.66	4.08	4.41	4.75	5.08	5.41	5.83	6.16	6.5	6.83	7.25	7.58	7.91	Moderate
c. catcher only	3.25	3.91	3.91	4.25	4.5	4.91	5.16	5.5	5.83	6.08	6.41	7.75	7	Moderate
Basketball														
a. nongame, ½ court, etc.	5.25	5.75	6.25	6.75	7.25	7.75	8.25	8.75	9.25	9.75	10.25	10.75	11.25	Mod/High
b. officiating	5.25	5.75	6.25	6.75	7.25	7.75	8.25	8.75	9.25	9.75	10.25	10.75	11.25	Mod/High
c. game (full court, cont.)	7.08	7.75	8.41	9.08	9.75	10.5	11.16	11.83	12.5	13.16	13.83	14.5	15.16	High
Bench stepping—30 steps per minute														
a. 7"	5.75	6.33	6.91	7.41	8.5	9.08	9.58	10.16	10.75	11.25	11.83	12.41	12.41	Mod/High
b. 12"	7.58	8.25	9	9.75	10.41	11.16	11.91	12.58	13.33	14	14.75	15.5	16.16	Very High
c. 16"	10.5	11.5	12.5	13.5	14.5	15.5	16.5	17.5	18.33	19.50	20.5	21.5	22.5	Very High
d. 18"	13.25	14.5	15.75	17	18.25	19.5	20.75	22.08	23.33	24.58	25.83	27.08	28.33	Very High
Bicycling														
a. 5½ mph	2.25	2.5	2.5	2.91	3.16	3.41	3.58	3.83	4.08	4.25	4.5	4.66	4.91	Mild
b. 10 mph	3.91	4.33	4.66	5	5.41	5.83	6.16	6.58	6.91	7.33	7.66	7.91	8.41	Moderate
c. 13 mph	6.16	6.83	7.41	8	8.58	9.16	9.75	10.33	10.91	11.5	12.08	12.66	13	High

Table 36
CALORIES USED FOR VARIOUS ACTIVITIES
Per Minute

Weight in Pounds

Activity	71 or less	72-82	83-93	94-104	105-115	116-126	127-137	138-148	149-159	160-170	171-181	182-192	193 or more	EXERCISE INTENSITY
Bowling														
a. continuous	2.5	2.83	3	3.25	3.5	3.75	4	4.25	4.5	4.75	5	5.16	5.41	Mild
b. regular	1.75	1.91	2.08	2.33	2.5	2.66	2.83	3	3.16	3.33	3.5	3.66	3.83	Mild
Boxing (sparing only)	5.16	5.66	6.16	6.66	7.16	7.66	8.16	8.66	9.16	9.66	10.16	10.66	11.16	Mod/High
Bricklaying	1.91	2.08	2.33	2.5	2.66	2.83	3	3.25	3.41	3.58	3.75	3.91	4.16	Mild
Calisthenics (general)	2.83	2.08	3.33	3.66	3.91	4.16	4.5	4.75	6.91	7.33	7.66	7.91	8.41	Moderate
Canadian 5Bx														
a. Chart 1A	4.83	5.25	5.75	6.25	6.66	7.16	7.58	8.08	8.5	9	9.41	9.91	10.33	Mod/High
b. Chart 2A	6.08	6.66	7.25	7.83	8.41	9	9.58	10.16	10.75	11.33	11.91	12.5	13.08	High
c. Charts 3A & 4A	9.08	10	10.83	11.66	12.58	13.41	15.16	16	16	16.83	17.75	18.58	19.5	Very High
d. Charts 5A & 6A	9.16	10	10.91	11.75	12.66	13.5	14.41	15.25	16.16	17	17.91	18.75	19.66	Very High
Canadian XBX														
a. Level 12	2.83	3.08	3.41	3.66	3.91	4.16	4.5	4.75	5	5.25	5.58	5.83	6.08	Moderate
b. Level 24	4.83	5.25	5.75	6.25	6.66	7.16	7.58	8.08	8.5	9	9.41	9.91	10.33	Mod/High
c. Level 36	6.16	6.83	7.41	8	8.58	9.16	9.75	10.33	10.91	11.5	12.08	12.66	13	High
d. Level 48	7.5	8.16	8.91	9.58	10.33	11	11.75	12.5	13.16	13.91	14.58	15.33	16	High
Canoeing														
a. 2 mph	2.83	3.08	3.33	3.66	3.91	4.16	4.5	4.75	5	5.25	5.58	5.83	6.08	Moderate
b. 4 mph	5.91	6.5	7.08	7.5	8.16	8.75	9.33	9.91	10.41	11	11.58	12.16	12.75	Moderate
Card Playing	.83	.91	1.08	1.16	1.25	1.33	1.33	1.41	1.5	1.58	1.66	1.75	1.83	Low
Carpentry work														
a. light	2.16	2.41	2.58	2.83	3	3.25	3.41	3.66	3.83	4.08	4.25	4.5	4.66	Mild
b. heavy	3.16	3.66	4	4.33	4.66	5	5.25	5.58	5.91	6.25	6.58	6.91	7.16	Moderate

Carrying trays, dishes, etc.														
a. waitress	2.33	2.5	2.75	3	3.16	3.41	3.58	3.83	4.08	4.25	4.5	4.66	4.91	Mild
b. busboy	2.83	3.08	3.41	3.66	3.91	4.16	4.5	4.75	5	5.25	5.58	5.83	6.08	Moderate
Checkout counter work	1.25	1.41	1.5	1.58	1.75	1.83	2	2.08	2.25	2.33	2.5	2.58	2.66	Low
Chess	.83	.91	1	1.08	1.16	1.25	1.33	1.41	1.5	1.58	1.66	1.75	1.83	Low
Chopping wood														
a. automatically (power saw)	2.08	2.33	2.5	2.66	2.91	3.08	3.33	3.5	3.66	3.91	4.08	4.33	4.5	Mild
b. hand	4.25	4.66	5.08	5.5	5.91	6.25	6.66	7.08	7.5	7.91	8.33	8.75	9.16	Moderate
Class work (sitting)	.83	.91	1	1.08	1.16	1.25	1.33	1.41	1.5	1.58	1.66	1.75	1.83	Low
Coffee Klatch	.91	1	1.08	1.16	1.25	1.33	1.41	1.5	1.58	1.66	1.75	1.83	1.91	Low
Crane operator	2.16	2.41	2.58	2.83	3	3.25	3.41	3.66	3.83	4.08	4.25	4.5	4.66	Mild
Cranking up dollies, hitching trailers operating large levers, jacks, etc.	2.41	2.66	2.83	3.08	3.33	3.58	3.83	4	4.25	4.5	4.75	4.91	5.16	Mild
Dancing														
a. Aerobic (low)	2.58	2.83	3.08	3.33	3.58	3.83	4.08	4.33	4.58	4.83	5.08	5.33	5.58	Mild
b. Aerobic (medium)	4.16	4.58	5	5.41	5.83	6.16	6.58	7	7.41	7.83	8.16	8.58	9	Moderate
c. Aerobic (high)	6.16	6.75	7.41	8	8.58	9.16	9.75	10.33	10.91	11.5	12.08	12.66	13.25	High
d. Fox trot	2.41	2.58	2.83	3.08	3.25	3.5	3.75	4	4.16	4.41	4.66	4.91	5.08	Mild
e. contemporary (rock)	2.41	2.58	2.83	3.08	3.25	3.5	3.75	4	4.16	4.41	4.66	4.91	5.08	Mild
f. Waltz	2.41	2.58	2.83	3.08	3.25	3.5	3.75	4	4.16	4.41	4.66	4.91	5.08	Mild
g. Rumba	2.83	3.08	3.41	3.66	3.91	4.16	4.5	4.75	5	5.25	5.58	5.83	6.08	Moderate
h. Square	4	4.33	4.75	5.08	5.5	5.83	6.25	6.66	7	7.41	7.75	8	8.5	Moderate
i. Polka	5.08	5.58	6.08	6.58	7.08	7.58	8	8.5	9	9.5	10	10.5	10.91	Mod/High
Digging	4.75	5.16	5.66	6.08	6.5	7	7.41	7.91	8.33	8.75	9.25	9.66	10.16	Mod/High
Dinner preparation	1.25	1.41	1.5	1.58	1.75	1.83	2	2.08	2.25	2.33	2.5	2.58	2.66	Mild

Table 36
CALORIES USED FOR VARIOUS ACTIVITIES
Per Minute

Weight in Pounds

Activity	71 or less	72–82	83–93	94–104	105–115	116–126	127–137	138–148	149–159	160–170	171–181	182–192	193 or more	EXERCISE INTENSITY
Domestic work (cleaning windows, mopping, scrubbing floors—no pause)	2.41	2.58	2.83	3.08	3.25	3.5	3.75	4	4.16	4.41	4.66	4.91	5.08	Mild
Driving a car														
a. standard—heavy traffic	1.25	1.41	1.5	1.58	1.75	1.83	2	2.08	2.25	2.33	2.5	2.58	2.66	Low
b. standard—light traffic	.91	1	1.16	1.25	1.33	1.41	1.5	1.58	1.66	1.75	1.83	1.91	2	Low
c. automatic—heavy traffic	.91	1	1.16	1.25	1.33	1.41	1.5	1.58	1.66	1.75	1.83	1.91	2	Low
d. automatic—light traffic	.91	1	1.08	1.16	1.25	1.33	1.41	1.5	1.58	1.66	1.75	1.83	1.91	Low
Driving a truck														
a. regular	1.33	1.5	1.58	1.75	1.91	2	2.16	2.25	2.41	2.5	2.66	2.83	2.91	Low
b. heavy rig—including getting on off frequently, & some arm work	2.16	2.41	2.58	2.83	3	3.25	3.41	3.66	3.83	4.08	4.25	4.5	4.66	Mild
Eating	.83	.91	1	1.08	.16	1.25	1.33	1.41	1.5	1.58	1.66	1.75	1.83	Low
Electric work (rewiring home)	2.41	2.58	2.83	3.08	3.25	3.5	3.75	4	4.16	4.41	4.66	4.91	5.08	Mild
Farming														
a. modern equipment	2.16	2.41	2.58	2.83	3	3.25	3.41	3.66	3.83	4.08	4.25	4.5	4.66	Mild
b. haying & plowing with horse	3.75	4.16	4.5	4.83	5.25	5.58	5.91	6.33	6.66	7	7.41	7.75	8.08	Moderate

Fencing														
a. recreational	2.83	3.08	3.41	3.66	3.91	4.16	4.5	4.75	5	5.25	5.58	5.83	6.08	Moderate
b. competitive (vigorous)	5.75	6.33	6.91	7.41	8	8.5	9.08	9.58	10.16	10.75	11.25	11.83	12.41	Mod/High
Fishing														
a. boat	1.25	1.41	1.5	1.58	1.75	1.83	2	2.08	2.25	2.33	2.5	2.58	2.66	Low
b. ice	1.66	1.83	2	2.16	2.33	2.5	2.66	2.83	2.91	3.08	3.25	3.41	3.58	Mild
c. standing (little movement)	1.5	1.58	1.75	1.91	2	2.16	2.33	2.41	2.58	2.75	2.83	3	3.16	Mild
d. surf	1.66	1.83	2	2.16	2.33	2.5	2.66	2.83	2.91	3.08	3.25	3.41	3.58	Mild
e. stream (wading)	2.83	3.08	3.41	3.66	3.91	4.16	4.5	4.75	5	5.25	5.58	5.83	6.08	Moderate
Fitness Finders Workout														
a. low	3	3.25	3.58	3.83	4.08	4.41	4.66	5	5.25	5.5	5.83	6.08	6.41	Moderate
b. medium	4.58	5	5.41	5.83	6.25	6.75	7.16	7.58	8	8.41	8.91	9.33	9.75	Mod/High
c. high	5.66	6.25	6.75	7.25	7.83	8.33	8.91	9.41	10	10.5	11.08	11.58	12.16	Mod/High
Football														
a. playground (touch)	5.66	6.25	6.75	7.25	7.83	8.33	8.91	9.41	10	10.5	11.08	11.58	12.16	Mod/High
b. officiating	5.25	5.75	6.25	6.75	7.25	7.75	8.25	8.75	9.25	9.75	10.25	10.75	11.25	Mod/High
c. tackle	7.91	8.66	9.41	10.16	11	11.75	12.5	13.25	13.91	14.75	15.5	16.25	17	Very High
Gardening (weeding, hoeing, digging, etc.)	3.66	4	4.33	4.75	5.08	5.41	5.75	6.08	6.5	6.83	7.16	7.5	7.83	Moderate
Gas Station attendant														
a. pump gas—wash windows	2.08	2.33	2.5	2.66	2.91	3.08	3.33	3.5	3.66	3.91	4.08	4.33	4.5	Mild
b. mechanic—car	2.16	2.41	2.58	2.83	3	3.25	3.41	3.66	3.83	4.08	4.25	4.5	4.66	Mild
c. wash cars	2.25	2.41	2.66	2.83	3.08	3.25	3.5	3.75	3.91	4.16	4.33	4.58	4.75	Mild
d. combination of above three	2.41	2.58	2.83	3.08	3.25	3.5	3.75	4	4.16	4.41	4.66	4.91	5.08	Mild
e. fix flats—wrecker work	3.16	3.66	4	4.33	4.66	5	5.25	5.58	5.91	6.25	6.58	6.91	7.16	Moderate

Table 36
CALORIES USED FOR VARIOUS ACTIVITIES
Per Minute

Weight in Pounds

Activity	71 or less	72–82	83–93	94–104	105–115	116–126	127–137	138–148	149–159	160–170	171–181	182–192	193 or more	EXERCISE INTENSITY
Golf														
a. 4-some 9 holes in 2 hrs. (carry clubs)	2.5	2.83	3	3.25	3.5	3.75	4	4.25	4.5	4.75	4.91	5.16	5.41	Mild
b. 4-some 9 holes in 2 hrs. (pull clubs)	2.41	2.58	2.83	3.08	3.25	3.5	3.75	4	4.16	4.41	4.66	4.91	5.08	Mild
c. cart	2.08	2.33	2.5	2.66	2.91	3.08	3.33	3.5	3.66	3.91	4.08	4.33	4.5	Mild
d. driving	2.41	2.58	2.83	3.08	3.25	3.5	3.75	4	4.16	4.41	4.75	4.91	5.08	Mild
e. putting	1.5	1.58	1.75	1.91	2	2.16	2.33	2.41	2.58	2.75	2.83	3	3.16	Mild
f. two some 9 holes in 1½ hrs. (carrying clubs)	3.58	3.91	4.25	4.58	4.91	5.33	5.66	6	6.33	6.66	7	7.33	7.66	Moderate
g. (two some 9 holes in 1½ hrs. (pull clubs)	3.16	3.41	3.75	4.08	4.33	4.66	4.91	5.25	5.58	5.83	6.16	6.41	6.75	Moderate
Gymnastics														
a. light	2.83	3.08	3.41	3.66	3.91	4.16	4.5	4.75	5	5.25	5.58	5.83	6.08	Moderate
b. medium	4.83	5.25	5.75	6.75	6.66	7.16	7.58	8.08	8.5	9	9.41	9.91	10.33	Mod/High
c. hard	6.75	7.33	8	8.66	9.25	9.91	10.58	11.16	11.83	12.5	13.08	13.5	14.41	High
Handball														
a. cut throat	5.66	6.25	6.75	7.25	7.83	8.33	8.91	9.41	10	10.5	11.08	11.58	12.16	Mod/High
b. 4	4.83	5.25	5.75	6.25	6.66	7.16	7.58	8.08	8.5	9	9.41	9.91	10.33	Mod/High
c. 2	7.33	8.08	8.75	9.41	10.16	10.83	11.58	12.25	12.91	13.66	14.33	15.08	15.75	High
Handtools—light assembly work—radio repair, etc.	1.33	1.5	1.58	1.75	1.91	2	2.16	2.25	2.41	2.5	2.66	2.83	2.91	Mild
Hiking														
a. 20 lb. pack, 2 mph	2.83	3.08	3.41	3.66	3.91	4.16	4.5	4.75	5	5.25	5.58	5.83	6.08	Moderate

b. 20 lb. pack, 3½ mph	3.66	3.91	4.25	4.66	5	5.33	5.66	6	6.33	6.66	7	7.33	7.75 Moderate
c. 20 lb. pack, 4 mph	4.25	4.66	5.08	5.5	5.91	6.25	6.66	7.08	7.5	7.91	8.33	8.75	9.16 Moderate
Hill climbing	5.66	6.25	6.75	7.25	7.83	8.33	8.91	9.41	10	10.5	11.08	11.58	12.16 Mod/High
Hockey													
a. ice	8.5	9.33	10.16	10.91	11.75	12.58	13.41	14.16	15	15.83	16.66	17.41	18.25 Very High
b. field	8.5	9.33	10.16	10.91	11.75	12.58	13.41	14.16	15	15.83	16.66	17.41	18.25 Very High
Horseback riding													
a. walk	1.58	1.75	1.91	2	2.16	2.33	2.5	2.58	2.75	2.91	3.08	3.25	3.41 Mild
b. trot	3.91	4.33	4.66	5	5.41	5.83	6.16	6.58	6.91	7.33	7.66	7.91	8.41 Moderate
c. gallop	5.66	6.25	6.75	7.25	7.83	8.33	8.91	9.41	10	10.5	11.08	11.58	12.16 Mod/High
Horseshoes	2.16	2.41	2.58	2.83	3	3.25	3.41	3.66	3.83	4.08	4.25	4.5	4.66 Mild
Housework (general) See also Dinner, Domestics, Telephone, Sitting, Standing, Washing													
Clothes, Shopping, Ironing	1.91	2.08	2.33	2.5	2.66	2.83	3	3.25	3.41	3.58	3.75	3.91	4.16 Mild
Hunting (not sitting)	4.25	4.66	5.08	5.5	5.91	6.25	6.66	7.08	7.5	7.91	8.33	8.75	9.16 Moderate
Isometrics	2.16	2.41	2.58	2.83	3	3.25	3.41	3.66	3.83	4.08	4.25	4.5	4.66 Mild
Jackhammer (pneumatic tools)	4.25	4.66	5.08	5.5	5.91	6.25	6.66	7.08	7.5	7.91	8.33	8.75	9.16 Moderate
Jogging (5.5 mph)	6.16	6.75	7.41	8	8.58	9.16	9.75	10.33	10.91	11.5	12.08	12.66	13.25 High
Judo	7.5	8.16	8.91	9.58	10.33	11	11.75	12.5	13.16	13.91	14.58	15.33	16 High
Karate	7.5	8.16	8.91	9.58	10.33	11	11.75	12.5	13.16	13.91	14.58	15.33	16 High
Kneeling	.75	.83	.91	.91	1	1.08	1.16	.25	1.33	1.33	.41	.5	1.58 Low
LaCrosse	8.5	9.33	10.16	10.91	11.75	12.58	13.41	14.16	15	15.83	16.66	17.41	5/18.25 Very High
Lawn mowing													
a. power—must push	2.5	2.83	3	3.25	3.5	3.75	4	4.25	4.5	4.75	5	5.16	5.41 Mild
b. power	2.41	2.58	2.83	3.08	3.25	3.5	3.75	4	4.16	4.41	4.66	4.91	5.08 Mild

Table 36
CALORIES USED FOR VARIOUS ACTIVITIES
Per Minute

Weight in Pounds

Activity	71 or less	72–82	83–93	94–104	105–115	116–126	127–137	138–148	149–159	160–170	171–181	182–192	193 or more	EXERCISE INTENSITY
c. sitting	1.33	1.5	1.58	1.75	1.91	2	2.16	2.25	2.41	2.5	2.66	2.83	2.91	Mild
d. push	4.33	4.75	5.16	5.58	6	6.41	6.83	7.25	7.66	8.08	8.5	8.91	9.33	Moderate
Lecturing														
a. standing	1.16	1.25	1.41	1.5	1.58	1.66	1.83	1.91	2	2.16	2.25	2.33	2.5	Low
b. sitting	.91	1	1.16	1.25	1.33	1.41	1.5	1.58	1.66	1.75	1.83	1.91	2	Low
Making Beds	2	2.16	2.33	2.5	2.75	2.91	3.08	3.25	3.5	3.66	3.83	4.08	4.25	Mild
Martial arts	7.5	8.16	8.91	9.58	10.33	11	11.75	12.5	13.16	13.91	14.58	15.33	16	High
Masonry (wall)	2	2.16	2.33	2.5	2.75	2.91	3.08	3.25	3.5	3.66	3.83	4.08	4.25	Mild
Mechanical work (truck, auto repair)	2.16	2.41	2.58	2.83	3	3.25	3.41	3.66	3.83	4.08	4.25	4.5	4.66	Mild
Metal work	2	2.16	2.33	2.5	2.75	2.91	3.08	3.25	3.5	3.66	3.83	4.08	4.25	Mild
Motorcycling														
a. regular	1.91	2.08	2.33	2.5	2.75	2.83	3	3.25	3.41	3.58	3.75	3.91	4.16	Mild
b. trail riding	2.16	2.41	2.58	2.83	3	3.25	3.41	3.66	3.83	4.08	4.25	4.5	4.66	Mild
c. racing	2.83	3.08	3.41	3.66	3.91	4.16	4.5	4.75	5	5.25	5.58	5.83	6.08	Moderate
Mountain climbing	5.66	6.25	6.75	7.25	7.83	8.33	8.91	9.41	10	10.5	11.08	11.58	12.16	Mod/High
Office work (secretary)	1.33	1.5	1.58	1.75	1.91	2	2.16	2.41	2.41	2.5	2.66	2.83	2.91	Mild
Orienteering	5.66	6.25	6.75	7.25	7.83	8.33	8.91	9.41	10	10.5	11.08	11.58	12.16	Mod/High
Painting House	2	2.16	2.33	2.5	2.75	2.91	3.08	3.25	3.5	3.66	3.83	4.08	4.25	Mild
Paperhanging	2	2.16	2.33	2.5	2.75	2.91	3.08	3.25	3.5	3.66	3.83	4.08	4.25	Mild
Personal Toilet	1.16	1.25	1.41	1.5	1.58	1.66	1.83	1.91	2	2.16	2.25	2.33	2.5	Low

Activity														Intensity
Personal Toilet (dressing, washing, showering, shaving, combing, etc.)	1.91	2.08	2.33	2.5	2.66	2.83	3	3.25	3.41	3.58	3.75	3.91	4.16	Mild
Piano playing	1.16	1.25	1.41	1.5	1.58	1.66	1.83	1.91	2	2.16	2.25	2.33	2.5	Low
Pick & shovel work (continuous)	3.75	4.16	4.5	4.83	5.25	5.58	5.91	6.33	6.66	7.	7.41	7.75	8.16	Moderate
Pool	1.5	1.58	1.75	1.91	2	2.16	2.33	2.41	2.58	2.75	2.83	3	3.16	Mild
Raking leaves and dirt	2.08	2.33	2.5	2.66	2.91	3.08	3.33	3.5	3.66	3.91	4.08	4.33	4.5	Mild
Resting	.75	.75	83	91		1.08	.08	1.16	.25	.33	.41	1.5	1.5	Low
Ropeskipping														
a. 50–60 skips left foot only (per min.)	4.83	5.25	5.75	6.25	6.66	7.16	7.58	8.08	8.5	9	9.41	9.91	10.33	Mod/High
b. 70–80 skips left foot only (per min.)	5.25	5.75	6.25	6.75	7.25	7.75	8.25	8.75	9.25	9.75	10.25	10.75	11.25	Mod/High
c. 90–100 skips left foot only (per min.)	6.16	6.75	7.41	8	8.58	9.16	9.75	10.33	10.91	11.5	12.08	12.66	13.25	High
d. 110–120 skips left foot only (per min.)	8.5	9.33	10.16	10.91	11.75	12.58	13.41	14.16	15	15.83	16.66	17.41	18.25	Very High
e. 130–140 skips left foot only (per min.)	11.33	12.41	13.50	14.58	15.66	16.75	17.83	18.91	20	21.08	22.16	23.25	24.33	Very High
Rowing														
a. pleasure 2 mph	2.83	3.08	3.41	3.66	3.91	4.16	4.5	4.75	5	5.25	5.58	5.83	6.08	Moderate
b. vigorous 4 mph	6.16	6.75	7.41	8	8.58	9.16	9.75	10.33	10.91	11.5	12.08	12.66	13.25	High
Rowing machine														
a. easy	2.83	3.08	3.41	3.66	3.91	4.16	4.5	4.75	5	5.25	5.58	5.83	6.08	Moderate
b. vigorous	6.16	6.75	7.41	8	8.58	9.16	9.75	10.33	10.91	11.5	12.08	12.66	13.25	High
Run in place														
a. 50–60 steps per min (left foot only)	4.83	5.25	5.75	6.25	6.66	7.16	7.58	8.08	8.5	9.75	9.41	9.91	10.33	Mod/High

Table 36
CALORIES USED FOR VARIOUS ACTIVITIES
Per Minute

Weight in Pounds

Activity	71 or less	72–82	83–93	94–104	105–115	116–126	127–137	138–148	149–159	160–170	171–181	182–192	193 or more	EXERCISE INTENSITY
b. 70–80 steps per min (left foot only)	5.25	5.75	6.25	6.75	7.25	7.75	8.25	8.75	9.25	9.25	10.25	10.75	11.25	Mod/High
c. 90–100 steps per min (left foot only)	6.16	6.75	7.41	8	8.58	9.16	9.75	10.33	10.91	11.5	12.08	12.66	13.25	High
d. 110–120 steps per min. (left foot only)	8.5	9.33	10.16	10.91	11.75	12.58	13.41	14.16	15	15.83	16.66	17.41	18.25	Very High
e. 130–140 steps per min. (left foot only)	11.33	12.41	13.50	14.58	15.66	16.75	17.83	18.91	20	21.08	22.16	23.25	24.33	Very High
Running														
a. 5.5 mph	6.2	6.8	7.4	8.0	8.6	9.2	9.8	10.3	10.9	11.5	12.1	12.7	13.3	High
b. 6.0 mph	6.3	6.9	7.6	8.2	8.8	12.7	9.9	10.5	11.2	11.8	12.3	12.9	13.5	High
c. 6.5 mph	6.4	7.1	7.8	8.3	8.9	9.5	10.2	10.8	11.4	12.0	12.6	13.2	13.8	High
d. 7.0 mph	6.6	7.3	7.9	8.5	9.2	9.8	10.4	11.0	11.7	12.3	12.9	13.5	14.2	High
e. 7.5 mph	7.1	7.8	8.5	9.1	9.8	10.4	11.2	11.8	12.5	13.2	13.8	14.5	15.2	High
f. 8.0 mph	7.6	8.3	9.0	9.8	10.4	11.2	11.9	12.6	13.3	14.1	14.8	15.5	16.3	Very High
g. 8.5	8.2	8.8	9.7	10.5	11.2	12.0	12.8	13.5	14.3	15.1	15.8	16.7	17.4	Very High
h. 9.0 mph	8.8	9.5	10.3	11.3	12.0	12.8	13.8	14.4	15.3	16.2	17.0	17.8	18.7	Very High
i. 9.5 mph	9.3	10.1	11.0	12.0	12.8	13.7	14.7	15.3	16.3	17.2	18.1	19.0	19.8	Very High
j. 10.0 mph	9.8	10.8	11.8	12.7	13.6	14.6	15.5	16.3	17.3	18.3	19.3	20.2	21.1	Very High
k. 10.5 mph	10.4	11.3	12.4	13.4	14.3	15.4	16.3	17.3	18.3	19.3	20.3	21.3	22.3	Very High
l. 11.0 mph	11.0	12.0	13.1	14.2	15.2	16.3	17.3	18.3	19.3	20.3	21.5	22.5	23.5	Very High
m. 11.5 mph	11.6	12.7	13.8	14.8	15.9	17.1	18.2	19.3	20.3	21.4	22.6	23.7	24.8	Very High
n. 12.0 mph	13.2	14.4	15.7	16.9	18.2	19.4	20.7	21.8	23.2	24.4	25.7	26.9	28.2	Very High
o. 12.5 mph	14.7	16.1	17.5	18.9	20.3	21.7	23.1	24.5	25.9	27.3	28.7	30.1	31.5	Very High

	2.16	2.41	2.58	2.83	3	3.25	3.41	3.66	3.83	4.08	4.25	4.5	4.66	
Sanding floors (power)														Mild
Sailing														
a. calm water	1.5	1.58	1.75	1.91	2	2.16	2.33	2.41	2.58	2.75	2.83	3	3.16	Mild
b. rough water	1.75	1.91	2.08	2.25	2.41	2.58	2.75	2.91	3.08	3.25	3.41	3.58	3.75	Mild
Sawing														
a. power	2.16	2.41	2.58	2.83	3	3.25	3.41	3.66	3.83	4.08	4.25	4.5	4.66	Mild
b. hand	3.66	4.08	4.41	4.75	5.08	5.41	5.83	6.16	6.5	6.83	7.25	7.58	7.91	Moderate
Scuba diving	4.25	4.66	5.08	5.5	5.91	6.25	6.66	7.08	7.5	7.91	8.33	8.75	9.16	Moderate
Sex														
a. foreplay	.91	1	1.16	1.25	1.33	.41	1.5	1.58	1.66	1.75	1.83	1.91	2	Low
b. submissor	1.25	1.41	1.5	1.58	1.75	1.83	2	2.08	2.25	2.33	2.5	2.58	2.66	Low
c. intercourse (agressor)	2.83	3.08	3.41	3.66	3.91	4.16	4.5	4.75	5	5.25	5.58	5.83	6.08	Moderate
Shining shoes	1.25	1.41	1.5	1.58	1.75	1.83	2	2.08	2.25	2.33	2.5	2.58	2.66	Low
Shopping	1.58	1.75	1.91	2	2.16	2.33	2.5	2.58	2.75	3	3.08	3.25	3.41	Mild
Shooting														
a. pistol	1.5	1.66	1.83	1.91	2.08	2.25	2.41	2.5	2.66	2.83	3	3.08	3.25	Mild
b. rifle	1.75	1.91	2.08	2.25	2.41	2.58	2.75	2.91	3.08	3.25	3.41	3.58	3.75	Mild
Sitting														
a. quietly	.75	.83	.91	.91	1	.08	1.16	1.25	1.33	1.33	.41	1.5	1.58	Low
b. reading	.83	.91	1	1.08	1.16	.25	1.33	1.41	1.5	1.58	1.66	1.75	1.83	Low
c. hand work—knitting, crocheting, sewing	.91	1	1.08	1.16	1.25	.33	1.41	1.5	1.58	1.66	1.75	1.83	1.91	Low
d. in truck or car	.58	.66	1	1.08	1.16	.25	1.33	1.41	1.5	.58	1.66	1.75	1.83	Low
Sprinting	23.08	25.33	27.5	29.66	31.91	34.08	36.33	38.5	40.66	42.91	45.08	47.33	49.5	Very High
Skating (leisure)														
a. ice	3.33	3.58	3.91	4.25	4.58	4.91	5.16	5.5	5.83	6.16	6.41	6.75	7.08	Moderate
b. roller	3.33	3.58	3.91	4.25	4.58	4.91	5.16	5.5	5.83	5.16	6.41	6.75	7.08	Moderate

Table 36

CALORIES USED FOR VARIOUS ACTIVITIES
Per Minute

Weight in Pounds

Activity	71 or less	72-82	83-93	94-104	105-115	116-126	127-137	138-148	149-159	160-170	171-181	182-192	193 or more	EXERCISE INTENSITY
Skating (vigorous)														
a. Ice	5.91	6.41	7	7.58	8.08	8.66	9.25	9.83	10.33	10.91	11.5	12	12.58	Mod/High
b. roller	5.91	6.41	7	7.58	8.08	8.66	9.25	9.83	10.33	10.91	11.5	12	12.58	Mod/High
Skiing														
a. downhill (continuous riding & lifts not included)	5.91	6.16	6.66	7.25	7.75	8.33	8.83	9.33	9.91	10.41	11	11.5	12	Mod/High
b. cross country 5 mph	6.58	7.25	7.91	8.5	9.16	9.75	10.41	11	11.66	12.25	12.91	13.33	14.16	High
c. cross country—9 mph	9.41	10.33	11.25	12.16	13.08	13.91	14.83	15.75	16.66	17.58	18.41	19.33	20.25	Very High
Skin diving	4.25	4.66	5.08	5.5	5.91	6.25	6.66	7.08	7.5	7.91	8.33	8.75	9.16	Moderate
Sledding	4	4.41	4.83	5.16	5.58	5.91	6.33	6.75	7.08	7.5	7.83	8.25	8.66	Moderate
Sleeping	.58	.66	.75	.83	.91	1.0	1.0	1.08	1.16	1.25	1.33	1.33	1.33	Low
Snowshoeing 2.2 mph	3.58	3.91	4.25	4.66	5	5.33	5.66	6	6.33	6.66	7	7.33	7.75	Moderate
Snowshoveling														
a. snowblower	2.41	2.58	2.83	3.08	3.25	3.5	3.75	4	4.16	4.41	4.66	4.91	5.08	Mild
b. light	5.75	6.33	6.91	7.41	7.91	8.5	9.08	9.58	10.16	10.75	11.25	11.83	12.41	Mod/High
c. heavy	10	10.91	11.83	12.83	13.75	14.75	15.66	16.58	17.58	18.5	19.5	20.41	21.33	Very High
Snowmobiling	1.91	2.08	2.33	2.5	2.75	2.83	3	3.25	3.41	3.58	3.75	3.91	4.16	Mild
Soccer	5.66	6.25	6.75	7.25	7.83	8.33	8.91	9.41	10	10.5	11.08	11.58	12.16	Mod/High
Stacking lumber	3.58	3.91	4.25	4.66	5	5.33	5.66	6	6.33	6.66	7	7.33	7.75	Moderate
Stacking shelves (packing & unpacking small or medium packages—														

	2.16	2.41	2.58	2.83	3	3.25	3.41	3.66	3.83	4.08	4.25	4.5	4.66	
grocery shelves														Mild
Standing														
a. light activity—														
dishwashing	.25	1.41	1.5	1.58	1.75	1.83	2	2.08	2.25	2.33	2.5	2.58	2.66	Low
b. normally	91	1	1.16	1.25	1.33	1.41	1.5	1.58	1.66	1.75	1.83	1.91	2	Low
Stationary bicycle-resistance sufficient to get pulse rate to rate to 130														
a. 10 mph	4	4.33	4.75	5.08	5.5	5.91	6.25	6.66	7	7.41	7.75	8.16	8.58	Moderate
b. 15 mph	6.16	6.75	7.41	8	8.58	9.16	9.75	10.33	10.91	11.5	12.08	12.66	13.25	High
c. 20 mph	8.41	9.16	10	10.83	11.66	12.41	13.25	14	14.75	15.58	16.41	17.16	18	Very High
Steward & stewardess work (unless sitting)	2.16	2.41	2.58	2.83	3	3.25	3.41	3.66	3.83	4.08	4.25	4.5	4.66	Mild
Stone Masonry	3.58	3.91	4.25	4.66	5	5.33	5.66	6	6.33	6.66	7	7.33	7.75	Moderate
Studying	.75	.83	.91	1	1.08	1.16	1.25	1.33	1.41	1.5	1.5	.58	1.66	Low
Swimming (crawl)														
a. 20 yards per minute	2.83	3.08	3.41	3.66	3.91	4.16	4.5	4.75	5	5.25	5.58	5.83	6.08	Moderate
b. 30 yards per minute	4	4.33	4.75	5.08	5.5	5.83	6.25	6.66	7	7.41	7.75	8	8.5	Moderate
c. 35 yards per minute	5.08	5.58	6.08	6.58	7.08	7.58	8	8.5	9	9.5	10	10.5	10.91	Mod/High
d. 40 yards per minute	5.66	6.25	6.75	7.25	7.83	8.33	8.91	9.41	10	10.5	11.08	11.58	12.16	Mod/High
e. 45 yards per minute	6.5	7.16	7.75	8.33	9	9.58	10.25	10.83	11.6	12.08	12.75	13.33	13.91	High
f. 55 yards per minute	7.91	8.66	9.41	10.16	11	11.75	12.5	13.25	13.91	14.75	15.5	16.25	17	Very High
Table tennis														
a. recreational	2.83	3.08	3.41	3.66	3.91	4.16	4.5	4.75	5	5.25	5.58	5.83	6.08	Moderate
b. vigorous	4.25	4.66	5.08	5.5	5.91	6.25	6.66	7.08	7.5	7.91	8.33	8.75	9.16	Moderate
Telephone														
a. sitting	.83	.91	1	1.08	1.16	1.25	1.33	1.4	1.5	1.58	1.66	1.75	1.83	Low

Table 36
CALORIES USED FOR VARIOUS ACTIVITIES
Per Minute

Weight in Pounds

Activity	71 or less	72–82	83–93	94–104	105–115	116–126	127–137	138–148	149–159	160–170	171–181	182–192	193 or more	EXERCISE INTENSITY
b. standing	1.08	1.16	1.25	1.33	1.41	1.58	1.66	1.75	1.83	1.91	2.08	2.16	2.25	Low
Tennis (singles)														
a. recreational	4	4.41	4.83	5.16	5.58	5.91	6.33	6.75	7.08	7.5	7.83	8.25	8.66	Moderate
b. competitive	5.66	6.25	6.75	7.25	7.83	8.33	8.91	9.41	10	10.5	11.08	11.58	12.16	Mod/High
Tennis (doubles)														
a. recreational	2.83	3.08	3.41	3.66	3.91	4.16	4.5	4.75	5	5.25	5.58	5.83	6.08	Moderate
b. competitive	4	4.41	4.83	5.16	5.58	5.91	6.33	6.75	7.08	7.5	7.83	8.25	8.66	Moderate
Trampolining	7.5	8.16	8.91	9.58	10.33	11	11.75	12.5	13.16	13.91	14.58	15.33	16	High
TV watching	.75	.83	.91	.91	1	1.08	1.16	1.25	1.33	1.33	1.41	1.5	1.58	Low
Typing														
a. electric	1	1.08	1.16	1.25	1.33	1.5	1.58	1.66	1.75	1.83	1.91	2	2.16	Low
b. manual	1.08	1.16	1.33	1.41	1.5	1.58	1.75	1.83	1.91	2.08	2.16	2.25	2.33	Low
Volleyball														
a. recreational	3.33	3.58	3.91	4.25	4.58	4.91	5.16	5.5	5.83	6.16	6.41	6.75	7.08	Moderate
b. competitive	5.66	6.25	6.75	7.25	7.83	8.33	8.91	9.41	10	10.5	11.08	11.58	12.16	Mod/High
Waitress work	2.33	2.5	2.75	3	3.16	3.41	3.58	3.83	4.08	4.25	4.5	4.66	4.91	Mild
Walking														
a. 2 mph	1.8	1.9	2.1	2.3	2.4	2.6	2.8	2.9	3.1	3.3	3.4	3.6	3.8	Mild
b. 2.5 mph	2.4	2.7	2.9	3.1	3.3	3.6	3.8	4.0	4.3	4.5	4.8	5.0	5.2	Mild
c. 3 mph	2.8	3.1	3.4	3.7	3.9	4.2	4.5	4.8	5.0	5.3	5.6	5.8	6.1	Moderate
d. 3.5 mph	3.0	3.3	3.6	3.8	4.1	4.4	4.7	5.0	5.3	5.5	5.8	6.1	6.4	Moderate
e. 4 mph	3.3	3.6	3.9	4.3	4.5	4.8	5.2	5.5	5.8	6.1	6.4	6.8	7.0	Moderate
f. 4.5 mph	4.3	4.7	5.1	5.5	5.9	6.3	6.7	7.1	7.5	7.9	8.3	8.8	9.2	Moderate

g. 5 mph	5.3	5.8	6.3	6.8	7.3	7.8	8.3	8.8	9.3	9.8	10.3	10.8	11.3	Mod/High
h. 5.5 mph	6.2	6.8	7.4	8.0	8.6	9.2	9.8	10.3	10.9	11.5	12.1	12.7	13.3	High
i. upstairs normal	4.3	4.7	5.1	5.5	5.9	6.3	6.7	7.1	7.5	7.9	8.3	8.8	9.2	Moderate
j. downstairs normal	4.3	4.7	5.1	5.5	5.9	6.3	6.7	7.1	7.5	7.9	8.3	8.8	9.2	Moderate
k. upstairs, 2 at a time, rapidly	9.4	10.3	11.3	12.2	8.7	13.9	14.8	15.8	16.7	17.6	18.4	19.3	20.3	Very High
Washing cars & polishing	2.16	2.41	2.58	2.83	3	3.25	3.41	3.66	3.83	4.08	4.25	4.5	4.66	Mild
Washing clothes														
a. modern methods	1.5	1.66	1.83	2	2.08	2.25	2.41	2.58	2.66	2.83	3	3.16	3.25	Mild
b. scrub board	2.16	2.41	2.58	2.83	3	3.25	3.41	3.66	3.83	4.08	4.25	4.5	4.66	Mild
c. drying clothes—clothes dryer	1.5	1.66	1.83	2	2.08	2.25	2.41	2.58	2.66	2.83	3	3.16	3.25	Mild
hanging clothes on line	2.33	2.5	2.75	3	3.16	3.41	3.58	3.83	4.08	4.25	4.5	4.66	4.91	Mild
Washing dishes														
a. by hand	1.25	1.41	1.5	1.58	1.75	1.83	2	2.08	2.25	2.33	2.5	2.58	2.66	Low
b. dishwasher	1.08	1.16	1.25	1.33	1.41	1.58	1.66	1.75	1.83	1.91	2.08	2.16	2.25	Low
Weeding	2.83	3.08	3.41	3.66	3.91	4.16	4.5	4.75	5	5.25	5.58	5.83	6.08	Moderate
Weight training (doesn't include super s)	2.83	3.08	3.41	3.66	3.91	4.16	4.5	4.75	5	5.25	5.58	5.83	6.08	Moderate
Welding (light)	1.5	1.66	1.83	1.91	2.08	2.25	2.41	2.5	2.66	2.83	3	3.16	3.25	Mild
Window Cleaning	2.16	2.41	2.58	2.83	3	3.25	3.41	3.66	3.83	4.08	4.25	4.5	4.66	Mild
Writing	.83	.91	1	1.08	1.16	1.25	1.33	1.41	1.5	1.58	1.66	1.75	1.83	Low
Yoga	2.16	2.41	2.58	2.83	3	3.25	3.41	3.66	3.83	4.08	4.25	4.5	4.66	Mild

APPENDIX E

Calorie Values of Various Foods

All calorie values listed here for the various foods must be regarded as approximate. Some bakeries, for example, put more sugar in cookies or cake than others. Some fruit juices have sugar added while others do not. And an apple grown in Washington does not necessarily contain the same number of calories as a similar-sized one grown in Pennsylvania.

In the listing that follows, the caloric equivalents of foods and beverages are given in terms of common household usage. Many of the portions are described as "average." I wish it were possible to be more specific as to just what "average" really amounts to. However, if you're a fairly big eater, it's pretty safe to assume that what looks like an "average" portion to you is larger and has more calories than the "average" portion listed, and you probably should take this into account when you compute your caloric income.

Table 37
CALORIE VALUES OF VARIOUS FOODS

Food	Amount	Calories
African Lobster Tail	4 ounces meat	100
Ale	1 cup	100
All-Bran	1 cup	100
Almond Cake	Average serving	250
Almond Coffee Cake	Average piece	250
Almond Cookies	2 medium	50
Almond Fudge	1-inch square	110
Almond Macaroons	1 large	100
Almonds, Salted	12 medium	75
Almonds, Shelled	12 medium	75
Ambrosia	Average serving	140
Anchovies	6	50
Angel Food Cake	2-inch section	125
Apple	1 small	75
Apple, Baked with Sugar	1 small	100
Apple, Baked with Sugar and Cream	1 small	150
Apple Butter	1 tablespoon	35
Apple Brown Betty	½ cup	200
Apple Cake, Dutch	1 average piece	250
Apple Cider	¾ cup	75
Apple, Cubed	1 cup	90
Apple, Dried	2 ounces	150
Apple Dumpling	1 medium	275

Food	Amount	Calories
Artichoke Heart	1 medium	50
Artichoke with 1 Tablespoon Hollandaise	1 medium	150
Artichoke, Stuffed with Mushrooms	1 medium	100
Asparagus	12 stalks	25
Asparagus Omelet	With 2 eggs	220
Asparagus Soufflé	Average serving	200
Asparagus Soup. Creamed	1 cup	200
Asparagus Tips	12 tips	25
Asparagus Vinaigrette	Average serving	175
Aspic, Tomato	Average serving	35
Avocado	1 small	425
Avocado Salad	Average serving	275
Bacardi Rum	1½ ounces	100
Bacon, Broiled	3 strips, crisp	100
Bacon, Canadian, Broiled	4 ounces	250
Bacon, Canadian, Fried	4 ounces	250
Bacon Fat	1 teaspoon	50
Bacon, Fried	3 strips, crsip	100
Bagel	1	110
Baked Alaska	Average serving	350
Baked Beans	1 cup	200

Food	Measure	Value
Apple Juice	1 cup	120
Apple Pandowdy	Average serving	375
Apple Pie	Average piece	400
Apple Pudding	½ cup	200
Apple Strudel	Average piece	225
Apple, Taffy	1	260
Apple Tapioca Pudding	½ cup	140
Apple Tart	1 medium	175
Apple Turnover	1 medium	250
Applesauce Bread	1 slice	110
Applesauce Cake	⅛ cake	420
Applesauce, Canned	½ cup	50
Capplesauce, Canned with Sugar	½ cup	115
Applesauce, Fresh	½ cup	50
Applesauce, Fresh with Sugar	½ cup	100
Apricots	5 medium	95
Apricot-Apple Compote	Average serving	75
Apricot Brandy	1 cordial glass	75
Apricot Butter Preserve	1 tablespoon	35
Apricots, Canned, No Syrup	3 halves	30
Apricots, Canned with Sugar	3 halves	50
Apricot Cordial	1 cordial glass	75
Apricots, Dried	3 halves	50
Apricots, Frozen	5 medium	100
Apricot Juice	6 ounces	120
Apricot Pie	Average piece	350
Apricots, Spiced	4 medium	100
Apricot Whip	Average serving	110
Arrowroot	1 tablespoon	30
Arrowroot Flour	2 ounces	225
Artichoke	1 large	75
Baked Beans, Canned with Pork and Molasses	½ cup	170
Baked Beans, Canned with Tomato	½ cup	140
Baking Powder Biscuits	2 small or 1 large	100
Bamboo Shoots	⅔ cup	40
Banana	1 medium	100
Banana Cake	Average serving	200
Banana Cream Pie	Average piece	400
Banana Custard	Average serving	200
Banana Fritter	1 average	200
Banana Shortcake	Average serving	350
Banana Split	1	450
Barbecue Sauce	1 tablespoon	50
Barbecued Beef	Average serving	300
Barbecued Chicken	Average serving	200
Barbecued Lamb	Average serving	350
Barbecued Spareribs	6 average ribs	250
Barley	½ cup	325
Barley-Mushroom Soup	1 cup	120
Barley Soup	1 cup	125
Barley Soup, Creamed	1 cup	200
Bass	¼ pound	100
Bavarian Cream, Orange	Average serving	300
Bean Soup	1 cup	225
Bean Sprouts, Mung	1 cup	20
Bean Sprouts, Soy	1 cup	50
Beans, Black, Soup	1 cup	225
Beans, Butter	½ cup, cooked	125
Beans, Kidney	1 cup	225
Beand, Kidney, Dried	½ cup	390

Item	Serving	Calories
Beans, Lima	1 cup	150
Beans, Lima, Canned	½ cup	75
Beans, Lima, Dried	½ cup	265
Beans, Navy	1 cup	200
Beans, Navy, Canned	½ cup	100
Beans, Navy, Dried	½ cup	350
Beans, Navy, Soup	8-ounce serving	175
Beans, Pinto, Soup	8-ounce serving	225
Beans, Snap, Green, Canned	1 cup	25
Beans, Snap, Green, Fresh	1 cup	25
Beans, Soybeans	½ cup	115
Beans, String	1 cup	25
Beans, String, Canned	1 cup	25
Beans, Wax, Canned	1 cup	30
Beans, Wax, Fresh,	1 cup	30
Beans, Yellow, Canned	1 cup	30
Beans, Yellow, Fresh	1 cup	30
Beef, Boiled	Average serving	250
Beef, Bouillon	1 cup	25
Beef, Broiled	Average serving	250
Beef, Broth	1 cup	35
Beefburgers	2-ounce patty	200
Beef, Chipped	3 ounces	175
Beef, Chipped, Creamed	3 ounces	225
Beef, Chopped	¼ pound	350
Beef, Chuck Pot Roast	Average serving	300
Beef Consomme	1 cup	35
Beer, Ginger	6 ounces	75
Beer, Root	6 ounces	75
Beet Borscht	1 cup	75
Beet Greens	1 cup cooked	40
Beets	½ cup	35
Beets, Buttered	½ cup	70
Beets, Canned	½ cup	35
Beets, Harvard	Average serving	70
Berry Pie	Average piece	350
Beverage, Carbonated	1 average	75
Biscuit, Baking Powder	2 small or 1 large	100
Biscuit, Buttermilk	2 small or 1 large	110
Biscuit, Shortcake	1	175
Biscuit, Tortoni	1 small	175
Biscuit, Yeast	1 large	100
Blackberries, Canned in Syrup	1 cup	230
Blackberries, Canned in Water	1 cup	100
Blackberries, Fresh	1 cup	100
Blackberry Brandy	Shot	75
Blackberry Cordial	Pony	100
Blackberry Pie	Average piece	350
Black-Eyed Peas, Canned,	½ cup	100
Blackstrap Molasses	1 tablespoon	45
Black Walnuts	11 halves	100
Blintz, Jelly	1 average	175
Blueberries, Canned with Sugar	½ cup	125

Beef, Corned	4 ounces	250
Beef, Corned, Hash	½ cup	150
Beef Croquettes	Average serving	250
Beef, Dried	3 ounces	175
Beef, Filet Mignon	Average serving	250
Beef Heart	3 ounces	100
Beef, Kidney	Average serving	225
Beef, Liver	Average serving	150
Beef Pie	Average	375
Beef, Porterhouse Steak	Average serving	400
Beef, Pot Roast	Average serving	200
Beef, Rib Roast, Rolled	Average serving	350
Beef, Rib Roast, Standing	Average serving	300
Beef Roast	Average serving	200
Beef Roast, Hash	½ cup	125
Beef, Round Steak	Average serving	200
Beef, Short Ribs, Braised	Average serving	200
Beef, Sirloin Tips	Average serving	200
Beef Steak	Average serving	200
Beef Steak, Flank	Average serving	200
Beef, Steak and Kidney Pie	Average serving	375
Beef, Steak, Planked	Average serving	200
Beef Stew	1 cup	250
Beef Stroganoff	Average serving	350
Beef, Swiss Steak	1½ ounces	150
Beef, Sweetbreads	Small serving	125
Beef, T-Bone Steak	Average serving	200
Beef, Tenderloin Steak	Average serving	200
Beef, Tongue	2 average slices	100
Beer	12-ounces	150
Beer, Bock	8-ounce glass	175
Blueberries, Canned, Water Packed	½ cup	50
Blueberries, Fresh	1 cup	100
Blueberry Cream Pie	Average piece	400
Blueberry Griddle Cakes	1 (4-inch diameter)	125
Blueberry Muffin	1 average	150
Blueberry Pie	Average piece	375
Blueberry Tart	1 medium	225
Bluefish, Baked	Average serving	200
Bluefish, Broiled	Average serving	185
Bluefish, Fried	Average serving	240
Bologna	2 ounces	125
Bon Bon	1 average	50
Bonita	Average serving	150
Bordeaux Wine	1 wine glass	125
Borscht, Plain	1 cup	75
Boston Brown Bread	3-inch square, ½-inch thick	75
Boston Brown Muffin	1 average	110
Boston Cream Pie	1 piece	400
Bouillabaise	Restaurant portion	525
Bouillon	1 cup	25
Bouillon, Beef	1 cup	25
Bouillon, Chicken	1 cup	25
Bourbon	1 shot	100
Bourbon Highball	Average	150
Boysenberries, Fresh	1 cup	100
Boysenberry Pie	Average piece	350
Bran Flakes	¾ cup	100
Bran Muffin	1 average	100
Brandy	1 shot	75
Brandy Alexander	1 cocktail	240

Brandy, Fruit	1 cordial	75
Brandy Punch	1 cup	225
Brazil Nuts	2 average	50
Bread, Applesauce	1 slice	110
Bread, Bran	1 slice	75
Bread with Butter	1 slice	90
Bread, Corn	2-inch square	200
Bread, Cracked Wheat	1 slice	55
Bread Crumbs, Dried	½ cup	170
Bread, Date Nut	Average Slice	90
Bread, Egg	1 slice	75
Bread, French	1 slice	50
Bread, Ginger	2-inch square	175
Bread, Gluten	1 slice	75
Bread, Graham	1 slice	75
Bread, Italian	1 slice	55
Bread, Protein	1 slice	40
Bread Pudding	½ cup	125
Bread, Raisin	1 slice	75
Bread, Rye	1 slice	75
Bread, Short	1 slice	125
Bread, White	1 slice	65
Bread, Whole Wheat	1 slice	65
Broccoli	1 cup	45
Broccoli, Baked	1 serving	50
Broccoli, Canned	1 cup	45
Bronx Cocktail	Average	225
Cabbage Soup	Average serving	50
Cabbage, Stuffed	Average serving	150
Cabbage, Sweet and Sour	1 cup	75
Cake, Almond	Average serving	250
Cake, Angel Food	2-inch section	125
Cake, Applesauce	⅙ cake	420
Cake, Banana	Average serving	200
Cake, Blueberry	Average piece	175
Cake, Bride's	Average piece	250
Cake, Buckwheat	1 (4-inch diameter)	90
Cake, Butter Sponge	Average Slice	150
Cake, Caramel	Average piece	250
Cake, Cheese	Average slice	350
Cake, Chocolate	Average serving	250
Cake, Chocolate Chip	Average piece	200
Cake, Cinnamon	Average piece	150
Cake, Coffee	2x4-inch piece	100
Cake, Coffee, with Icing	2x4-inch piece	150
Cake, Crumb	Average piece	100
Cake, Devil's Food	Average slice	275
Cake, Egg Nog	Average piece	175
Cake, Fruit	2½ ounces	250
Cake, Ice Box	Average piece,	300
Cake, Jelly Roll	Average serving	200
Cake, Marble	1-inch slice	125
Cake, Pound	½-inch slice	125
Cake, Rich	Average slice	300

Food	Measure	Calories
Brownies	2-inch square	150
Brussels Sprouts	1 cup cooked	60
Buckwheat Cake	1 (4-inch diameter)	90
Buckwheat Flour	½ cup	170
Bun, Cinnamon	1 average	100
Bun, Hot Cross	1 average	150
Burgundy Wine	1 wine glass	85
Butter	Average pat	40
Butter	1 tablespoon	100
Butter, Apple	1 tablespoon	35
Butter, Apricot Preserve	1 tablespoon	35
Butter Cookies	6	100
Butter Crackers	3 small	50
Butter Frosting	1 tablespoon	50
Butter, Peanut	1 tablespoon	100
Butter Sauce, Lemon	1 tablespoon	20
Butter, Sweet	1 tablespoon	100
Buttermilk	1 cup	85
Buttermilk Biscuits	2 small or 1 large	110
Butternut Squash	1 cup	35
Butternuts	5	100
Butterscotch Candy	Wafer	75
Butterscotch Frosting	1 tablespoon	50
Butterscotch Pudding	½ cup	175
Butterscotch Sauce	1 tablespoon	25
Butterscotch Sundae	Average serving	400
Cabbage, Green, Boiled	1 cup	40
Cabbage, Green, Raw	¾ cup	20
Cabbage, Red, Boiled	1 cup	40
Cabbage, Red, Raw	¾ cup	20
Cake, Sponge	Average piece	125
Cake, Strawberry Cream	Average piece	275
Cake, Upside Down, Apricot	Average piece	275
Cake, Upside Down, Blueberry	Average piece	275
Cake, Upside Down, Cherry	Average piece	275
Cake, Upside Down, Pineapple	Average piece	225
Cake, Washington Cream	Average piece	225
Cakes, Rice	2 ounces	225
Cantaloupe	½ medium	50
Capers	1 teaspoon	3
Capon, Roasted	Average serving	225
Caramel	1 average	50
Caramel Cake	Average piece	250
Caramel Frosting	1 tablespoon	50
Caramel Sundae	Average serving	350
Caramel Syrup	1 tablespoon	60
Caraway Roll	1 average	125
Carbonated Beverages	1 average	75
Carp	Average serving	100
Carrot Juice	1 cup	50
Carrots, Cooked	½ cup	25
Carrots, Raw	1 medium	25
Cashew Nuts	7	75
Catsup	1 tablespoon	25
Cauliflower	1 cup	30
Caviar	1 tablespoon	50
Celery, Cooked	1 cup	25
Celery, Raw	2 stalks	15
Celery Soup, Clear	1 cup	100
Celery Soup, Creamed	⅔ cup	150
Chablis	1 wine glass	75

Food	Portion	Calories
Champagne, Domestic	1 glass	85
Champagne, Imported	1 glass	100
Champagne Cocktail	1 glass	100
Chard, Cooked	1 cup	50
Cheese, American	1 slice	100
Cheese, Bleu	1½ ounces	150
Cheese Blintz	1 average	175
Cheese, Brick	1½ ounces	150
Cheese, Brie	1½ ounces	140
Cheese Cake	Average slice	350
Cheese Cake, Pineapple	Average piece	350
Cheese Cake, Strawberry	Average piece	350
Cheese, Camembert	1½ ounces	125
Cheese, Cheddar	1½ ounces	150
Cheese, Cheshire	1½ ounces	150
Cheese, Cottage	1 cup	215
Cheese, Cottage, Low-Fat	1 cup	165
Cheese, Crackers	3 small	50
Cheese, Cream	1 tablespoon	50
Cheese, Edam	1½ ounces	150
Cheese, Emmenthaler	1½ ounces	150
Cheese, Farmers	½ cup	200
Cheese, Goat	1½ ounces	175
Cheese, Gouda	1½ ounces	150
Cheese, Gruyere	2 ounces	225
Cheese, Jack	1½ ounces	150
Cheese, Liederkranz	1½ ounces	125
Chicken Giblets	Average serving	150
Chicken Gumbo	1 cup	125
Chicken Livers	Each	50
Chicken Livers, Chopped	1 ounce	125
Chicken Noodle Soup	1 cup	125
Chicken Paprika	Average serving	200
Chicken Pot Pie	4 ounces	350
Chicken, Roasted	Average serving	250
Chicken Rice Soup	1 cup	125
Chicken Salad	Average serving	225
Chicken Soup	1 cup	100
Chicken Soup with Matzoth Balls	1 cup	175
Chicken Soup, Creamed	1 cup	200
Chicken, Stewed	Average serving	300
Chicken Won Ton	4 average	150
Chicory	Average serving	10
Chiffon Pie, Orange	Average piece	300
Chili Con Carne	½ cup	250
Chili Con Carne with Beans, Canned	½ cup	175
Chili Sauce	1 tablespoon	25
Chives	½ cup	25
Chocolate Bar	Average	250
Chocolate Bar with Almonds	Average	250
Chocolate Butter Frosting	1 tablespoon	55
Chocolate Cake	Average serving	250
Chocolate Chip Cookies	3 small	65

Food	Measure	Calories
Cheese, Limburger	1½ ounces	150
Cheese and Macaroni	½ cup	225
Cheese, Muenster	1½ ounces	150
Cheese, Neufchatel	1½ ounces	110
Cheese Omelet	2 eggs	250
Cheese, Parmesan	1½ ounces	170
Cheese, Pot	½ cup	200
Cheese, Provolone	1½ ounces	150
Cheese, Reggiano	1½ ounces	170
Cheese, Romano	1½ ounces	170
Cheese, Roquefort	1½ ounces	150
Cheese Souffle	¾ cup	150
Cheese, Stilton	1½ ounces	150
Cheese Strudel	Average piece	225
Cheese, Swiss	1½ ounces	150
Cherries, Canned	20 small	75
Cherries, Fresh, White	½ cup	100
Cherries, Fresh	25 small	75
Cherries, Maraschino	2 average	35
Cherry Pie	Average piece	350
Chestnuts, Roasted	8	50
Chewing Gum	1 stick	6
Chicken a la King	½ cup	230
Chicken, Barbecued	Average serving	250
Chicken Bouillon	1 cup	25
Chicken, Broiled	Average serving	200
Chicken Broth	1 cup	35
Chicken, Canned	4 ounces	225
Chicken Fat	1 teaspoon	45
Chicken Fricassee	Average serving	225
Chicken, Fried	Average serving	325

Food	Measure	Calories
Chocolate Cookies	3 small	50
Chocolate Creams	1 average	75
Chocolate Cream Pie	Average piece	400
Chocolate Eclair	1	275
Chocolate Fudge	1-inch square	110
Chocolate Hot, with Whipped Cream	1 cup	150
Chocolate Milk	1 cup	225
Chocolate Mints	3 small	125
Chocolate Pudding	½ cup	250
Chocolate Sauce	1 tablespoon	25
Chocolate Sundae	Average serving	350
Chocolate Syrup	1 tablespoon	50
Chop Suey, Beef	½ cup	275
Chop Suey, Chicken	½ cup	250
Chop Suey, Pork	½ cup	300
Chop Suey, Vegetable	½ cup	225
Chow Mein, Beef	½ cup	150
Chow Mein, Chicken	½ cup	125
Chow Mein, Pork	½ cup	175
Chuck Steak, with Bone	Average serving	285
Chutney	1 teaspoon	25
Cider	1 cup	100
Cinnamon Bun	1 average	100
Cinnamon Cake	Average piece	150
Cinnamon Muffin	1 average	110
Cinnamon Roll	1 average	100
Cinnamon Toast	1 slice	200
Citron, Candied	1 ounce	100
Clam Broth	6 ounces	50
Clam Chowder, Manhattan	Average portion	125

Food	Portion	Calories
Clam Chowder, New England	Average portion	225
Clam Juice	6 ounces	50
Clams	12 medium	100
Clams, Cheerystone, Raw	12 medium	125
Clams, Fried	6	175
Clams, Steamed	12 medium	100
Claret Wine	1 wine glass	75
Cobbler, Fruit	Average serving	300
Cocoa, Powdered	1½ tablespoons	50
Cocoa with Milk	1 cup	235
Cocoa with Half-Milk, Half-Water	1 cup	150
Cocoamalt	1 cup	275
Coconut Cake	Average slice	275
Coconut Cake with Icing	Average serving	350
Coconut Cream Pie	Average piece	450
Coconut Custard Pie	Average piece	400
Coconut, Dried	2 tablespoons	50
Coconut, Fresh	2x1x½-inch slice	100
Coconut Fudge	1-inch square	110
Coconut Macaroon	1 large	100
Coconut Milk	1 cup	605
Codfish	Average serving	100
Codfish Ball	1 average	100
Codfish, Creamed	½ cup	150
Cod Liver Oil	1 tablespoon	120
Coffee, Black	1 cup	0
Coffee Cake	2x4-inch piece	100
Corn, Niblets	½ cup	70
Corn Oil	1 tablespoon	120
Corn on Cob	1 average ear	100
Corn Pone	2-inch square	200
Cornstarch	1 tablespoon	30
Cornstarch, Chocolate	1 tablespoon	100
Cornstarch Pudding	½ cup	150
Corn Syrup	2 tablespoons	115
Corned Beef	4 ounces	250
Corned Beef Hash	½ cup	150
Cottage Cheese	1 cup	215
Cottage Cheese, Low-Fat	1 cup	165
Cotton Seed Oil	1 tablespoon	120
Crab Apple	2 ounces	45
Crab, Deviled	½ cup	225
Crab, Hard Shell, Atlantic	3 ounces meat	90
Crabmeat	½ cup	65
Crab, Soft Shell	1 medium crab	200
Cracked Wheat Bread	1 slice	55
Crackers, Animal	6	50
Crackers, Butter	3 small	50
Crackers, Cheese	3 small	50
Crackers, Graham	3 medium	75
Crackers, Matzoth	1	75
Crackers, Oatmeal	3	125
Crackers, Oyster	½ cup or 14	60
Crackers, Saltines	6 2-inch squares	100

Food	Portion	Calories
Coffee Cream	1 tablespoon	30
Coffee with Cream	1 tablespoon cream	30
Coffee Eclair	1 average	275
Coffee Espresso	1 cup	0
Coffee with Sugar	1 teaspoon sugar	18
Coffee, Turkish	5 teaspoons sugar	90
Cognac	1 shot	75
Cola	6 ounces	75
Cole Slaw	6 ounces	20
Consomme	1 cup	25
Cookies, Almond	1 ounce	125
Cookies, Anise	3 small	50
Cookies, Butter	6	100
Cookies, Chocolate	3 small	50
Cookies, Chocolate Chip	3 small	65
Cookies, Date	2 average	100
Cookies, Oatmeal	1 large	100
Cookies, Raisin	1 ounce	125
Cookies, Walnut	1 ounce	125
Cooking Oil, Vegetable	1 tablespoon	120
Corn Bread	2-inch square	200
Corn, Canned	½ cup	70
Corn Soup, Creamed	1 cup	225
Corn Flakes	1 ounce or 1 cup	100
Corn, Fresh Frozen	1 cup	140
Corn Fritter	1 average	175
Corn Grits	1 cup	120
Corn Meal, Cooked	½ cup	60
Corn Meal Flour	½ cup	240
Corn, Mexican Style	½ cup	75
Corn Muffin	1 average	100
Crackers, Soda	6	100
Cranberry Sauce	3 tablespoons	100
Crappies, Baked	Average serving	150
Crappies, Fried	Average serving	250
Cream, 20%	3 tablespoons	100
Cream Cheese	1 tablespoon	50
Cream Pie, Banana	1 piece	400
Cream Pie, Blueberry	1 piece	400
Cream Pie, Boston	1 piece	400
Cream Pie, Cherry	1 piece	400
Cream Pie, Coconut	1 piece	450
Cream Pie, Huckelberry	1 piece	400
Cream Pie, Peach	1 piece	400
Cream Pie, Strawberry	1 piece	400
Cream Puff	1 average	175
Cream Sauce, Medium	2 tablespoons	50
Cream, Sour	¼ cup	100
Cream of Wheat	¾ cup	100
Cream, Whipped, 40%	1 tablespoon	50
Creme de Cacao	1 Pony	75
Creme de Menthe	1 Pony	75
Crepe Suzette	1	225
Croutons	6 average cubes	25
Crumb Cake	2x4-inch piece	100
Cube Steak	1½ ounces	150
Cucumber	1 8-inch	20
Cupcake	1 small	100
Cupcake, with Icing	1 small	150
Currants, Dried	¼ cup	150
Curried Beef	Average serving	400
Curried Chicken	Average serving	325

Curried Duck	Average serving	400
Curried Eggs	Average serving	250
Curried Fish	Average serving	225
Curried Lamb	Average serving	400
Curried Pork	Average serving	400
Custard	½ cup	125
Custard Pie	Average piece	300
Custard, Rice	½ cup	200
Daiquiri	1 cocktail	125
Dandelion Greens, Cooked	½ cup	40
Dandelion Greens, Fresh	½ cup	50
Danish Pastry	Average piece	200
Danish Pastry, Cheese	Average piece	250
Danish Pastry, Prune	Average piece	250
Date Cookies	2 average	100
Date and Nut Bread	Average slice	90
Date Pudding	Average serving	150
Dates, Dried or Fresh	4	100
Dates, Stuffed	2	100
Devil's Food Cake	Average slice	275
Doughnut	Average	150
Doughnut, French	Average	200
Doughnut, Jelly	Average	250
Doughnut, Sugared	Average	175
Dressing, French	1 tablespoon	100
Dressing, Oil and Vinegar	1 tablespoon	65

Egg, Shirred	1 average	75
Egg White	1 average	15
Egg Whites, Dried	1 ounce	115
Egg Yolk	1 average	60
Egg Yolks, Dried	1 ounce	200
Eggplant	1 cup	50
Eggplant, Baked, Italian Style	Average serving	475
Eggplant, Parmigiana	Average serving	600
Eggplant, Scalloped	Average serving	250
Eggs Creole	Average serving	175
Elderberry Cordial	1 cordial glass	75
Elderberry Pie	Average piece	350
Elderberry Wine	1 wine glass	125
Enchilada	1 average	200
Endive	Small	10
English Muffin	1 average	150
English Toffee	Average piece	25
Escarole	½ heart	10
Farina	¾ cup	100
Fig Bars	2	100
Fig Muffin	1 average	125
Figs, Canned	½ cup	125
Figs, Dried	1 medium	50
Figs, Fresh	4 small (1½-inch)	120
Filberts	6	50
Filet of Sole, Broiled	Average serving	125

Food	Measure	Calories
Dressing, Roquefort Cheese	1 tablespoon	125
Dressing, Russian	1 tablespoon	100
Dressing, Thousand Island	1 tablespoon	100
Duck	Average serving	300
Duck, Roasted with Dressing	Average serving	375
Duck Soup	1 cup	125
Duck Soup, Creamed	1 cup	225
Dumpling, Apple	1 medium	275
Eel, Baked	1 average serving	185
Eel, Broiled	1 average serving	185
Egg	1 average	75
Egg, Boiled	1 average	75
Egg, Bread	1 slice	75
Egg, Coddled	1 average	75
Egg, Cream	1 cup	200
Egg Cream, Chocolate	1 cup	250
Egg, Deviled	2	225
Egg Drop Soup	1 cup	60
Egg Foo Yung, Chicken	Average portion	350
Egg Foo Yung, Ham	Average portion	475
Egg Foo Yung, Lobster	Average portion	275
Egg Foo Yung, Pork	Average portion	475
Egg Foo Yung, Shrimp	Average portion	275
Egg, Fried	1 average	100
Egg Nog	1 cup	300
Egg Nog Cake	Average piece	175
Egg, Poached	1 average	75
Egg Roll, Chinese	1 average	175
Egg, Scrambled	1 average	110
Egg, Scrambled with Milk	1 average	150
Filet Mignon	Average serving	250
Finnan Haddie	Average serving	125
Fish, Bluefish, Baked	Average serving	200
Fish, Bluefish, Broiled	Average serving	185
Fish, Bluefish, Fried	Average serving	240
Fish, Buffalofish, Broiled	Average serving	115
Fish, Butterfish, Fried	Average serving	200
Fish, Catfish	Average serving	100
Fish, Cod	Average serving	100
Fish, Cod, Ball	1 average	100
Fish, Cod, Cake	1 average	100
Fish, Cod, Creamed with 2 Tablespoons Sauce	Average serving	150
Fish, Cod, Dried	2 ounces	210
Fish, Cod, Steak	Average serving	100
Fish, Gefilte	Average serving	150
Fish, Sweet and Sour	Average serving	200
Fish, Smoked	½ fish	150
Fish, Swordfish	Average serving	150
Fish, Tuna, Canned in Oil	½ cup	250
Fish, Tuna, Cooked	¾ cup	100
Fish, Whitefish, Broiled	Average serving	125
Fish, Whitefish, Fried	Average serving	225
Fish, Whitefish, Smoked	Average serving	150
Fish, Whitefish, Steamed	Average serving	125
Flounder	Average serving	150
Flour, All-Purpose	1 cup	400
Flour, Arrowroot	2 ounces	225
Flour, Buckwheat	½ cup	170
Flour, Corn Meal	½ cup	240
Flour, Soybean, Medium Fat	1 cup	230

Frankfurter	1 average	125
Frankfurter Roll	1	125
French Garlic Dressing with Olive Oil	1 tablespoon	100
French Onion Soup with Croutons	1 cup	150
French Roll	1 average	100
French Salad Dressing	1 tablespoon	100
French Toast	1 slice	125
Frijoles, Pinto Beans	½ cup cooked	125
Fritter, Apple	1 average	200
Fritter, Banana	1 average	200
Fritter, Corn	1 average	175
Frogs Legs	4 large	50
Frosting, Boiled	1 tablespoon	35
Frosting, Brown Sugar	1 tablespoon	40
Frosting, Butter	1 tablespoon	50
Frosting, Butterscotch	1 tablespoon	50
Frosting, Chocolate Butter	1 tablespoon	55
Frosting, Fudge	1 tablespoon	42
Frosting, Lemon	1 tablespoon	35
Frosting, Maple	1 tablespoon	40
Frosting, Mocha, Chocolate	1 tablespoon	45
Frosting, Orange	1 tablespoon	35
Frosting, Pineapple	1 tablespoon	50
Frosting, Seven-Minute	1 tablespoon	42
Fruitcake	2½ ounces	250
Fruit Cobbler	Average serving	300
Gin Rickey	1 glass	150
Gin and Tonic	1 glass	125
Ginger Ale	6 ounces	75
Ginger Beer	6 ounces	75
Ginger, Candied	1 ounce	100
Ginger Snaps	5	100
Gingerbread	2-inch square	175
Gnocchi (No Sauce)	½ cup	140
Goat Milk	1 cup	165
Goose Fat	1 tablespoon	145
Goose Liver	Average serving	150
Goose, Roasted	Average serving	300
Goose, Roasted with Dressing	Average serving	375
Gooseberries, Fresh	1 cup	60
Gorgonzola Cheese	1 ounce	100
Goulash, Hungarian	Average serving	350
Graham Crackers	3 medium	75
Grape Juice	½ cup	75
Grape Nuts	2 ounces	200
Grapefruit	½ small	50
Grapefruit, Canned	½ cup	75
Grapefruit Juice	6 ounces	75
Grapefruit Juice, Canned, Sweetened	1 cup	130
Grapefruit Juice, Canned, Unsweetened	6 ounces	70
Grapes, Concord	1 cup or 5½ ounces	85

Food	Measure	Calories
Fruit Cocktail, Canned	Average serving	100
Fruit Cocktail, Fresh	Average serving	75
Fruit Jam	1 tablespoon	50
Fruit Jelly	1 tablespoon	50
Fruit Preserves	1 tablespoon	50
Fruit Punch	6 ounces	150
Fruit Sherbet	Average scoop	100
Fruit Sundae	Average serving	400
Fruit Syrup	1 tablespoon	60
Fudge	1-inch square	110
Fudge, Almond	1-inch square	110
Fudge, Brown Sugar	1-inch square	100
Fudge Cake	2-inch piece	42
Fudge Frosting	1 tablespoon	110
Fudge, Milk Chocolate	1 piece	100
Fudge, Raisin	1-inch square	25
Fudge Sauce	1 tablespoon	400
Fudge Sundae, Hot	Average serving	400
Garbanzos (Chick Peas) Dried, Uncooked	¼ cup	175
Garlic	1 clove	2
Garlic French Dressing	1 tablespoon	100
Gefilte Fish	Average serving	150
Gelatin, Processed, Sweetened	Average serving	100
German Pancake	1	225
Giblets, Chicken	Average serving	150
Giblets, Turkey	Average serving	150
Gin	2 ounces	150
Gin Collins	1 glass	150
Gin Fizz	1 glass	125
Grapes, Delaware	1 cup or 5½ ounces	85
Grapes, Green, Seedless	1 cup or 5½ ounces	90
Grapes, Malaga	1 cup or 5½ ounces	100
Grapes, Muscat	1 cup or 5½ ounces	100
Grapes, Niagara	1 cup or 5½ ounces	85
Grapes, Scuppernong	1 cup or 5½ ounces	85
Grapes, Tokay	1 cup or 5½ ounces	100
Gravy, Thick	1 tablespoon	50
Green Gage Plums	1 cup	95
Green Pepper, Cooked	1 medium	25
Green Pepper, Stuffed	1 medium	125
Green Tea, Plain	1 cup	0
Grenadine Syrup	1 teaspoon	55
Griddle Cake	1 (4½-inch diameter)	100
Griddle Cake, Blueberry	1 (4-inch diameter)	125
Grits, Hominy	½ cup	60
Grits, Soybean, Medium Fat	1 cup	365
Grog, Hot	6 ounces	175
Guava	1 medium	50
Guava Butter	1 tablespoon	40
Gum Drops	3 large	100
Haddock, Baked	Average serving	180
Haddock, Broiled	Average serving	180
Haddock, Fried	Average serving	250
Hake, Broiled	Average serving	125
Halibut, Baked	Average serving	200
Halibut, Broiled	Average serving	200
Halibut, Creamed	Average serving	250
Halvah	1 ounce	125
Ham, Baked	Average slice	350

Food	Serving	Calories
Ham, Boiled	Average slice	350
Ham Butt, Boiled	Average slice	100
Ham, Deviled	1 tablespoon	100
Ham, Fried	2 average slices	200
Ham Hock	Average serving	400
Ham, Smoked	Average serving	450
Ham Steak	Average serving	400
Ham, Virginia Baked	Average serving	375
Hamburger, Broiled	2-ounce patty	200
Hamburger, Fried	2-ounce patty	225
Hamburger Steak	Average serving	400
Hard Candy	1 ounce	110
Hard Roll	1 average	100
Hard Salami	1 ounce	125
Hard Sauce	1 tablespoon	100
Hasenpfeffer	Average serving	250
Hash, Corned Beef	½ cup	150
Hash, Roast Beef	½ cup	125
Hash, Turkey	Average serving	175
Hashed Brown Potato	1 medium	225
Hazel Nuts	10 average	100
Head Cheese	1½ ounces	150
Herring, Bismarck	Average serving	225
Herring, Kippered	Average serving	225
Herring, Pickled	Average serving	150
Herring, Smoked	Average serving	225
Hickory Nuts	8 average	50

Food	Serving	Calories
Jam, Fruit	1 tablespoon	50
Jello	Average serving	100
Jelly Beans	15 average	100
Jelly Blintz	1 average	175
Jelly Doughnut	1 average	250
Jelly, Fruit	1 tablespoon	50
Jelly Omelet	2 eggs, 1 tablespoon jelly	235
Jelly Roll	Average serving	200
Juice, Apple	1 cup	120
Juice, Apricot	6 ounces	120
Juice, Carrot	1 cup	50
Juice, Clam	6 ounces	50
Juice, Grape	½ cup	75
Juice, Grapefruit	6 ounces	75
Juice, Grapefruit, Canned, Sweetened	6 ounces	100
Juice, Grapefruit, Canned, Unsweetened	6 ounces	70
Juice, Orange, Fresh	4 ounces	55
Juice, Passion Fruit	½ cup	75
Juice, Papaya	6 ounces	75
Juice, Pear (Nectar)	4 ounces	55
Juice, Pineapple	1 cup	125
Juice, Prune, Canned	½ cup	85
Juice, Raspberry	6 ounces	100
Juice, Sauerkraut	6 ounces	5
Juice, Tomato	1 cup	50

Lemon Drops	7	100
Lemon Frosting	1 tablespoon	35
Lemon Juice	½ cup	30
Lemon Juice, Canned	½ cup	30
Lemon Meringue Pie	Average piece	350
Lemon Peel, Candied	1 ounce	100
Lemon Sauce	1 tablespoon	25
Lemon Whip	Average serving	40
Lemonade	1 cup	100
Lentil Soup	1 cup	300
Lentils	½ cup	110
Lentils, Dried	½ cup cooked	100
Lettuce	¼ head	10
Lettuce Heart	½ head	20
Lettuce, Romaine	½ head	20
Lettuce, Shredded	1 cup	10
Lichi Nuts	6 nuts	50
Licorice Candy	1 ounce	100
Licorice Stick	1 ounce	100
Lima Beans, Canned	½ cup	75
Lima Beans, Dried	½ cup (4 ounces)	265
Lima Beans, Fresh	½ cup (4 ounces)	100
Lime	1 medium	20
Lime Chiffon Pie	Average piece	300
Lime Juice	1 cup	60
Liver, Beef	Average serving	150
Liver, Calves	Average serving	160
Mango	1 average	100
Manhattan	1 cocktail	175
Maple Nut Sundae	Average	400
Maple Sugar	1 teaspoon	20
Maple Syrup	1 tablespoon	60
Maraschino Cherries	2 average	35
Marble Cake	1-inch slice	125
Margarine	1 tablespoon	100
Marmalade	1 tablespoon	50
Marshmallow	1 average	25
Marshmallow Sundae	Average	400
Marshmallow Topping	2 tablespoons	100
Martini	1 cocktail	125
Matzoth	1	75
Matzoth Ball	1 average	125
Mayonnaise	1 tablespoon	100
Meal, Whole	1 cup	175
Meal, Whole, Wheat-Germ	1 cup	150
Meat Gravy, Medium	1 tablespoon	50
Meat Loaf	Average serving	225
Meatball	1 2-ounce ball	200
Melba Toast	1 slice	30
Melon, Casaba	⅛ average	65
Melon, Honeydew	¼ average	65
Mexican Rice	1 cup	225
Milk, Buttermilk	1 cup	85
Milk, Coconut	1 cup	605

Food	Serving	Calories
Liver, Chicken, Broiled	Each	50
Liver, Chicken, Chopped	Average serving	200
Liver, Goose	Average serving	150
Liver Paste	1 tablespoon	50
Liverwurst	1 slice, 3-inch diameter, ¼-inch thick	75
Loaf, Meat	Average serving	225
Loaf, Salmon	Average serving	225
Lobster	Average serving	100
Lobster, Canned	Average serving	100
Lobster, Cocktail	½ cup	90
Lobster, Creamed with 2 Ounces Sauce	Average serving	150
Lobster Egg Foo Yung	Average portion	275
Lobster Newburg	Average serving	350
Lobster Sauce	1 tablespoon	40
Lobster Tails	Average serving	100
Loganberries, Canned	½ cup	45
Loganberries, Fresh	½ cup	45
Loganberry Pie	1 piece	350
London Broil	Average serving	200
Lox	2 ounces	200
Macaroni and Cheese	½ cup	225
Macaroni, Cooked	1 cup	200
Macaroon	1 large	100
Mackerel	Average serving	150
Mackerel, Canned	Average serving	175
Mackerel, Salt	Average serving	175
Madeira Wine	1 wine glass	75
Malted Milk, with Ice Cream	1	400
Milk, Condensed	1 tablespoon	60
Milk, Dried, Skim	1 tablespoon	25
Milk, Dried, Whole	1 tablespoon	40
Milk, Evaporated, Skim	¼ cup	50
Milk, Evaporated, Whole	¼ cup	85
Milk, Goat	1 cup	165
Milk, Malted, with Ice Cream	1	400
Milk Shake	1	350
Milk, Skim	1 cup	85
Milk, Whole	¾ cup	125
Mince Pie	1 piece	350
Minestrone	1 serving	100
Mint Jelly	1 tablespoon	50
Mint Sauce	1 tablespoon	50
Mints, Chocolate	3 small	125
Mocha Frosting	1 tablespoon	45
Mock Turtle Soup	1 cup	125
Molasses	1 tablespoon	50
Molasses, Blackstrap	1 tablespoon	45
Mousse, Apricot	1 serving	350
Mousse, Banana	1 serving	350
Mousse, Peach	1 serving	350
Mousse, Pineapple	1 serving	350
Mousse, Strawberry	1 serving	350
Muffin, Blueberry	1 average	150
Muffin, Boston Brown	1 average	110
Muffin, Boston Brown Bran	1 average	100
Muffin, Bran	1 average	100
Muffin, Cinnamon	1 average	110
Muffin, Corn	1 average	100
Muffin, English	1 average	150

Muffin, Fig	1 average	125
Muffin, Whole Wheat	1 average	125
Mulligatawny	1 cup	175
Muscatel Wine	1 wine glass	150
Mushroom-Barley Soup	1 cup	120
Mushroom Pizza	⅙ 12-inch diameter	200
Mushroom Soup, Creamed	1 cup	200
Mushrooms	½ cup	15
Mushrooms, Button	½ cup	15
Mushrooms, Canned	½ cup	15
Mushrooms, Cooked	½ cup	15
Mushrooms, Creamed, with 2 Tablespoons Sauce	1 cup	80
Muskmelon	½ medium	50
Mussles	12	125
Mustard, Dry	1 teaspoon	5
Mustard Greens	1 cup	30
Mustard, Prepared	1 tablespoon	10
Mutton, Boiled	Average serving	200
Mutton Chop	½-inch thick	125
Mutton, Leg Roast	4x3x¼-inch slice	200
Napoleon	Average serving	300
Nectarine	1 medium	50
Nesselrode Pie	1 piece	375
Noddle Soup	1 cup	125
Noodles	¾ cup	125
Onion, Boiled	1 large	50
Onion, Creamed with 2 Tablespoons Sauce	½ cup	140
Onion, French Fried	1 large	150
Onion, Fried	1 large	100
Onion, Raw	1 large	50
Onion Roll	1 average	150
Onion Soup, Clear	1 cup	100
Onion Soup, French	8-ounch cup	150
Orange	1 medium	75
Orange Ambrosia	1 serving	140
Orange Bavarian Cream	Average serving	300
Orange Chiffon Pie	Average piece	300
Orange Juice	6 ounces	75
Orange Juice, Canned, Sweetened	4 ounces	70
Orange Juice, Canned, Unsweetened	4 ounces	55
Orange Peel, Candied	1 ounce	100
Oxtail Soup	1 cup	200
Oyster Cocktail, Raw	6 medium	75
Oyster Crackers	½ cup or 14	60
Oyster Stew with Milk	1 cup	200
Oysters, Baked	1 dozen	85
Oysters, Blue Point	12	100
Oysters, Fried	6	175
Oysters, on the Half Shell	6 medium	50

Food	Quantity	Calories
Nuts, Brazil	2 average	50
Nuts, Butter	5 average	100
Nuts, Cashew	7 average	75
Nuts, Hazel	10 average	100
Nuts, Hickory	8 average	50
Nuts, Indian	1 tablespoon	25
Nuts, Lichi	6 average	50
Nuts, Pine	1 teaspoon	25
Nuts, Pistachio	16	50
Oatmeal, Cooked	½ cup	75
Oatmeal Cookies	1 large	100
Oil and Vinegar Dressing	1 tablespoon	65
Oil, Cod Liver	1 tablespoon	120
Oil, Corn	1 tablespoon	120
Oil, Cotton Seed	1 tablespoon	120
Oil, Peanut	1 tablespoon	120
Oil, Salad	1 tablespoon	120
Okra	1 cup	50
Old Fashioned	1 cocktail	150
Olive Oil	1 tablespoon	120
Olives	6 small	50
Omelet	2 eggs, 1 teaspoon butter	185
Omelet, Asparagus	2 eggs	220
Omelet, Cheese	2 eggs	250
Omelet, Fluffy	2 eggs	185
Omelet, Jelly	2 eggs, 1 tablespoon jelly	235
Omelet, Mushroom	2 eggs	190
Omelet, Onion	2 eggs	200
Omelet, Spanish	Average	225
Omelet, Western	Average	325
Oysters, Raw	12 medium	100
Oysters Rockefeller	6	180
Pancake, Blueberry	1 (4-inch diameter)	125
Pancake, Buckwheat	1 (4-inch diameter)	90
Pancake, German	1	225
Pancake, Griddle	1 (4-inch diameter)	100
Pancakes, with 2 Teaspoons Butter, 2 Tablespoons Syrup	3 (4-inch diameter)	470
Papaya	½ cup	35
Papaya Juice	6 ounces	75
Parfait, Coffee	1 average	250
Parfait, Maple	1 average	250
Parfait, Peach	1 average	250
Parkerhouse Roll	1 average	100
Parsnip, Cooked	1 large	75
Passion Fruit Juice	½ cup	75
Pastry, Danish	1 average piece	250
Pea Soup	1 cup	140
Pea Soup, Creamed	1 cup	275
Pea Soup, Split	1 cup	200
Peach Brandy	1 shot	75
Peach, Fresh	1 medium	50
Peach Parfait	1 average	250
Peach Pie	Average piece	375
Peach Shortcake	1 average serving	350
Peaches, Canned in Syrup	2 halves	125
Peaches, Canned in Water	2 halves	50
Peaches, Spiced	2 halves	75
Peanut Brittle	1x3-inch piece	75
Peanut Butter	1 tablespoon	100

Peanut Oil	1 tablespoon	120
Peanuts	10	100
Pear, Alligator	½ small	125
Pear, Dried	½	50
Pear, Fresh	1 medium	75
Pear Nectar	4 ounces	55
Pears, Canned or Cooked	2 halves	75
Pears, Spiced	2 halves	75
Peas, Canned or Cooked	1 cup	110
Peas, Black-Eyed, Canned	½ cup	100
Pecans	3	50
Pepper, Green	1 large	25
Pepper, Red, Fresh	1 medium	40
Pepper Steak	Average serving	225
Pepper Steak, Chinese	Average serving	275
Pepper, Stuffed	1	125
Peppermint Candy, Chocolate Covered	1 ounce	110
Peppermint Stick Candy	1 ounce	100
Perch	Average serving	100
Persian Melon	⅛ average	65
Persimmon	1 medium	100
Picalilli	1 tablespoon	15
Picalili Beets	1 serving	60
Pickerel	4-ounce serving	75
Pickle, Dill or Sour	1 large	15
Pickle, Sweet	1 small	25

Pie, Raisin	Average piece	400
Pie, Raspberry	Average piece	350
Pie, Rhubarb	Average piece	400
Pie, Strawberry	Average serving	375
Pie, Strawberry Cream	Average piece	400
Pie, Sweet Potato	Average piece	350
Pie, Youngberry	Average piece	350
Pike	Average serving	100
Pimiento	1 average	15
Pimiento Cheese	1½ ounces	150
Pineapple, Canned	1 slice	75
Pineapple Cheese Cake	Average piece	350
Pineapple Cheese Pie	Average piece	350
Pineapple Cream Pie	Average piece	400
Pineapple, Crushed, Canned	½ cup (4 ounces)	200
Pineapple, Fresh	1 cup	75
Pineapple Frosting	1 tablespoon	50
Pineapple Ice Cream Soda	Average serving	350
Pineapple Juice	1 cup	125
Pineapple Pie	Average piece	350
Pineapple Sundae	Average serving	400
Pineapple Upside Down Cake	Average piece	250
Pine Nuts	1 teaspoon	25
Pistachio Nuts	16	50
Pizza, Anchovy	1 piece	225
Pizza, Mushroom	⅛ 12-inch diameter	200
Pizza, Sausage	⅛ 12-inch diameter	250

Pickled Beets	½ cup	40
Pickled Herring	Average serving	150
Pie, Beef	1 average	375
Pie, Blackberry	Average piece	350
Pie, Blueberry	Average piece	375
Pie, Blueberry Cream	Average piece	400
Pie, Boston Cream	Average piece	400
Pie, Boysenberry	Average piece	350
Pie, Butterscotch	Average piece	350
Pie, Cheese	Average piece	350
Pie, Cherry	Average piece	350
Pie, Chocolate Cream	Average piece	400
Pie, Coconut Cream	Average piece	450
Pie, Coconut Custard	Average piece	400
Pie, Custard	Average piece	300
Pie, Elderberry	Average piece	350
Pie, Gooseberry	Average piece	360
Pie, Huckleberry	Average piece	400
Pie, Huckleberry Cream	Average piece	400
Pie, Kidney	Average serving	225
Pie, Lemon Cream	Average piece	350
Pie, Lemon Meringue	Average piece	350
Pie, Loganberry	Average piece	350
Pie, Mince	Average piece	350
Pie, Nesselrode	Average piece	375
Pie, Peach	Average piece	375
Pie, Peach Cream	Average piece	400
Pie, Pineapple	Average piece	350
Pie, Pineapple Cheese	Average serving	350
Pie, Pineapple Cream	Average serving	400
Pie, Pumpkin	Average piece	325

Pizza, Shrimp	⅛ 12-inch diameter	225
Pizza, Tomato	⅛ 12-inch diameter	200
Plain Cake	Average piece	120
Planters Punch	1 glass	175
Plum, Fresh	1 medium	30
Plum, Pudding	Average servi.	225
Plums, Canned	2 medium	75
Pollack, Broiled	Average serving	125
Pomegranate	1 average	100
Pompano	Average serving	125
Popcorn, Plain	1 cup	50
Popover	1 average	75
Porgy	Average serving	100
Pork Chop, Baked	1 medium	225
Pork Chop, Broiled	1 medium	225
Pork Chop, Fried	1 medium	250
Pork Chop Suey	½ cup	300
Pork Egg Foo Yung	Average Portion	475
Pork, Kidney	Average serving	130
Pork, Liver	Average serving	150
Pork, Loin Roast	1 slice	100
Pork Roast	Average serving	200
Pork Sausage	2 3-inch links	150
Pork Sausage Patty	Average patty	175
Pork, Sweet and Sour, Chinese	Average serving	250
Pot Roast	Average serving	200
Pot Roast, Chuck	Average serving	300
Potato, American Fried	1 medium	240
Potato Au Gratin	Average serving	225
Potato, Baked	1 medium	125
Potato, Boiled	1 medium	125

Food	Measure	Calories
Potato, Browned	1 medium	150
Potato Chips	½ cup	100
Potato, French Fried	6 average	100
Potato, Hashed Brown	1 medium	225
Potato, Idaho, Baked	1 medium	125
Potato, Irish, Boiled	1 medium	125
Potato, Julienne	1 medium	225
Potato, Lyonnaise	1 medium	225
Potato, Mashed with 1 Teaspoon Butter and 2 Tablespoons Milk	1 medium	180
Potato, Pan Browned	1 medium	175
Potato Pancake	Average serving	175
Potato Salad	½ cup	175
Potato Soup	1 cup	175
Potato Soup, Creamed	1 cup	275
Potato, Sweet, Baked	1 medium	200
Potato, Sweet, Boiled	1 medium	200
Potato, Sweet, Candied	6 ounces	300
Potato, Sweet, Canned	1 cup	235
Pound Cake	Average slice	125
Powdered Sugar	1 tablespoon	30
Praline	1 average	300
Preserves, Fruit	2 tablespoons	100
Pretzel Sticks	5 medium sticks	20
Pretzels	6 average	100
Protein Bread	1 slice	40
Prune Juice	½ cup	85
Raisin Pie	1 piece	400
Raisins, Seeded	½ cup	225
Rarebit, Welsh	½ cup	200
Raspberries, Canned	½ cup	100
Raspberries, Fresh	½ cup	50
Raspberry Pie	Average slice	350
Ravioli	1	75
Red Pepper, Fresh	1 medium	50
Red Snapper, Baked	Average serving	100
Red Snapper Creole	Average serving	150
Red Wine	1 glass	75
Rhine Wine	1 glass	75
Rhubarb Pie	Average piece	400
Rhubarb, Stewed, No Sugar	1 cup	35
Rhubarb, Stewed, with Sugar	½ cup	190
Rib Roast, Standing	Average serving	300
Rib Steak	Average serving	200
Rice, Boiled, White	¾ cup	100
Rice, Brown	¾ cup	100
Rice Cakes	2 ounces	225
Rice Custard	½ cup	200
Rice Flakes	1 cup	120
Rice Flakes, Puffed	1 cup	55
Rice Flour	½ cup	350
Rice, Fried, Chinese	1 cup	200
Rice, Fried, with Chicken	1 cup	200
Rice, Fried, with Pork	1 cup	225

Food	Measure	Calories
Prune Strudel	Average piece	225
Prune Whip	1 cup	100
Prunes, Cooked	3	100
Prunes, Dried	4	100
Pudding, Apple	½ cup	200
Pudding, Bread	½ cup	125
Pudding, Butterscotch	½ cup	175
Pudding, Cornstarch	½ cup	150
Pudding, Date	Average serving	150
Pudding, Peach	Average serving	200
Pudding, Plum	Average serving	225
Pudding, Rice	½ cup	175
Pudding, Tapioca	½ cup	140
Pudding, Yorkshire, No Meat	Average serving	200
Puffed Oats	½ cup	50
Puffed Rice	¾ cup	50
Puffed Wheat	¾ cup	50
Pumpkin	1 cup	85
Pumpkin Pie	Average piece	325
Punch, Brandy	1 cup	225
Punch, Fruit	6 ounces	150
Puree, Tomato	1 cup	90
Rabbit, Baked	Average serving	175
Rabbit Fricassee	Average serving	225
Rabbit, Fried	Average serving	275
Rabbit Stew	Average serving	175
Radishes	7	15
Raisin Bread	1 slice	75
Raisin Cookies	1 ounce	125
Raisin Fudge	1-inch square	100
Rice, Mexican	1 cup	225
Rice Pudding	½ cup	175
Rice, Spanish	Average serving	125
Rice, Spanish, with Meat	Average serving	200
Rice, Wild, Cooked	¾ cup	110
Rice, Steamed	½ cup	100
Riesling Wine	1 glass	75
Rock & Rye	1 drink	225
Roll, Caraway	1 average	125
Roll, French	1 average	100
Roll, Hard	1 average	100
Roll, Kaiser	1 average	125
Roll, Onion	1 average	150
Roll, Parkerhouse	1 average	100
Roll, Plain	1 small	75
Roll, Whole Wheat	1 average	90
Rolled Oats, Cooked	½ cup	75
Romaine Lettuce	½ head	20
Root Beer	6 ounces	75
Roquefort Dressing	1 tablespoon	125
Rum, Bacardi	1 shot	100
Rum Cooler	1 average	225
Rum, Hot Buttered	1 glass	150
Russian Dressing	1 tablespoon	100
Rutabaga	½ cup	30
Rye Bread	1 slice	75
Rye Whiskey	1 shot	100
Salad Dressing, Boiled	¼ cup	100
Salad Dressing, French	1 tablespoon	100
Salad Dressing, Oil and Vinegar	1 tablespoon	65

Salad Dressing, Roquefort Cheese	1 tablespoon	125
Salad Dressing, Russian	1 tablespoon	100
Salad Oil	1 tablespoon	120
Salami, Hard	1 ounce	125
Salmon, Baked	1 serving	250
Salmon, Boiled	4 ounces	140
Salmon, Broiled	Average serving	225
Salmon, Canned	½ cup	200
Salmon, Canned, Chinook	Average serving	235
Salmon, Canned, Chum	Average serving	160
Salmon, Canned, Humpback	Average serving	160
Salmon, Canned, Pink	Average serving	160
Salmon, Canned, Sockeye	Average serving	190
Salmon Loaf	Average serving	225
Salmon, Nova Scotia	2 ounces	200
Salmon, Smoked	2 ounces	200
Salt Pork (Fat)	1 ounce	200
Salted Almonds	12 medium	75
Saltine Crackers	6	100
Sardines, Canned	4	100
Sauce, Barbecue	1 tablespoon	50
Sauce, Butterscotch	1 tablespoon	25
Sauce, Chili	1 tablespoon	25
Sauce, Cranberry	3 tablespoons	100
Sauce, Cream	2 tablespoons	50
Sauce, Fudge	1 tablespoon	25
Sauce, Garlic	1 tablespoon	100
Shallot	1 clove	2
Sherbet, Fruit-Flavored	Average scoop	100
Sherry Wine	1 glass	125
Shish Kebab	Average serving	350
Short Bread	1 slice	125
Shortcake, Banana	Average serving	350
Shortcake Biscuit	1	175
Shortcake, Peach	Average serving	350
Shortcake, Strawberry	Average serving	350
Shortening, Vegetable	1 tablespoon	100
Shrimp	10 average	100
Shrimp, Boiled	4 ounces	120
Shrimp, Canned	4 ounces	145
Shrimp Cocktail	6 medium size	75
Shrimp Creole	Average serving	175
Shrimp Egg Foo Yung	Average portion	275
Shrimp, French Fried	10 average	200
Skim Milk	1 cup	85
Sloe Gin	1 ounce shot	75
Sloe Gin Fizz	1 glass	150
Smelts, Broiled	7 medium	100
Smelts, Fried	7 medium	200
Snap Beans, Green, Canned	8 ounces	25
Snap Beans, Green, Fresh	8 ounces	25
Soda Pop	6 ounces	75
Sole, Filet, Broiled	Average serving	125
Sole, Filet, Fried	Average serving	200

Item	Serving	Value
Sauce, Hard	1 tablespoon	100
Sauce, Hollandaise	1 tablespoon	75
Sauce, Lemon	1 tablespoon	25
Sauce, Lobster	1 tablespoon	40
Sauce, Soy	1 teaspoon	5
Sauce, Tartar	1 tablespoon	100
Sauce, Tomato	1/4 cup	50
Sauce, White	1 tablespoon	25
Sauce, Wine	1 tablespoon	35
Sauce, Worcestershire	1 tablespoon	15
Sauerbraten	Average serving	375
Sauerkraut	1/2 cup	25
Sauerkraut Juice	6 ounces	5
Sausage, Bologna	2 ounces	125
Sausage, Frankfurter	1 average	125
Sausage, Knockwurst	1 average	250
Sausage, Liver	3x1/4-inch slice	75
Sausage, Pork	2 3-inch links	150
Sausage, Pork, Patty	Small patty	175
Sauterne Wine, Dry	1 glass	75
Sauterne Wine, Sweet	1 glass	100
Scallions	5	25
Scallops	Average serving	100
Scotch	1 shot	100
Scotch Broth	Average serving	100
Sea Bass	4 ounces	100
Seafood Cocktail	1	90
Seafood Cocktail Sauce	1 tablespoon	50
Shad, Baked	Average serving	190
Shad, Broiled	Average serving	125
Shad Roe	Average serving	100
Souffle, Asparagus	Average serving	200
Souffle, Cheese	3/4 cup	150
Soup, Asparagus, Creamed	1 cup	200
Soup, Barley	1 cup	125
Soup, Bean	1 cup	225
Soup, Beef Broth	1 cup	35
Soup, Black Bean	1 cup	225
Soup, Cabbage	Average serving	50
Soup, Celery Clear	1 cup	100
Soup, Celery, Creamed	2/3 cup	150
Soup, Chicken	1 cup	100
Soup, Chicken, Creamed	1 cup	200
Soup, Chicken Gumbo	1 cup	125
Soup, Chicken with Matzoth Balls	1 cup	175
Soup, Chicken Noodle	1 cup	125
Soup, Chicken Rice	1 cup	125
Soup, Corn, Creamed	1 cup	225
Soup, Duck	1 cup	125
Soup, Duck, Creamed	1 cup	225
Soup, Egg Drop	1 cup	60
Soup, French Onion, with Croutons	1 cup	150
Soup, Lentil	1 cup	300
Soup, Mock Turtle	1 cup	125
Soup, Mulligatawny	1 cup	175
Soup, Mushroom-Barley	1 cup	120
Soup, Mushroom, Creamed	1 cup	200
Soup, Noodle	1 cup	125
Soup, Onion, Clear	1 cup	100
Soup, Oxtail	1 cup	200
Soup, Pea, Creamed	1 cup	275

Food	Portion	Calories
Soup, Split Pea	1 cup	220
Soup, Pepperpot	1 cup	125
Soup, Pinto Bean	8-ounce serving	225
Soup, Potato	1 cup	175
Soup, Potato, Creamed	1 cup	275
Soup, Spinach, Creamed	8-ounce cup	175
Soup, Tomato	1 cup	100
Soup, Tomato, Creamed	1 cup	225
Soup, Turkey, Creamed	1 cup	200
Soup, Vegetable	1 cup	100
Soup, Won Ton	Average portion	250
Sour Balls	6 balls or 1 ounce	100
Sour Cream	¼ cup	100
Soybeans	½ cup	115
Soy Sauce	1 teaspoon	5
Soybean Flour, Medium Fat	1 cup	230
Soybean Grits, Medium Fat	1 cup	365
Spaghetti, Cooked, Tender	1 cup	155
Spaghetti with Butter	4 ounces	220
Spaghetti with Cheese	4 ounces	200
Spaghetti with Clam Sauce and 1 Tablespoon Olive Oil	4 ounces	200
Spaghetti with 2 Meatballs	4 ounces	370
Spaghetti with Meat Sauce	4 ounces	275
Spaghetti with Tomato Sauce	Average serving	235
Spanish Rice	Average serving	125
Spanish Rice, with Meat	Average serving	200
Steak, Veal	Average serving	250
Stew, Beef	1 cup	250
Stew, Irish	1 cup	250
Stew, Lamb, Breast	Average serving	250
Stew, Oyster, with Milk	1 cup	200
Stew, Rabbit	Average serving	175
Stew, Veal, Breast	Average serving	250
Strawberries, Fresh	1 cup	50
Strawberries, Cooked or Canned, Sweetened	1 cup	225
Strawberries, Frozen, Sweetened	½ cup	115
Strawberry Cheese Cake	Average piece	350
Strawberry Chiffon Pie	Average piece	300
Strawberry Cream Pie	Average serving	400
Strawberry Pie	Average serving	375
Strawberry Shortcake	Average serving	350
Strawberry Soda, Ice Cream	1 average	350
Strawberry Sundae	Average serving	400
Strawberry Tart, Deep	1 average	300
Stroganoff, Beef	Average serving	350
Strudel, Apple	Average piece	220
Strudel, Cheese	Average piece	225
Strudel, Prune	Average piece	225
Sturgeon	2 ounces	175
Succotash, Canned	½ cup	150
Succotash, Fresh	½ cup	150
Sugar, Beet	1 teaspoon	18

Food	Measure	Calories
Spareribs, Barbecued	6 average ribs	250
Sparkling Burgundy Wine	1 glass	90
Spinach	½ cup	25
Spinach, Canned	1 cup	50
Spinach, Frozen	8 ounces	60
SPinach Soup, Creamed	8-ounce cup	175
Split Pea Soup	1 cup	220
Sprouts, Soybean	1 cup	50
Sprouts, Brussels	1 cup cooked	60
Squash, Acorn	½ cup	50
Squash, Butternut	1 cup	35
Squash, Hubbard	½ cup	50
Squash, Summer	1 cup	35
Squash, Winter, Baked, Mashed	8 ounces	100
Squid	Average serving	125
Steak, Beef	Average serving	200
Steak, Chopped	¼ pound	350
Steak, Chuck, with Bone	Average serving	285
Steak, Cube	1½ ounces	150
Steak, Flank	Average serving	200
Steak, Ham	Average serving	400
Steak, Pepper	Average serving	225
Steak, Porterhouse	Average serving	400
Steak, Rib	Average serving	200
Steak, Round	Average serving	200
Steak, Salisbury	Average serving	400
Steak, Sirloin	Average serving	200
Steak, Spencer	Average serving	200
Steak, Swiss	1½ ounces	150
Steak, T-Bone	Average serving	200
Steak, Tenderloin	Average serving	200
Sugar, Brown	1 teaspoon	18
Sugar, Cane	1 teaspoon	18
Sugar, Granulated	1 teaspoon	18
Sugar, Maple	1 ounce	100
Sugar, Powdered	1 tablespoon	30
Sukiyaki	Average serving	375
Sundae, Butterscotch	1 average	400
Sundae, Caramel	1 average	350
Sundae, Chocolate	1 average	350
Sundae, Fudge	1 average	375
Sundae, Hot Fudge	1 average	400
Sundae, Maple Nut	1 average	400
Sundae, Marshmallow	1 average	400
Sundae, Walnut	1 average	400
Sweetbreads	Small serving	125
Sweetbreads, Broiled	Small serving	125
Sweetbreads, Creamed with 2 Tablespoons Sauce	Small serving	175
Sweet Potato, Baked	5 ounces	215
Sweet Potato, Boiled	6 ounces	210
Sweet Potato, Candied	6 ounces	300
Sweet Potato, Canned	1 cup	235
Sweet Potato Pie	Average piece	350
Sweet Roll	Average	125
Sweet and Sour Cabbage	1 cup	75
Sweet and Sour Fish	Average serving	200
Sweet and Sour Pork, Chinese	Average serving	250
Swiss Chard	1 cup cooked	50
Swiss Steak	1½ ounces	150
Swordfish	Average serving	150
Syrup, Brown Sugar	1 tablespoon	60

Food	Measure	Calories
Syrup, Caramel	1 tablespoon	60
Syrup, Chocolate	1 tablespoon	50
Syrup, Corn	2 tablespoons	115
Syrup, Grenadine	1 tablespoon	55
Syrup, Maple	1 tablespoon	60
Taffy, Apple	1 average	260
Taffy Candy	1-inch cube	40
Tangerine	1 large	35
Tapioca Pudding	½ cup	140
Tapioca Pudding, Apple	½ cup	140
Tart with Filling	1 medium	225
Tartar Sauce	1 tablespoon	100
Tea, No Sugar or Cream	1 cup	0
Terrapin	Average serving	150
Thousand Island Dressing	1 tablespoon	100
Toast, Cinnamon	1 slice	200
Toast, French	1 slice	125
Toast, Melba	1 slice	30
Toast, Milk	1 slice	170
Toast, Raisin	1 slice	75
Toast, Rye	1 slice	75
Toast, White	1 slice	65
Toast, Whole Wheat	1 slice	65
Toddy, Hot	1 cup	150
Toffee, English	Average piece	25
Tokay Wine	1 wine glass	70
Tom Collins	1 tall glass	175
Veal Cutlet, Broiled	Average serving	125
Veal Loaf	Average serving	250
Veal Marsala	Average serving	300
Veal Roast	Average serving	150
Veal Scallopini	Average serving	375
Veal Steak	Average serving	250
Veal Stew	Average serving	250
Vegetable Juice	6 ounces	75
Vegetable Soup	1 cup	100
Vermicelli	¾ cup	125
Vermouth, French	2 ounces	35
Vermouth, Italian	2 ounces	50
Vichysoisse	1 cup	275
Vinaigrette, Asparagus	Average serving	175
Vinegar	1 ounce	0
Vodka	1 ounce	125
Waffle	1	225
Waffle, Cheese	1	350
Waffle, Ham	1	325
Walnut Cookies	2 ounces	250
Walnuts	4	100
Walnuts, Black	11 halves	100
Walnut Caramel Square	1 average	50
Walnut Sundae	Average serving	400
Washington Cream Cake	Average piece	225
Watercress	1 cup	10

Tom and Jerry	Average	175
Tomato Aspic	Average serving	35
Tomato Catsup	1 tablespoon	25
Tomato, Fresh	1 medium	25
Tomato Juice	1 cup	50
Tomato Pizza	1/6 12-inch diameter	200
Tomato Puree	1 cup	90
Tomato Soup	1 cup	100
Tomato Soup, Creamed	1 cup	225
Tomatoes, Stewed or Canned	1 cup	50
Tongue, Canned	2 average slices	100
Tongue, Pickled	2 average slices	100
Tortilla	5-inch diameter	50
Tortoni, Biscuit	1 small	175
Trout, Brook	1/2 pound	225
Trout, Fried	Average serving	220
Tuna, Canned in Oil	1/4 cup	125
Tuna, Cooked	3/4 cup	100
Turkey	Average serving	175
Turkey, Canned, Boned	4 ounces	300
Turkey Hash	Average serving	175
Turkey Soup, Creamed	1 cup	200
Turnip Greens, Cooked	1 cup	45
Turnips, Cooked	1 cup diced	45
Turnover, Apple	1 medium	250
Turtle Soup, Mock	1 cup	125
Vanilla Extract	1 teaspoon	10
Vanilla Wafer	Average size	25
Veal Birds	2 average	350
Veal Chop	1 medium	150

Watermelon	Medium slice	100
Watermelon Rind, Pickled	1/2 cup	40
Watermelon Rind Relish	1/2 cup	60
Welsh Rarebit	1/2 cup	200
Western Omelet	Average	325
Wheat, Cream of	3/4 cup	100
Wheat FLour, All-Purpose	1 cup	400
Wheat Flour, Self-Rising	1 cup	385
Wheat Flour, Whole 80%	1 cup	400
Wheat Germ Flakes	1/4 cup	100
White Sauce, Medium	1 tablespoon	25
White Wine	1 glass	135
Whiting	Average serving	125
Whole Meal, Cooked	8-ounce cup	175
Whole Meal, Cooked, Wheat Germ	8-ounce cup	150
Whole Wheat Bread	1 slice	65
Whole Wheat Muffin	1 average	125
Wienerschnitzel	Average serving	400
Wine, Bordeaux	1 wine glass	125
Wine, Burgundy	1 wine glass	85
Wine, Burgundy, Sparkling	1 wine glass	90
Wine, Chablis	1 wine glass	75
Wine, Champagne, Domestic	1 wine glass	85
Wine, Champagne, Imported	1 wine glass	100
Wine, Claret	1 wine glass	75
Wine, Elderberry	1 wine glass	125
Wine, Madeira	1 wine glass	75
Wine, Red	1 wine glass	75
Wine, Rhine	1 wine glass	75
Wine, Riesling	1 wine glass	75

Wine Sauce	1 tablespoon	35
Wine, Sauterne, Dry	1 wine glass	75
Wine, Sauterne, Sweet	1 wine glass	100
Wine, Sherry	1 wine glass	125
Wine, Tokay	1 wine glass	70
Wine, White	1 wine glass	135
Won Ton	1	85
Won Ton Soup	Average portion	250
Worcestershire Sauce	1 tablespoon	15
Yam	1 small	150
Yam, Baked	5 ounces	190
Yam, Boiled	6 ounces	185
Yam, Canned	8 ounces	225
Yam, Candied	1 medium	325
Yeast, Bakers	1 ounce	25
Yeast Biscuit	1 large	100
Yogurt	1 cup	165